Becoming a Model Warden: Striving for Excellence

Clemens Bartollas, Ph.D.

American Correctional Association
Lanham, Maryland

Mission of the American Correctional Association

The American Correctional Association provides a professional organization for all individuals and groups, both public and private, that share a common goal of improving the justice system.

Printed in the United States of America by Kirby Lithographic Company, Inc., Arlington, VA

For information on publications and videos available from ACA, contact our worldwide web home page at: http://www.aca.org

ISBN: 1-56991-204-1
This publication may be ordered from:
American Correctional Association
4380 Forbes Boulevard
Lanham, Maryland 20706-4322
1-800-222-5646

Library of Congress Cataloging in Publication Data
Bartollas, Clemens.
Becoming a model warden : striving for excellence / Clemens Bartollas.
p. cm.
Includes bibliographical references.
ISBN 1-56991-204-1
Prison wardens—United States. 2. Prison administration—United States. I. Wood, Frank W. II Title.

HV9470.B37 2003
364'.068'4—dc21

2003056321

Table of Contents

ACKNOWLEDGMENTS

Frank W. Wood has my profound gratitude for his willingness to have a book based on his philosophy, principles, and leadership. Somewhat embarrassed by the possibility of a book framed around the principles and philosophy of his career, he reluctantly agreed to participate and help in any way he could with the project. I am also pleased that Dr. David Ward was willing to participate in the project. The chapter that he wrote is critical in evaluating the effectiveness of the philosophy and principles of Frank Wood as they are translated into everyday prison life. I am grateful that Roy D. King, professor at the University of Wales, was willing to write the preface.

A number of individuals were willing to be interviewed for this book. This includes: Dennis Benson, Alvin J. Bronstein, James Bruton, Mary Leftridge Byrd, Burl Cain, Norman C. Carlson, Jack Cowley, David Crist, Lynn Dingle, John Hurley, W. L. Kautzky, Patrick McManus, Pat Noland, Steven H. Norris, Orville Pung, Chase Riveland, Kathryn Hawk Sawyer, William Sondervan, and Reginald Wilkinson.

In all my publications, I like to give a special thanks to my wife, Linda Dippold Bartollas. She has always supported me in my various projects. Karla DeVries, Diane Kaufmanmy, Ali Reicks, and Lucas Bee, my work-study students at the University of Northern Iowa, were particularly helpful in transcribing tapes of interviews. Finally, I am grateful to Alice Heiserman, manager of publications and research for the American Correctional Association, who has been supportive and helpful throughout this project.

Foreword

We are pleased to present this book because it describes a method for making prisons more humane for both staff and prisons. This is a goal that we endorse. We recently met at ACA headquarters with national and international prison reform organizations to discuss how we might best accomplish this.

At the same time, this work outlines a proactive and anticipatory management philosophy of running an institution that exemplifies the fundamental beliefs that you should treat others as you would want your sibling or child to be treated were they incarcerated.

This book is about far more than one person—though that person, Frank Wood, was an outstanding warden and administrator. Rather, this book is about a way of approaching life. The author, Clemens Bartollas, has written a large number of books about corrections and this work allows him to test out his ideas by getting input from some of the best and brightest who are administering departments or institutions today. So, this book is no mere history of one man; it is a cookbook offering recipes showing how to run a model prison—even in a time of stringent budget cutbacks and repressive philosophy.

"We hope all wardens and aspiring wardens will read this and give it to those they mentor. It offers hope and a proof that "good guys [and gals] can win."

James A. Gondles, Jr., CAE
Executive Director
American Correctional Association

Preface

It is a great pleasure to be given the opportunity to write this brief foreword in tribute to Frank Wood, the proactive warden par excellence. I first met Frank Wood late in 1983 when I was on study leave at the University of Wisconsin, Madison and for several months undertook a weekly commute to Minnesota to pursue research at the recently opened facility at Oak Park Heights. I had come to the United States to explore the operation of maximum-security custody at a time when I was frustrated at not being able to pursue research in the so-called English dispersal prisons—maximum-security institutions to which both the most serious escape risks and the worst control problems were dispersed—among lower-security and less difficult-to-manage prisoners. It was a policy I had been extremely critical of, on the basis of research which I had carried out at one of the first of a growing number of such prisons that had become beset by riots and disturbances.

Although I had become part of a small working group which met with prison officials on a regular and very constructive basis, the politics was such that the time was not right for me to do further research. In fact, the dispersal policy had been introduced in Britain following a visit to the United States by our Advisory Council on the Penal System, during which, under Myrl Alexander, the Federal Bureau had flirted with an element of dispersal after the closure of Alcatraz. Not for the first time the English prison system followed what it thought was the American lead, but on this occasion, shortly after the dispersal policy had been introduced in England, the Federal Bureau returned to the policy of concentration, and Marion began to evolve into what was to become the first Level Six penitentiary.

Denied access to English maximum-security facilities, I resolved to look at how these matters were dealt with in the United States. A couple of trans-Atlantic telephone calls and Professor David Ward put me in touch with Frank Wood and Orville Pung, then Commissioner of Corrections in Minnesota, and also with Norman Carlson, then Director of the Federal Bureau of Prisons. There were minor hurdles to jump over, in the form of submitting research proposals and dealing with ethics committees, but with a minimum of fuss and in a few short weeks, I was given the kind of access which years of patient nurturing and negotiations had failed to produce in my own country. I had permission to study all the Federal penitentiaries with a view to exploring the hypothesis that concentrating federal (and many state) bad apples in Marion offered relief to the other institutions and systems.

That project floundered in part because of the terrible murders of two prison officers in Marion, but also because developing a reliable and effective methodology for assessing the impact of Marion proved well beyond the possibilities of a single-handed researcher to accomplish within a period of study leave. Nevertheless, I did visit all those establishments, including Marion very shortly after the murders—a quite remarkable testament to the openness of the American system at that time compared to the almost obssessional secrecy which then prevailed in the United Kingdom—and I was able to produce an impressionistic report. I was also given a very high degree of access to Oak Park Heights. And that project prospered—indeed it became one of the most rewarding experiences of my professional life. My thanks to Dave Ward for making the introductions and to all those who contributed so much to that program.

So much for the background. My first recollection of Frank Wood was sitting in his office and being given my initial briefing. After outlining the history of Stillwater and Oak Park Heights and his philosophy in managing the prison, we discussed which prisoners I might wish to interview. Warden Wood had one of those systems of index cards on his desk giving brief details of every prisoner in the facility. In the course of the afternoon, he must have referred me to between fifty and sixty prisoners rehearsing their names, why they were in Oak Park Heights, and so on. In some prisons, I might have felt that I was being steered towards prisoners who would present the prison to me in the most favorable light. Instead, I had the distinct impression that he was picking out his worst offenders, possibly because he was sensitive to the suggestion that Minnesota, of all states, did not really need such a secure facility. But what impressed me was the fact that he clearly knew all these prisoners and in many cases their families also, giving me a degree of personal detail that could not possibly have been recorded on three-by-five inch cards. This was already suggesting to me a hands-on style of management that is quite rare in my experience.

Later, we toured the facility with his remarkable Captain Michael McGrath—the first prison captain I ever encountered whose desk was adorned by the *New York Review of Books*—and whose companionship and wisdom I came also greatly to value. As the weeks of observation and interviews, the sitting in on management meetings, and working my way through records turned into months, I came to realize that Frank Wood knew his staff, many of them college graduates, all of them handpicked after interviews with Wood and McGrath, every bit as well as he did his prisoners.

The English prison system, in those days before new-managerial procedures had turned prison governors (wardens) into deskbound auditors and accountants, had thrown up a good number of charismatic and inspirational leaders: clever, articulate, caring, and well intentioned, though sometimes a little eccentric. But none that I had met added to those characteristics a well thought out and systematically applied philosophy of what, how, and why things should be done in the way that Frank Wood did. If he sometimes seemed a driven man, in what appeared to be a determination to know everything that went on within his facility, it is probably because he was.

Over the last ten years or so, I have spent much of my time advising governments in the former Soviet Union and more recently in Brazil on how to develop their prison systems with respect for human rights. The process of development and training in human rights is long and complex and invades every aspect of the running of the prison, but the essence could not be simpler. If you want to know what human rights in prisons means, I tell them, I have never found a better message than Frank Wood's dictum—that you must treat prisoners in the way in which you would want your father, your brother, or your son to be treated if they were in prison. It is a message so simple and yet so far-reaching and profound.

By the time my first period of research in Oak Park Heights was complete, things in the United Kingdom prisons had deteriorated still further and the Home Secretary at the time, Leon Brittan, began talking up some rather draconian measures, which would have impacted heavily on our long-term prison population. The Prison Service set up the Control Review Committee to consider the problems of the dispersal policy. I met two of its most enlightened members, Anthony Langdon and Ian Dunbar, in New York, after I had advised them to visit Oak Park Heights, and we discussed the issues. When the Control Review Committee published its report, it stopped just short of recommending the ending of the dispersal policy, but it noted that two prisons such as Oak Park Heights would serve as a better substitute for the eight creaky and costly-to-maintain dispersal prisons then in operation, and they hoped that that would be the direction in which things developed.

But it was not to be. This is not the place to discuss the costs and benefits of different policies, or to go into the intricacies of differences between the English system and what happens in the United States. I raise the matter rather because it marked the beginning of a continuing fascination with Oak Park Heights by the English authorities. For that matter, not just the English authorities because I would hazard a guess that Oak Park Heights has received more official visits from more countries and had more television documentaries made about it than any other prison in the world.

I finally regained research access to an English dispersal prison and several other lower-security establishments in the mid to late 1980s. As a result, as David Ward has noted in Chapter Three of this volume, I was able to do what still remains the only cross-national study of maximum-security custody, using the same techniques and data collection instruments. The findings were not published until 1991, but it was clear that Oak Park Heights provided much higher levels of safety, as well as a much richer environment with much longer hours out of cells, and better work, education, and other facilities than did Gartree, its English counterpart. This occurred despite the fact that Gartree was based on the dispersal philosophy of a relaxed regime within a secure perimeter and that it was run by one of the best of English prison governors, who went on to become Director General of the Prison Service.

It is perhaps appropriate here that I should take slight issue with points made by both Professor Ward and Warden Wood in this volume and elsewhere. In my view, it is not appropriate, as David Ward does, to pose management and architecture as if they were at war with one another, with one triumphing over the other. Nor do I think Frank Wood's choice of a tent with good staff over a well-designed prison with bad staff is particularly meaningful. Yes, both make the rhetorical point of the absolutely central importance of good staff and good management. No one would disagree with that.

Nor am I aware of anybody arguing the case that prison problems can be designed out of existence without the need for good staff and good management—though this may be simply that I have not been exposed to some of the arguments that might have gone on in the United States. I have certainly heard some administrators express the view that expenditure on architecture, electronics, and hardware would enable them to reduce the numbers of staff employed—in my view a disastrous mistake that could only store up trouble for the future if it were taken much beyond trimming out a very few redundant tasks.

But my point is simply this: nobody who has ever tried to manage a maximum-security prison such as Gartree, or for that matter Marion, could fail to appreciate the value of good prison design. Surely prison staff deserve good training, good management, and good prison design. These things should work hand in hand. After all, we would ask no less for our cars and our houses and any other part of the built environment, so why not our prisons? I made the same point in my response to Gerry Northam's BBC documentary on Mecklenburg, *Buried Alive*, to which David Ward also refers, and I also noted that the history of imprisonment is littered with examples of the most atrocious events being committed in prisons of every conceivable design—from Devil's Island to Carandiru in Sao Paulo.

Gartree, together with some other prisons of a similar design, was eventually taken out of the English dispersal system, though the system continues albeit in a somewhat more compact fashion. By 1995, however, dispersal policy was again in trouble, this time through high profile escapes rather than riots. But, by then, things had moved on dramatically in the United States with the remarkable proliferation of so-called "supermax" facilities. On this occasion, a major public inquiry asked the question whether or not the English Prison Service should develop two American-style supermax facilities, each of 400 beds—one for escape risks and one for control problems. I was appointed to a working party to consider the feasibility of developing supermax facilities in the English system. Once again, politicians and officials looked to the United States. It is no secret that the prison service officials were once again attracted to the Oak Park Heights model, though by this time, Frank Wood had moved on and Jim Bruton was the warden. The politicians, however, preferred the ADX at Florence, which had replaced Marion as the federal level six facility.

The working party was minded to recommend the building of one 400-bed facility but only if this were funded by further reductions in the size of the dispersal system. In principle, the working party was opposed to the concentration of control risk prisoners, because a system of small units initiated by the Control Review Committee several years earlier and remodeled into what are now called Close Supervision Centres was working quite well. However, since it could not envisage a need for more than 200 beds for escape risks, it suggested a compromise proposal whereby the close supervision centres might move into the remaining half of the 400-bed unit as separate but related units. In truth, it was a somewhat half-hearted recommendation, and it took some time to move from one political desk to another, especially in the run up to a general election. By the time the politicians were ready to consider it, so much money had been spent reinforcing the security at the dispersal prisons that a new Director General was able to say that the need for a supermax no longer existed.

My membership in the working party greatly facilitated new research, which I conducted on supermax facilities in nine states of the union, between 1996 and 1999, including once again at Oak Park Heights—some fifteen years on from my first visitation. It is ironic that the Federal Bureau of Prisons, once so hospitable and among whose researchers I remained well known, was the only authority approached who denied me access, despite the direct intervention, among others, of the Director General of the Prison Service for England and Wales. It is a further irony that despite being the most visited prison in the world, I know of no prison system which has copied the Oak Park Heights' design nor any administration that has fully committed itself to embracing the Frank Wood philosophy, despite the fact that countless individual visitors and a remarkable group of colleagues have been massively influenced by it—as the contributions to this volume bear testimony. It is as though people do not quite believe what they see. Fellow Americans think that sort of thing could only happen in Minnesota. Other visitors seem to intuit that their own system would not have the strength or single-mindedness to carry it through.

Nevertheless, Oak Park Heights had changed over the fifteen years that had elapsed since my first research, perhaps not surprisingly so, given the sea change in American corrections that had taken place. Despite the early work on the addition of eighty new beds explicitly seen for supermax control unit purposes, in circumstances where few could think of more than a handful of possible candidates to be housed there, and despite the whittling away of workshop and education facilities, I had the clear sense that the Minnesota Department of Corrections and the staff at Oak Park Heights had resisted to a very considerable extent the baleful pressures that have oppressed American corrections for so long.

I have no hesitation in saying that Oak Park Heights remained the best example of American maximum-security facilities—in no small measure because it was supported by people at the Department of Corrections and managed by others at the institutional level who had received their professional training under the influence of Frank Wood. If I cannot quite bring myself to share the same sense of optimism for the future of the proactive warden, which is expressed in this volume, I am quite sure that such men and women are sorely needed and that for them, Frank Wood has been a beacon.

I think it is fitting for me to end this foreword with an anecdote not directly about Frank himself, but about his protégé and sometime successor, Jim Bruton. During the course of my research there in 1999, there was an incident in one of the workshops whereby a prisoner attacked an instructor hitting him on the head with, I think, a hammer. Another prisoner wrested the weapon away from him and pressed the alarm. Other prisoners did not involve themselves and upon instruction went to the far end of the workshop while the injured officer was removed. Such incidents have been rather rare in the history of Oak Park Heights, but when they occur, they cause anger and anxiety among staff. In most prisons, staff would probably call not just for punishment for the perpetrator, but for the closure of the workshop—if not permanently then at least on a temporary basis.

Having been briefed, and together with senior managers having considered some options, Bruton called an emergency meeting of all the staff. They were given a clear account of the incident and Bruton asked for suggestions as to how such an incident might be avoided in future. He then put in his own suggestions and a checklist of some seven or eight possible changes to the routine to ensure the safety of staff. There was then some pressure to make doubly sure that no member of staff be put at risk by closing the workshop.

Bruton asked his staff to consider what had actually happened and what the consequences of such a response would be. He pointed out that only one prisoner had been involved in the attack and he was now in segregation and would be dealt with by the courts in due course. Another prisoner had actually come to the rescue of the member of staff (who was, before too long, able to return to work). None of the remaining prisoners had involved themselves and all had obeyed instructions as soon as they were given.

The meeting had already agreed on measures for preventing a recurrence. Closing the workshop or other measures would simply punish all the other prisoners for doing precisely the things that the administration would want them to do. He pointed out that it was to the credit of the other prisoners that they had behaved well and that that, in turn, reflected credit upon the staff. The following morning, the workshop reopened.

I think that Frank Wood would be pleased with that as a small indication of his legacy at work.

Roy King
Professor of Criminology and Director of the Centre for Comparative Criminology and Criminal Justice at the University of Wales, Bangor, and Professorial Fellow at the Institute of Criminology, Cambridge

Introduction

In the early 1980s, as I was preparing a book on corrections, I traveled around the nation visiting a cross section of prisons. I also interviewed their wardens or superintendents. The most intriguing prison which I visited was in Oak Park Heights, Minnesota in a prototype facility that was still under construction. Its warden was Frank W. Wood. A friend of mine, John P. Conrad, a noted corrections authority, told me that if I talked with anybody, it should be Frank Wood. John said that he is something really special.

Warden Wood was very gracious to my wife and me as he took us around the facility. We were very impressed with him as a person and with what he was accomplishing with this prison. Subsequent to our initial conversation, Frank Wood has supplied materials for two other corrections books I have written.

When I reflected on his tenure as warden of Minnesota's largest prison at Stillwater and Minnesota's most secure prison at Oak Park Heights, and the time he spent as a federal court-appointed evaluator/consultant and commissioner of corrections in Minnesota, I became aware that he was espousing a proactive and principled managerial philosophy. I became convinced that his tactical way of managing a prison had a great deal to say to bring significant change to corrections, even when the political agenda in some states and financial restrictions in most states have brought repressive measures to correctional facilities.

Significantly, what Frank Wood accomplished at Stillwater and Oak Park Heights has been recognized by a number of publications, including three monographs on prisons, five textbooks on corrections, a formal study on incarceration, and Tom Lagana's *Chicken Soup for the Prisoners' Soul.* In addition to a number of articles in Minnesota's newspapers praising Wood's career and achievements, an article in the *New York Times* highlighted the architecture of Oak Park Heights, and *Life Magazine* compared what was taking place at Stillwater to Walla Walla prison in Washington State. Furthermore, a 1985 television special contrasted the quality of life at Oak Park Heights to that of a prison in Mecklenburg, Virginia.

This book came together from two day-long interviews with Frank Wood, from his supplying me with considerable information and newspaper articles about his years as warden, from his review of the manuscript, and from my framing what he has done in a corrections format. Throughout the chapters of this book, I examine the various aspects of becoming a proactive and humane warden. My goal was to flush out what Frank means by the term "proactive warden." This term concerns the anticipatory, strategic, tactical, and preventative management of a prison and this work shows how this form of management is different from the management styles of those wardens who are disillusioned and overwhelmed by their jobs.

What is encouraging is not only that there is a person of the stature of Frank Wood and what he has contributed to corrections in the state of Minnesota and as a federal court-appointed evaluator/consultant, but an increasing number of proactive wardens and superintendents are now in prisons across the United States. I have interviewed several of these individuals, and their contributions are included within this discussion of the proactive warden. I also have included comments of others who have played significant roles in the development of corrections.

The book begins with a glimpse into the three well-respected autocratic wardens of the twentieth century: Lewis E. Lawes, warden of Sing Sing Prison; Clinton Duffy, warden at San Quentin Correctional Center; and Joseph Ragen, warden of Stateville Penitentiary and Joliet Correctional Center. Contemporary proactive wardens have a number of commonalities with these heroes of the past.

The second chapter documents the bureaucratization of corrections following World War II. This changing approach to correctional administration brought new challenges and frustrations. In the final three decades of the twentieth century, the approaches to operate a prison varied from one decade to another. Then, in the 1980s, a new type of correctional administrator arose—the proactive warden—and the remainder of the book examines this type of administrator.

Chapter 3 offers an overview of the major events and significant changes in policy, practice, and leadership in the Minnesota Department of Corrections from the late 1960s to the present. Dr. David Ward, a nationally and internationally respected criminologist and corrections expert, wrote this chapter. The author's long career at the University of Minnesota provided an opportunity to observe events, to participate in several major planning events, and to conduct research at Stillwater Prison and at the High Security Facility at Oak Park Heights. The author's twenty-five year acquaintance with Frank Wood allowed him to talk with and see Wood in action in both an old and a new penitentiary and as Commissioner of Corrections. Innumerable informal conversations were supplemented by four wide-ranging interviews with Wood from 1987–1989. Chapter 3 is drawn from these observations, conversations, interviews, and dozens of visits to Stillwater and Oak Park Heights.

Chapter 4 presents the background of Frank Wood, his definition of what it means to be a proactive warden, how proactive wardens are different from those who are disillusioned, the characteristics of Frank Wood's style of leadership, and it examines the uniqueness of Wood compared with wardens elsewhere.

Chapter 5 begins to flush out the proactive model of prison administration. It describes background experiences that are helpful for those who aspire to be a proactive warden. The second part of the chapter provides the theoretical underpinnings of the proactive philosophy and practice. This chapter suggests that proactive wardens use a learning metaphor and employ power rather than force in prison administration. The final section of the chapter examines insights that are helpful in the proactive management of a prison.

Chapter 6 emphasizes the importance of integrity for a proactive warden. It examines such issues as the relationship of integrity to several factors: treating others with dignity and respect, behaving as a proactive warden, having a strong belief system, relating to politicians, and taking a stand on issues in which you feel strongly.

Chapter 7 focuses on staff development and the proactive approach to prison management. Beginning with the type of staff members that proactive wardens need on their management team, this chapter looks at the role of participative management, including how staff can be motivated to be proactive, helpful processes to be used in the training of new staff members, inappropriate behaviors for prison staff, and the issue of job enrichment for correctional officers.

Chapter 8 explores the topic of how to thrive in correctional leadership. It considers the problems that wardens encounter and examines the various strategies that will better ensure that wardens thrive in their jobs, including using a hands-on approach, having a clean institution, being predictable, and avoiding surprises. The author considers disillusionment and suggests how a warden can handle the difficulty of working in a repressive political environment such as we have today.

Chapter 9 examines what it means to manage a humane institution. It considers the ingredients of a humane prison, how wardens can make a difference in creating a humane prison, and how it is possible to have a humane prison in the present "make prisoners suffer" mood.

Chapter 10 brings the thesis of the book to a conclusion. It reviews the success of Frank Wood in Minnesota and the encouraging leadership of other proactive wardens in Minnesota and elsewhere in the United States. Noting the critics who contend that proactive philosophy and practice will not have any long-term effects on corrections, the book closes with the hopeful note that a critical mass will be changed and that proactive management will contribute to corrections so that we can realize a new day in the twenty-first century.

Readers should note that this book focuses on the management of maximum-security prisons. These high-security facilities are clearly the most difficult to manage because of their acute problems with violence, crowding, prison gangs, and racial conflicts. Although little discussion takes place on the management of women's prisons or minimum- or medium-security men's prisons, those who have managed these facilities are quick to say that the philosophy and principles of proactive management is equally, or even more, adaptable to these institutions.

Unquestionably, corrections has emerged from its Dark Ages, even with the repression and "get tough" measures of the 1990s and the fiscal constraints of the early years of the twenty-first century. In the century to come, I propose that the journey to an era of significant change and hope rides on the shoulders of anticipatory and proactive leadership.

Clemens Bartollas
Professor Of Sociology
University of Northern Iowa

Chapter One:

Heroes of the Past

Prison administration is not easy. The job of the warden demands enormous physical and emotional stamina from those engaged in it. A warden in North Carolina put it this way: "There is no question that the prison has taken its toll on me. I had ulcers at twenty-eight, heart problems at thirty-nine, and have hypertension now."[1] A warden in Illinois noted, "It is a hard struggle, and you just have to be prepared for it. Any decision you make takes a toll on you. If you make a mistake, you may not have a job tomorrow. If you make a mistake, the [prison] population won't let you forget it."[2] Another Illinois warden added, "The pressure is heavy duty, and I feel numb when I leave the institution at night. I don't think any warden can make it three years in this [maximum-security] institution."[3] In addition, a warden in Iowa commented, "I make good money, but is the cost worth it? My family takes a great deal of abuse. You are likely to be moved several times if you want to move up the correctional ladder."[4]

Dr. Reginald Wilkinson, Director of Ohio's Department of Rehabilitation and Correction, suggested in a 2002 interview that the job of the warden is not for the faint of heart:

> *The job of a warden is not a job just for anybody. When you get to be a warden, I think you have already demonstrated that you are a special person. I could probably pick two or three examples in the country where that is not the case, which is to be expected. But I think that when you look at persons who have the title 'warden' in front of their name, I think by and large they have earned that title, and they've paid their dues. So I have generally very good things to say about wardens across the country.*[5]

In a national survey about the satisfaction of prison wardens, 375 wardens of the 512 state and federal prisons returned their surveys. The data revealed that compared with other occupational groups, wardens had a high level of job satisfaction. To the question, "All in all, how satisfied would you say you are with your job?," 66 percent answered "very satisfied" and 30.5 percent responded "somewhat satisfied." To the question, "With regard to the kind of job you'd most like to have: If you were free to go into any kind of job you wanted, what would your choice be?," 72.6 percent indicated, "I would keep the job I now have." To the question, "Knowing what you know now, if you had to decide all over again whether to take the job you now have, what would you decide?," 78.4 percent responded, "I would decide without hesitation to take the same job."

Surprisingly, individual characteristics, organizational conditions, previous work experiences, and a prison's regional location did not influence satisfaction scores. What did make a difference is that the most satisfied wardens had supportive relations, emphasized humane services to inmates, and exercised administrative autonomy within the prison.[6]

How do the findings of this survey make sense when many wardens seem to feel overwhelmed and frustrated? You can argue that those who failed to return the survey were those who looked upon their jobs as overwhelming and exhausting, requiring various forms of crisis-centered management. It also can be argued that what wardens would put in a survey might be dramatically different from what they actually feel; that is, they might be afraid that negative statements about their jobs could become public information and be costly to them. The claim also can be made that there is a difference between reported general feelings of satisfaction and at times feeling frustrated, experiencing high levels of stress, and simply attempting to survive from one month to another, without major or career-altering incidents. Yet, it just might be that there are many satisfied wardens who love their jobs.

Feature 1.1 Chief Executive Officer of a Prison: Reactions of One Warden, Mary Leftridge Byrd

"I absolutely love this work. What an opportunity to intercede in someone's life. I'm talking about both staff and inmates now. I'm thinking about my staff being so young. Here's an opportunity to actually raise a young professional, and we've gotten to the point I think in this country where somebody may actually say they want to be a warden when they grow up. When I got into this two decades ago, you never heard anybody talk about working in corrections. So, it's great to think about leaving a legacy of influencing young people and trying to bring some enthusiasm about this profession with them and for them. . . .

"Why do I like being a warden? Where else could I have the opportunity to be a psychologist and deal with people's needs? Where else could I have the opportunity to be involved in providing medical care? Where else could I have the opportunity to learn a lot about facilities, management, and physical plant maintenance? Where else could I have the opportunity to become an educator, without a certificate? Where else would I have the opportunity to bring art works into the institution? Where else could I have the opportunity to be involved in the financial administration of a large organization? Where else could I have the opportunity to be involved with the culinary arts on such a large scale? Where else could I get involved in law enforcement as we are here? (We have a drug dog! We do sweeps, we do lock downs, and we search inmates and their cells.) Where else could I be involved in ministry? I do a lot of ministry. In sum, I have a really exciting job, and it propels me on a stimulating journey—learning and teaching this profession is certainly life-defining for me.

"My work is spiritual. I think that I am doing the Lord's work, and I'm called to do this. It's really hard for me to do this without acknowledging that it is spiritual. I acknowledge it pretty frequently, more through behavior than through spoken words."

Source: Interviewed in October of 2002.

Significantly, in the 1990s and early 2000s, some wardens not only were satisfied but thrived in their jobs. They were described by fellow wardens, by the commissioner or director of corrections in their states, and by staff and inmates in their institutions as proactive, innovative, resourceful, fair, and resilient. They remained ten, fifteen, or more years at the same institution. To them, correctional administration was challenging and engaging, and they spoke with pride when they discussed their careers. They usually understood management theory, had a good handle on correctional law, and were skillful in public relations. But most of all, they were effective managers within their facilities. They did their best to anticipate and prevent problems rather than constantly engaging in crisis management. In Feature 1.1, Mary Leftridge Byrd, then superintendent of the Chester Correctional Institution in Pennsylvania, has positive words to say about being the chief executive officer of a prison.

This book examines the art of becoming a proactive warden. The experiences, as well as the principles and philosophy behind what it means to become a proactive warden thriving on the job, are taken from the career of Frank W. Wood. He was warden of the Minnesota's Correctional Facility at Stillwater and the Minnesota's Correctional Facility Oak Park Heights, the state's largest and most secure prison. He also was the Commissioner of Corrections in Minnesota, before he retired in 1996. In addition, this book contains the insights of other proactive wardens and heads of corrections agencies. The author hopes that this book will be helpful to those aspiring to become a warden or superintendent of a correctional facility, to those who already are wardens who want to do a better job, and to those who may be responsible for selecting and appointing effective wardens.

How Did Autocratic Wardens Run Their Prisons?

From the birth of the penitentiary in Pennsylvania until the years following World War II, institutional wardens were sovereign. As long as they kept in favor with the governor's office, their word was law. Believing that no one else could run their organizations, these autocratic wardens took total responsibility for planning, controlling, and staffing the institution. The worst of these autocrats refused to accept either staff or inmate resistance and prisoners, like slaves, were denied nearly every human right beyond survival. These wardens mixed terror, incentives, and favoritism to keep their subjects "fearful but not desperate, hopeful but always uncertain." Guards[7] were subject to their absolute power and depended on their favor for their security and promotion.[8]

The most disturbing of these autocrats was the notorious Captain Elam Lynds, a nineteenth-century warden of Auburn and Sing Sing Prisons in New York. Feature 1.2 describes his leadership.

The three most admired autocratic wardens of the twentieth century were Lewis E. Lawes, warden of Sing Sing Prison in New York; Clinton Duffy, warden of San Quentin Prison in California; and Joseph E. Ragen, warden of Stateville and Joliet Penitentiaries in Illinois. As time changes and with the rise of statewide bureaucracy, their means of managing the prison were put aside. They also did not need to deal with federal court oversight of prisons that took place in the 1970s and has continued to

Feature 1.2: Captain Elam Lynds' Leadership

Captain Elam Lynds (1784–1855) is a memorable figure in American penological history. An army captain in the War of 1812, he returned to Auburn, his hometown, when he was demobilized, and he joined the staff of the new prison as warden, or—to use the terminology of the time—as "agent and principal keeper."

Lynds would not stand for individual treatment of convicts. Each was to be treated exactly like all the others. Prisoners were known only by number. Good behavior was not to be rewarded in any way. In Lynds' opinion and in the opinion of the Auburn Board of Inspectors, executive clemency or pardon mocked justice. According to Lynds, a prisoner's good behavior was no sign of a change of character: "Men of the most artful, desperate, and dangerous character are the most orderly, submissive, and industrious when confined." No one should be offered an incentive to behave according to penitentiary rules, he believed.

Lynds and his staff made every effort to systematically divest prisoners of self-respect and personality. Prisoners were dressed in black-and-white striped uniforms, and no visitors were permitted. Prisoners were not allowed to send or receive letters; indeed, they could read nothing but the Bible. To add to the prisoners' humiliation, citizens could pay admission to look them over, as if the prison were a zoo. Punishment for rule infraction was immediate and administered with a lash on the spot. Captain Lynds' discipline was criticized for severity, but flogging was standard in the military, and Lynds believed that convicts were not entitled to better treatment than defenders of the nation.

When Lynds was asked whether he thought flogging might be dispensed with, he was forthright: "I consider chastisement by the whip the most efficient, and at the same time, the most humane that exists. . . . I consider it impossible to govern a large prison without a whip. Those who know human nature from books only, may say the contrary." Lynds insisted that flogging "was necessary to begin with curbing the spirit of the prisoner, and convincing him of his weakness. This point attained, everything becomes easy, whatever may be the construction of the prison or the place of labor."

Sources: W. David Lewis. 1965. From Newgate to Dannemora: The Rise of the Penitentiary in New York, *1796-1848. Ithaca, New York: Cornell University Press; Gustave de Beaumont and Alexis de Tocqueville. 1883/1964.* On the Penitentiary System in the United States and Its Application in France, *trans. Francis Lieber. Carbondale, Illinois: Southern Illinois University Press.*

the present. Yet, although their ways of doing things varied, some of their basic principles of administration have been adapted by the proactive wardens highlighted in this book. We are fortunate that each of these wardens wrote or coauthored books, and along with what has been written about them, we have a good sense of how they ran their prisons.

What Was Unique about Lewis E. Lawes?

Lewis E. Lawes grew up near the New York State Penitentiary at Elmira. He lived only a half mile from the penitentiary, and he and his peers looked forward to the Saturday afternoon military drill. With the shooting of the canon, they rushed to get a good view of the parade grounds:

> *. . . We would listen with rapt attention to the commands of the officers and the steady march of the "solider boys" and never left until, with the bugle call at sunset, the flag was lowered and the day was done. It was our weekly treat.*[9]

Lawes was further fascinated when he watched the reformatory inmates work on the front lawns of the institution and on the farms. He observed that the inmates did not seem to be so dangerous nor did they appear to be unhappy. He added: "They joked among themselves and appeared rather neat and clean. I admired, too, the neatly uniformed officers."[10]

Early Days as a Prison Guard

On March 1, 1905, Lewis Lawes began his prison career. He reported to duty at Clinton Prison in Dannemora, New York, which was twenty miles from the Canadian border. Lawes was not impressed by his early experiences within the prison walls. Clinton Prison, as the other New York correctional facilities, was run on the silent system. The rules were clear in this depressing atmosphere: "No talking in shops, or at mess, or during the march to mess or shops; limited rations of tobacco, hardly any recreation and hundred and one other rules."[11]

Prisoners wore gray uniforms and, other than first-time offenders, there were stripes on them. Second-time offenders had [illegible] third-time offenders had three [illegible] gibles wore four stripes and we[illegible] because of their many stripes.

On his first day, Lawes was taken aside by some of the other guards and given counsel on how to survive on the job:

> *"Tough place," said one. "Toughest place in the State. We've got the most dangerous criminals here. You never know what they're up to. So you've got to watch your step. They haven't any respect for the new guards."*
>
> *"You've got to have eyes in the back of your head," cautioned another. "It's nothing for one of them to hit you on the back of the head when you're not looking."*
>
> *"Don't trust any of them," a white haired, solemn-looking keeper warned him. "Like it or not, they'll put a knife into you if they get a notion."*[12]

Lawes started out making $55 a month. He worked twelve hours every day, with two weeks' vacation a year. Frequently, he worked fourteen hours to fill in for vacation relief. He was expected to pay the dominant political party $25 a year to insure his job. Refusing to pay, he expected his walking papers but somehow managed to continue.[13]

On March 1, 1906, Lawes left Clinton Prison for Auburn. He had been married in Elmira and could not afford to turn down a job that paid $61.00 a month instead of $55.00. The extra $6 had a lot of purchasing power in those days. He discovered the famous Auburn Silent System. But in addition to the silence, the Auburn System had dark cells, bread and water diets, and other repressive measures.

After a few months at Auburn, Lawes took a civil service examination for reformatory guard and received a job at Elmira in October 1906. Zebulon R. Brockway, the founder of this reformatory, brought many reform ideas, but his iron-fisted administration also led to many abuses. Lawes found a repression about this reformatory that was as intensive as that of the other prisons of the day. During Lawes' eight years at Elmira, he struggled continually to find answers to the repression and the problems of the penitentiary.

In 1912, Lewis Lawes obtained a leave of absence and enrolled in the New York School of Social Work. Through contact and study with Dr. Katherine B. Davis, Burdette G. Lewis, and Dr. Orlando F. Lewis, Lawes saw himself as a practical penologist whose job was to guide and instruct rather than coerce inmates in a prison setting.[14]

Lawes returned to Elmira, where he was now the chief guard. His chance to put his ideas in practice came when he was appointed superintendent of the reformatory, which was located on Hart's Island. In the year he spent there, he treated the inmates with respect and had no trouble with them. However, he had troubles with staff, who never liked his appointment, and by the end of the year most of the unhappy staff had transferred out. Then, a decision was made to move the entire population of 547 inmates to New Hampton, New York to a prison without walls where Lawes instituted the honor system.[15]

Promoted to the Big House

On December 5, 1919, Lawes received a telegram that promised to be a significant career move. C. F. Rattigan, superintendent of prisons, invited him to meet with the governor in New York City. Lawes knew that he was being considered to become the warden of Sing Sing Prison, but he went to New York determined to turn the job down if it were offered. But after talking to the governor, he decided to become warden.[16]

Feature 1.3 The Philosophy of Lewis E. Lawes

"The Inaugural ceremonies were simple. I arrived on the first of January, 1920, and met the prisoner population for the first time, as a group, in the old mess hall at the noon hour. The then Superintendent of Prisons introduced me to the men. I was invited to address them from an improvised platform in the center of the hall. I refused. 'I'd rather talk to you men on the level,' I told them, 'I hope to stay here.'

"I explained to my audience that though I was willing to meet them half way and give them all the breaks they were entitled to on their records, there would be no 'you be a good boy and I'll be a good warden' policy. What they would get in the line of privileges they would have to earn. On the other hand, if their conduct justified it, they would get as much leeway as was consistent with their status as prisoners in a State Prison. That has been my theory and practice during the twelve years of my wardenship. I have never had occasion to regret the theory nor to seriously modify the practice."

Source: Lewis E. Lawes. 1932. Twenty Thousand Years in Sing Sing. *New York: A. L. Burt Company, p. 109.*

When the new warden realized that he did not know much about Sing Sing Prison, he began to study its history. He discovered that the name Sing Sing was derived from the Indian words "Sint Sings," a local tribe and a variation of the term "Ossine Ossine," which means stone upon stone. Intended to replace the mild prison in New York City known as Newgate Prison, Sing Sing actually was built and fashioned on the plan of the Auburn Prison.[17]

Lawes repeatedly heard that the "quickest way to get out of Sing Sing is to come in as warden." What contributed to this feeling is that prior to his administration, the average term of service had been about eleven months. Yet, Lawes became one of the most highly influential American wardens and stayed nearly twenty years. In Feature 1.3, he explains some of the basic philosophy that directed his tenure as warden of Sing Sing.

Lawes also had other beliefs that were critical to the ways in which he ran the prison. When he was faced with inmate self-government, as found in the Mutual Welfare League and its elected representatives, he stated that inmate self-government "cannot work at cross purposes with the administration."[17] He then proceeded to strip the Mutual Welfare League and its leaders of their power at Sing Sing. The warden believed that the only influence rightfully belonging to the League was to be a moral influence in the institution.

Lawes accepted the job with the belief that he had a free hand to run the prison in the light of his own conscience and judgment. He wished to develop his own policy and did not want interference from anyone. When challenged by the superintendent of prisons who wanted to be the censor of what would be printed in the prison newspaper, Lawes made an appointment to see Governor Alfred E. Smith in New York City. After explaining the problem, Governor Smith responded:

> Then he looked up at me and said, 'Now, Warden, you go back and tell that crowd that you're to run that prison as I said you should. Without any interference. We've got to get this thing on a sensible basis. I won't let politics interfere with our prisons any longer. Now, you go back and tell 'em that, will you, like a good fellow?'[18]

Warden Lawes ran the prison without opposition from that point. The warden had nearly total control over prisoners. In those days, prisoners had only two legal rights. The first was to attend whichever religious service they chose, and the second was the right to a specific food allowance. All other rights belonged to the warden, including engaging in recreation in the yard, watching all forms of entertainment, purchasing supplies from the commissary, receiving packages of goods and clothing from relatives and friends, writing and receiving letters, receiving newspapers and magazines, wearing articles of apparel not supplied by the state, and smoking in the yard and in the cells.[19]

Lewis E. Lawes is further known for his opposition to the death penalty. Two of his books dealt with this subject, *Man's Judgment of Death* (1924) and *Life and Death in Sing Sing* (1928). He says: "Capital punishment has never been and never can be anything but an uncertainty. It is a punishment for revenge, for retaliation, not for protection."[20] He then explains why we can abolish capital punishment: "We can have a punishment that is possible of application with both certainty and celerity, that presents an opportunity for individualization of treatment, and that is in accord with modern criminological methods."[21]

In 1941, after twenty-one years at Sing Sing, Warden Lawes retired. In the meantime, two other autocratic wardens, Clinton Duffy in California and Joseph E. Ragen in Illinois, were already establishing national reputations for correctional leadership.

Why Is Clinton Duffy Remembered?

Clinton Duffy was successful in gaining national press publicity on what took place in the prison at San Quentin. Two movies were made of the prison by San Francisco Bay, featuring Duffy and his leadership.[22] Duffy was featured in major magazines, including Life Magazine, and he wrote The San Quentin Story. His wife also contributed a book of her own, *Warden's Wife.*[23]

Clint Duffy grew up at San Quentin. He was four months old when his father, like his grandfather, became a prison guard there. Duffy, along with a lot of other youngsters, went to the one-room schoolhouse at the south end of Prison Town. Gladys Carpenter, one of his childhood playmates, later became his wife.

Clint and Gladys married on December 31, 1921, and for the first year of their marriage, they lived in Sausalito. Then, Duffy applied for and received a job at San Quentin. Working as the warden's secretary, later as prison historian and clerk of the parole board, he slowly began the movement up the prison ladder.

Duffy was appointed warden in 1940, but Court Smith, the current warden, refused to leave his office. Duffy managed the prison from a small office outside the facility. His first act was to call his wife. His second act was to dispose of "Rough-house" New, who was head of security and a person with a long career of knocking prisoners around. He walked down the street to New's house and knocked on the door. New opened it, and Duffy informed him, "I've just been appointed warden."

New said, "I heard that."

"All right," Duffy added, "I'm making some changes, and as of this minute, you're through."[24]

Duffy's Reforms

From the first days in office, Duffy staked his career on the theory that prison should be a place of rehabilitation. He viewed the prison as a modern laboratory for the study of criminals and crime. His doctrine of rehabilitation emphasized education, sports, religion, and psychiatry.

Duffy's reforms were very much the fruits of a reform movement elsewhere in corrections. The broad-based support given rehabilitation made it easier to gain support from the public. Duffy did not have the support from the governor's office that Lawes did, but as long as San Quentin did not "blow up," the politicians remained supportive of Duffy's style of leadership.

His first official act was to abolish the dungeon, a foul, fifty-foot cage where hundreds of inmates had suffered unbelievable tortures. He banned the use of whips, straps, rubber hoses, and other forms of corporal punishment. He had an inmate painting crew remove the nine-inch circles in one of the cell blocks where offending inmates had been forced to stand for hours at a stretch without moving or talking.

He issued an order abolishing head shaving for new prisoners. Another order eliminated the big numbers stamped in black on every prisoner's clothing.[25]

The changes shocked both staff and inmates. Before the day proceeded very far, five guards stomped into the warden's office and quit. They informed the warden that he was turning San Quentin into a playground and that they did not want to stick around for the riot.[26]

Shortly before noon, Duffy left his office and walked over to the old towered building that served as a control point. Six officers were waiting at the first gate when the warden got there. Duffy told them that he was going into the big yard.

"All right, Warden," one answered, "These men will go with you."

"No thanks," Duffy said, "I'm going alone."

"But you can't do that, Warden."

Duffy thought that he was kidding and so he said, "Why not?"

The officer looked at him with total surprise. "No warden ever goes into the yard alone," he responded. "None of 'em ever have. It's too risky. If you'll excuse me for saying so, Dr. Duffy, you've been around here long enough to know that."

"Well, there's always a first time," Duffy retorted, "Unlock the gate."

The officer twisted a big brass key and let him out reluctantly, muttering that he was not responsible for his safety.[27] Duffy spent a lot of time in the mess hall. He had witnessed a couple of major riots over food, and he was determined to serve decent food even at the cost of other important changes that he wanted to make.

Many expected Duffy to be "the thirty-day wonder," assuming that he would be gone after the first month. However, 3,000 inmates signed a petition requesting that the board give Duffy a permanent appointment. On September 1, he was given a four-year appointment.

Duffy had headsets installed in the cells so inmates could listen to the radio. The prison showed movies on a weekly basis. Duffy started a weekly question-and-answer program, "Interview Time." During this program, he would respond to the notes that he had received from inmates.

When late one night the U.S. Forest Service called requesting help in fighting a serious blaze in the mountains, Duffy and his staff picked 200 men. The inmates went, did the job, and all came back. This eventually led to the development of forestry camps in California in which inmates, among their other duties, fight forest fires.

Duffy approved the establishment of an Alcoholics Anonymous (AA) chapter at the prison. This movement soon was in full swing, with an average membership of 200 men. The San Quentin program was such a success that it soon spread across correctional institutions in the United States and Canada.

The prison published a weekly newsletter and established a hobby program to help the inmates to earn money. The warden oversaw the establishment of a canteen to reduce gambling and traffic in contraband goods. "San

Quentin on the Air" debuted from the prison on January 12, 1942. In a few weeks, it had spread to more than 300 stations on Mutual's coast-to-coast network.[28]

Duffy also began night classes at the prison. This program eventually had an average night enrollment of eighteen men, with all of the teachers certified and paid by the State Board of Education. He also expanded the educational and religious programs and built a larger library.

Duffy believed that "if you want men to respond like men, you've got to treat them like men."[29] However, he was willing to show force if it were necessary. In one such incident, he showed his strong hand with the jute-mill gang strike. Duffy's typical approach was to say that if there were inmate's resistance, then all his reforms would be taken away, including the radio outlets in cells and weekly movies.

Governor Earl Warren ordered an investigation of Folsom and San Quentin prisons because of the rumors of scandals. The investigating committee spoke critically of some aspects of Duffy's management. One consequence of their findings was a reorganization bill, creating a Department of Corrections. Richard A. McGee was appointed to be the first Director of the Department of Corrections.

In 1951 Governor Warren announced Duffy's appointment to the Adult Authority. There is some debate about why Warren promoted Duffy. Some argue that his experiences and talents were needed on the parole board, but there is also reason to believe that this was a convenient strategy to put a new warden in San Quentin. The latter theory was expressed most succinctly by Jackson Doyle, Sacramento's *Chronicle* correspondent:

> *It is no secret that Duffy, while at San Quentin, had basic differences in matters of prison administration with his boss, Richard A. McGee of the Department of Corrections. Warren sided with McGee, and when the opportunity permitted, elevated Duffy out of the San Quentin wardership.*[30]

Why Is Joseph E. Ragen Considered Such a Giant in Corrections?

Ragen, like the two other autocratic wardens discussed in this chapter, grew up interested in law and order.[31] His father was elected sheriff of Clinton County, Illinois, when Ragen was seven years old in 1902. Joe followed his father whenever he was permitted to do so. Later, after a hitch in the Navy during World War I, he returned home and served as his father's deputy sheriff from 1922 to 1926. In 1926, he married Lorett Heyer. Shortly before his marriage, the deputy ran for sheriff and was elected, serving until 1930.

In 1930, Ragen ran for County Treasurer, was elected, and served until 1933 when the post of warden at the Southern Illinois Penitentiary became vacant. The governor received hundreds of letters urging him to appoint Ragen. The letter writers pointed out that his record as a sheriff qualified him to be a prison warden. Ragen was appointed warden, but it was not long before he was given a second job—Superintendent of Prisons for the State of Illinois. The second job required Ragen to make a tour of all state prisons every four weeks. He knew that it was only a matter of time before Stateville, the big prison at Joliet, blew sky-high.

In 1935, Joe Ragen was sitting in his office at Menard when he received a call from Governor Henry Horner wanting him to come to Springfield right away. Upon arriving at the governor's office, Ragen was offered the job of warden at both Stateville and the older prison in Joliet. He tried to protest, but the governor refused to listen:

> *Don't argue, Joe. I've given this a great deal of thought, and as far as I'm concerned, the appointment is already made. You're the only man I know who can handle that place. I'm giving you a free hand to move in and remake it. Joe Montgomery, your assistant at Menard, can take over down there. Now go and make that phone call to Loretta."*[32]

The new warden's first official act was to read the court orders that directed him to carry out an execution. He, as the two other autocratic wardens in this chapter, found the affair extremely distasteful because he did not believe in capital punishment.[33] He then called the captain in charge of the night guard shift. He questioned, "What's the inmate count?"

"Haven't got it yet, warden," the captain responded, "we're still missing a few."

Ragen exploded, "Missing a few?" He looked at his watch and saw that it was 9:30 in the evening. "This is a prison," he retorted, "not a hotel where they check in at any hour they please. From now on, get every convict into his cell in fifteen minutes or somebody will be out of a job tomorrow."[34]

The warden shook his head and realized that his first task would be to tighten up discipline all around. But he also knew that the disorganized and poorly trained staff and gang-organized inmates would not make it easy. The notebook he carried with him the first day still exists and contains his thoughts on how inmates were in control of the penitentiary and they had absolutely no discipline.[35]

It did not take the warden long to discover that three powerful gangs dominated the prison. In addition, there were eight or nine lesser gangs. The gangs used strong-arm methods to maintain their power and control. Knifings, assaults, and sluggings commonly took place throughout the prison. Gang members bullied the guards.

Early on, he developed a plan of action on which he based his administration:

- Eliminate politics from the hiring of guards and prison personnel.
- Build an efficient guard force through careful selection and set up training facilities for new guards.
- Keep the inmates working. Allow no idle gangs, where trouble develops.
- Keep close regulation on all movements of all prisoners.
- Enforce tight restrictions on the things which an inmate may possess. Allow no money in the prison yard at any time, for any reason.
- Give every prisoner equal treatment, regardless of name or crime, as long as he cooperates with the prison authorities.
- Permit no prison bargaining groups or other intercession parties. Each prisoner shall be allowed to approach the warden directly with requests and complaints. At no time should inmates be allowed any organization of any kind.

- Anticipate trouble and, when possible, deal with it beforehand. If trouble occurs, deal with it in quick, direct measures and no show of weakness. At no time, even during a time of trouble, allow inmates to have a voice in the operation of the prison.
- Operate the prison with a maximum of cleanliness and neatness—both as a matter of health and as an essential part of security.[36]

Ragen took daily trips through the prison yard, often walking alone and always unarmed. He broke the power of the cliques, shipping them to other institutions. Before shipping out the big shot inmates who thought that they ran the prison, Ragen said, "Tomorrow, nobody will have influence around here but me."[37]

Ragen also had great control over the guard force in the prison. He created a labyrinth of rules and regulations (89 general rules and 1,222 specific ones) to control the guards. He was quick to punish the guards for even the most minor violation, such as being on friendly terms with inmates, and 5 to 10 percent of the guards each month were punished.[38]

After a prison killing, Ragen ordered a shakedown of the prison. He found 250 truck-loads of contraband in the five cell houses: one barrel of knives, boxes of brass knuckles, a saw, butcher knives, and straight razors.

In October of 1940, Governor Henry Horner died. Ragen decided to submit his resignation. He felt that a change in political leadership would mean that political factors would play into how he ran the prison. The new governor wrote and asked him to reconsider. But Ragen left to accept an appointment in the U.S. Department of Justice. After a number of weeks of special training in Washington, D.C., he was assigned to the Chicago office, in charge of a special investigating unit within the Immigration Department. Ragen also was appointed to open detention camps for aliens in both Chicago and Milwaukee.[39]

After a prison escape from Stateville in October of 1941, Ragen heard from prominent citizens in Chicago, asking him to consider returning as warden. He agreed to meet with Governor Green and a few other citizens. The governor asked him to return. Ragen agreed with the following stipulations:

- that he would have a free hand in discharging employees who did not come up to the standards and requirements of good employees
- that all prison employees would come from the Civil Service lists
- that certain employees who had been with him at the prison and who had left shortly after he did be permitted to come back.[40]

Ragen appeared to mellow with age, but no officer or inmate had any illusions about this mellowness. They knew that in the event of trouble it would disappear. As one convict expressed it, "He's strict, but if you serve your time easy—you know, obey the regulations—he's easy to get along with. But you always know that he's bigger and tougher than you and this whole place put together."[41]

He insisted on absolute cleanliness and order, with heavy emphasis on "absolute." He was always inspecting to see if he could discover anything out of place. For example, even in the tailor shop, when there were bits and scraps on the floor of the tailor shop, the correctional officer would make certain that they were swept up before the men were mustered for lunch.[42]

Ragen also felt that there was a place for "reforming, rehabilitating, and reclaiming inmates rather than punishing them."[43] However, every employee's job is first and foremost custody. He felt that a program of fair treatment and close supervision is the most successful way of averting major disturbances and riots. He had rules for nearly everything, but he felt that guards should not impose corporal punishment at any time.[44]

Ragen did not trust outsiders, which meant, in his mind, anyone who did not work for him. After having been briefed in the morning, he would conduct his personal inspection. Accompanied by his two boxer dogs, he would make his personal inspection of Stateville and the Joliet prison.

James Jacob's able study of Stateville defined the Ragen years of 1936 to 1961 as "the establishment of an authoritarian prison regime under the growing personal dominance of Warden Joseph Ragen." According to Jacobs, Ragen created a stable social order at Stateville because he was able to gain a large measure of economic, political, and moral autonomy.[45] In Feature 1.4 James Jacobs evaluates Ragen's effect on Stateville:

In the vocabulary of both employees and prisoners, Ragen ran the prison.[46] The "old boss" devoted his life to perfecting the orderly prison regime at Stateville. He exercised personal control over every detail, regardless of how insignificant. Ragen maintained "that if you stress the small things, you will never have to worry about the big ones." Thus, under his elaborate system of administration, prisoners were subjected to intense supervision under innumerable rules that blanketed every aspect of prison life. It can be argued that while some inmates suffered emotionally and psychologically from this intense supervision, they still were physically safer, better fed, and provided with more programs than prisoners of most other prisons of the period.[47]

Ragen tolerated no challenges from employees, outside interest groups, or inmates. He cultivated an image that made him seem invincible to subordinates as well as to inmates. He was feared as well as respected, beloved as well as despised. The elite who were close to him

Feature 1.4 Ragen's Organization at Stateville

"In place of a system where order was based upon the rule of inmate bosses and gang leaders, Ragen established a patriarchal organization based upon his own charismatic authority. Later the perfection and perpetuation of this organization became a goal in itself. Under Ragen, Stateville was transformed from an organization without a stable goal to an institution infused with independent moral value. Stateville was Joseph Ragen's answer to *Walden Two*. Every person and every object had its place. From the award-winning gardens to the clocklike regularity of the movement of prisoners in precise formations from assignment to assignment, the prison reflected its warden's zeal for order and harmony. Indeed, Ragen and the organization's elite looked on the prison as morally superior to the outside society with its petty politics and debilitating corruption."

Source: James B. Jacobs. 1977. Stateville: The Penitentiary in Mass Society. *Chicago: The University of Chicago Press, p. 31.*

gave him intense loyalty, but many among the rank and file deeply resented his authoritarian and arbitrary leadership.[48]

In 1961, Ragen took over management of the entire Illinois prison system. He appointed Stateville's captains and administrators as wardens, and his influence on the Illinois system continued long after his retirement in the mid-1960s.

What Were the Commonalities in the Leadership of These Three Autocratic Wardens?

These three twentieth-century wardens had a number of similar traits in how they ran their prisons. They were in charge, and staff and inmates were both aware of their absolute control. They had secure prisons, with few riots, little violence among inmates, almost no violence directed toward staff, and a low rate of escapes. They believed in keeping politics out of prison and, for the most part, were successful in this objective.[49] Even when the governor of the state changed, they were not replaced as warden, a common practice in those days. They had long tenures at their "toughest prison," and resigned, rather than being fired. Indeed, none of the three were ever fired from a position in corrections.

Early in their administrations, these three wardens developed a plan on how to run the prison and a strategy to enforce their plan. This plan and strategy, modified somewhat as the years went on, contributed to their successes. Their public approval was usually very high. For most of their administration, they had the strong support of staff. They generally had the approval of inmates who viewed them as fair but firm. None of the three believed in the death penalty and found the enforcement of the death penalty an extremely toxic aspect of the role of a warden.

The style of leadership demonstrated by Lawes, Duffy, and Ragen became the model for other correctional administrators. Ragen, especially, had a following who attempted to operate their prisons the way Joe ran Stateville and Joliet. These three wardens had a profound effect on correctional administrators at the time. And highly effective wardens today use some of the same strategies to be the chief executive officer, or warden, of a prison.

However, all three autocrats featured in this chapter were flawed in operating a humane prison. For instance, none of the three autocrats believed in corporal punishment; yet, there were charges that prisoners were beaten at both San Quentin and Stateville during Duffy's and Ragen's administrations. Critics also viewed the administrations of the three autocrats, especially the one of Ragen, as a dictatorship which held both staff and inmates under total control, partly because he was so quick to crush any opposition to him.[50]

Another valid criticism is that none of them believed in capital punishment, but they continued to execute prisoners. Indeed, Lewis E. Lawes executed 150 male prisoners and one female prisoner while he was warden. At some point, personal integrity would seem to require they take a stand and say: If we are going to have capital punishment, then I am not going to be your warden. In addition, these three autocrats supported dark cells, and a bread and water diet for prisoners placed in segregation. Furthermore, they were quite content in stripping inmates of nearly all their rights, except food (providing they were keeping the rules) and religious guidance. Finally, Ragen made the statement that if a staff member were friendly at all with an inmate, even though he had not shown any favoritism or violated any rules, he would be fired. Obviously, staff members can be friendly with inmates without in any way compromising their honesty, integrity, or violating any rules.

What Commonalities Exist Between the Autocrat and the Proactive Warden?

One of the reasons why it is important to turn back the pages of correctional history to begin the examination of the proactive warden is that there are significant similarities in both of these approaches to managing a prison. In other words, readers will see a number of commonalities in the careers of the autocrats that are helpful in becoming a proactive correctional administrator.

- The autocrats wanted full control of their facility. When Frank Wood accepted the job of warden of the Correctional Facility at Stillwater, one of the conditions was that he would have full control of the facility. Other proactive wardens and superintendents have found this to be an absolute imperative.
- The autocrats knew what they wanted to change, and they put plans and actions into motion to effect and maintain the changes. Proactive wardens also have found that such a plan is necessary to effect meaningful institutional change.
- Autocratic wardens were anticipatory and preventative in their management styles and, as a result, were somewhat effective in avoiding institutional problems. Proactive wardens, as one of their basic principles, emphasize the importance of anticipating and preventing problems before they occur.
- Autocratic wardens placed a high priority on direct communication with inmates and less so with staff. Proactive wardens hold that direct communication with both staff and inmates is crucial in running a prison. Proactive administrators want everyone in the prison to understand the priorities and the goals that the warden and staff are attempting to accomplish.
- Autocratic wardens placed importance on accountability, attention to detail, and timely and rigid compliance with schedules and movement. Frank Wood and other proactive wardens place this same importance on accountability, attention to detail, and following the schedule.
- Cleanliness and orderliness were priorities with autocratic wardens, as they are with proactive wardens.
- Autocratic wardens realized the importance of selecting, recruiting, and training staff. Proactive wardens even more so than autocrats see the importance of staff development in effective prison management.
- Both the autocrats from the past and the proactive wardens from the present are against idleness in the prison.
- Both the autocrats and the proactive wardens realize that inmate government is not consistent with the effective management of a prison.
- The autocrats resisted the intrusion of politics in how they ran a prison. At a much different time, proactive wardens

also would like to keep politics out of prison management as much as possible.

- The autocrats made their changes, and the institution was stable after they left. This was certainly true with the two prisons in which Wood was warden. Institutional stability and the permanence of positive changes also have been true of the administrations of most other proactive wardens after they leave.

Summary

This chapter examined the autocratic warden by featuring the widely respected correctional leadership of Lewis E. Lawes, warden of Sing Sing for twenty-one years; Clinton Duffy, warden of San Quentin for eleven years; and Joseph E. Ragen, warden of Stateville for twenty years. Wardens at the time had more control of their institutions than subsequent wardens would have, especially if they were able to maintain political autonomy. Both Lawes and Ragen were able to establish this type of political autonomy. Yet, there were clouds on the horizon that would make the autocrat a relic of the past. Duffy experienced the changing waves of corrections when a corrections director was hired in California and, not surprisingly, it was not long before the governor moved San Quentin's warden. Another cloud on the horizon was the federal courts' oversight of prisons that began in the 1960s.

Yet, these three autocratic wardens are worthy of study today because so many of their strategies of correctional administration have proven successful. Proactive wardens, like the autocrat of old, also hold to the close connection between security and safety, a focus on the cleanliness of the institution, a commitment to their jobs, and a concern about anticipating rather than reacting to institutional problems.

ENDNOTES

[1] Interviewed in 1978.

[2] Interviewed in February 1983.

[3] Interviewed in January 1988.

[4] Interviewed in March 1990.

[5] Interviewed in October 2002.

[6] Francis T. Cullen, Edward J. Latessa, Renee Kopache, Lucien X. Lombardo, and Velmer S. Burton, Jr., 1993. "Prison Wardens' Job Satisfaction," *The Prison Journal.* 73(June): 141-161.

[7] The correct contemporary term is correctional officer. *See* the resolution from the American Correctional Association on this topic, January 1999.

[8] This section on the role of the autocratic warden is adapted in part from John Conrad and Simon Dinitz. 1977. "Position Paper for the Seminar on the Isolated Prisoner," presented at the Academy for Contemporary Problems, National Institute of Corrections, Columbus, Ohio, December 8–9, pp. 4-11.

[9] Lewis E. Lawes. 1932. *Twenty Thousand Years in Sing Sing.* New York: A. L. Burt Company, pp. 12-13.

[10] *Ibid.*, p. 13.

[11] *Ibid.*,p. 12.

[12] *Ibid.*, p. 17.

[13] *Ibid.*, p. 18.

[14] *Ibid.*, p. 44.

[15] *Ibid.*, p. 55.

[16] *Ibid.*, pp. 65-66.

[17] *Ibid.*, pp. 68-69.

[18] *Ibid.*, p. 129.

[19] *Ibid.*, pp. 186-187.

[20] Lewis E. Lawes. 1928. *Life and Death in Sing Sing.* Garden City, New Jersey: Garden City Publishing Company, Inc., p. 157.

[21] *Ibid.*

[22] The movie San Quentin and its warden, "Warden Kelly," and the movie *The San Quentin Story* both depict a fictitious account of Warden Duffy at San Quentin.

[23] Gladys Duffy with Blaise Whitehead Lane. 1950. *Warden's Wife.* New York: Appleton-Century-Crofts, Inc., pp. 3-4.

[24]Kenneth Lamont. 1961. *Chronicles of San Quentin.* New York: Ballantine Books, p. 42.

[25]Clinton T. Duffy, as told to Dean Jennings. 1968. *The San Quentin Story.* New York: Greenwood Press, pp. 68.

[26]*Ibid.*, p. 69.

[27]*Ibid.*, p. 232.

[28]*Ibid.*, pp. 238-239.

[29]Lamont, *Chronicles of San Quentin*, p. 190.

[30]Quoted in *Ibid.*, p. 197.

[31]There are three main sources on the life and accomplishments of Joseph E. Ragen. A biography that inflated Ragen's accomplishments and minimized his flaws is Gladys A. Erickson. 1957. *Warden Ragen of Joliet.* New York: E. P. Dutton and Company. She was a Chicago newspaper reporter who got to know and admire Ragen and, subsequently, wrote a book on his management of Stateville. A second source is Ragen's autobiography. *See* Joseph E. Ragen and Charles Finston. 1962. *Inside the World's Toughest Prison.* Springfield, Illinois: Charles C Thomas. A book that is much more critical of Ragen's administration than the other two is Nathan Kantrowitz. 1996. *Close Control: Managing a Maximum Security Prison -The Story of Ragen's Stateville Penitentiary.* Guilderland, New York: Harrow and Heston. For six years, Kantrowitz worked as a sociologist-actuary to the Illinois Parole Board at the Stateville facility while Ragen was warden.

[32]Erickson, *Warden Ragen of Joliet*, pp. 30-31.

[33]Ragen and Finston, *Inside the World's Toughest Prison.*

[34]Erickson, *Warden Ragen of Joliet*, p. 43

[35]Ragen and Finston, *Inside the World's Toughest Prison.*

[36]Erickson, *Warden Ragen of Joliet*, p. 50.

[37]*Ibid.*, p. 56.

[38]Kantrowitz, Close Control, pp. 80-82.

[39]Kantrowitz's account of the early years of Ragen's administration at Stateville is quite different from Erickson or Ragen and Finston's accounts. According to Kantrowitz, Ragen's early years at Stateville were ones in which he did not have nearly the control that he did after his return. *See* Kantrowitz, *Close Control*, p. 21.

[40]Erickson, *Warden Ragen of Joliet*, pp. 233-234.

[41]Ragen and Finston, *Inside the World's Toughest Prison*, p. 53.

[42]*Ibid.*, p. 45.

[43]James B. Jacobs. 1977. *Stateville: The Penitentiary in Mass Society.* Chicago: The University of Chicago Press, p. 28.

[44]Inmates would not be beaten unless they hit or fought with a guard, and the beatings would take place in the isolation-segregation building and be administered by lieutenants. *See* Kantrowicz, *Close Custody*, p. 135.

[45]Jacobs, *Stateville*, p. 29.

[46]Kantrowicz is very critical of how Ragen ran the prison. He calls his management approach "storm trooper" tactics. *See* Kantrowicz, *Close Control*, p. 12.

[47]Jacobs, *Stateville*, p. 31.

[48]For the antagonism with which some viewed Ragen, *see* Kantrowicz, *Close Custody*, pp. 80-86, 125-126.

[49]Unlike the other two autocratic wardens featured in this chapter, Ragen was very much involved in the world of Illinois politics. *See* Kantrowicz, *Close Custody*, p. 193.

[50]Kantrowicz, *Close Custody.*

Chapter Two:

Changing Approaches to Correctional Administration

Following War World II, corrections discovered, as did other departments of state government, that no organization, private or pubic, could survive without bureaucratization. However, bureaucratization has been a dubious blessing. The volume of paper generated in any professional bureaucracy far exceeds that of the simpler generations of management. All that paperwork must be read, initialed, and shuffled off to other desks or to accessible files. Many wardens complain that they spend far too much time in their offices, coping with e-mails, memoranda, and urgently required reports. They say that they are too busy to inspect their cellblocks from one week to the next.

The head of the corrections department—whether titled director, commissioner, secretary, or administrator—serves at the pleasure of the governor and runs the department from the state capital. His or her responsibility is to make certain that there are no cracks, and that all categories or decisions are governed by regulations. As an appointee of the governor, this person is also responsible for supervising wardens of state institutions, and supervising public relations, making political contacts with the legislature, supervising fiscal management, ensuring policy implementation, and developing long-range planning.

Directors may supervise wardens directly, or they may turn that responsibility over to a subordinate, who then reports back to the director. Others also have ongoing contact with institutions. Headquarters staff are involved in interaction with institutions; they include the deputy director for operations, the deputy director for programs, the business manager and the budget analysts, the supervisor of classification, the personnel officer, and the staff attorney.

Other changes also have limited the warden's power:

- Civil service rules set limits for hiring and firing professionals.
- Associations hold the warden responsible for meeting their requirements.
- Unions and employee associations impose rules about working conditions and promotions by seniority for their members.
- Courts insist on inmate due process rights.

Today, top managers are more professional and more knowledgeable about managerial concepts. They are usually college graduates and even may have advanced degrees; some have studied correctional administration. The percentage of women who have been wardens or superintendents continues to rise, and several women have been directors of state systems and many are wardens or superintendents of state

Feature 2.1: Women as Correctional Administrators

The first woman correctional administrator in the United States was Mary Weed, who was named principal keeper of the Walnut Street Jail in Philadelphia in 1793. Nineteenth-century leaders included Eliza W. B. Farnham, head matron at New York's Sing Sing Prison between 1844 and 1848, and Clara Barton, who served as superintendent of the Massachusetts Reformatory Prison for Women at Farmingham in 1882.

In the early decades of the twentieth century, Kate Barnard was elected to be the first Commissioner of Charities and Corrections in Oklahoma in 1907 and served for two terms. Katherine Davis was appointed to be superintendent of the Bedford Hills Prison from 1901 to 1914, and Mary Bell Harris became the first superintendent of the Federal Women's Prison at Alderson, West Virginia. Kate Richard O'Hare was the first inmate sentenced for violation of the Federal Espionage Act and, following her pardon, eventually became assistant director of the California Department of Penology. Mabel Walker Willebrandt oversaw the administration of federal prisons from 1921 to 1929, and Dr. Mirian van Waters served as superintendent of the Massachusetts Reformatory for Women from 1932 to 1957.

More recently, Elayn Hunt was appointed to be Director of Corrections in Louisiana in 1972, but died four years later before she could implement many of her reforms. In the 1980s, Ward Murphy in Maine, Ali Klein in New Jersey, and Ruth L. Rushen in California became directors of state systems. In 1990, Alaska, North Dakota, South Dakota, and Puerto Rico had women commissioners of adult corrections, a record number. In 1992, Kathleen M. Hawk was appointed director of the Federal Bureau of Prisons and became the sixth director of the Bureau and its first woman director since its establishment in 1930.

Women also have made some inroads as administrators of male institutions, but the road has not been easy. By 1997, women represented about 10 percent of wardens and superintendents of the 900 statewide correctional facilities for men. Camille Graham Camp was one such groundbreaker who in 1977 became warden of the Maximum Security Center in South Carolina. As the first woman to head such a facility, she was responsible for the state's most violent inmates.

Source: Katherine van Wormer and Clemens Bartollas. 2000. Women and the Criminal Justice System. *Needham Heights, Massachusetts: Allyn and Bacon, pp. 214-215. Current information on women wardens is available from the Association of Women Executives in Corrections (AWEC) care of sjohnrion@aol.com. In 2002, almost 25 percent of all wardens were women (ACA, 2003).*

institutions. For a brief sweep of the history of women who have served as correctional administrators, see Feature 2.1. Correctional administrators also appear to be younger than in the past. Associate wardens are now often appointed when they are in their early thirties and become wardens or superintendents before they are forty.

What Are the Changing Roles of Bureaucratic Wardens?

Directors and commissioners of corrections expect wardens or superintendents in the bureaucratic model to comply with both the law and the spirit of administrative regulations they receive from the central office and to keep the director informed about what is taking place within the correctional institution. If there is a problem, the director wants to know about it, so he or she can help the warden take appropriate action. The warden also is expected to do the following things:

- prevent institutional escapes and maintain good security practices
- maintain a safe environment for inmates and staff
- be an effective fiscal manager
- promote good personnel practices in hiring and firing
- maintain affirmative action goals
- settle employee grievances
- negotiate effectively with union officials
- establish good communications with staff and inmates (this does not mean that the director wants wardens making deals with inmate gangs or inviting inmates to make managerial decisions)[1]

Directors differ in their views on the weight they expect wardens to give to each of these duties and responsibilities. Directors' interpretations of how wardens should order their priorities depend largely on how the governor and legislature define the correctional mission of that state and on the groundrules that directors have developed for working in corrections. Nevertheless, directors do not like to be surprised by institutional crises and, therefore, one of the most important responsibilities of wardens is to keep directors informed about institutional problems.

Richard A. McGee, who became director of the California Department of Corrections in the early 1940s, did much to shape the role of directors or commissioners of corrections across the United States. In Feature 2.2, John P. Conrad, who worked as a staff member on McGee's staff, evaluates why McGee had so much influence in shaping California's corrections.

In the bureaucratic model that emerged in corrections in the final decades of the twentieth century, the warden or superintendent knew that he or she must please the director or commissioner of corrections. One Midwestern warden put it this way: "I know what the director is looking for, and this state is in compliance with his administrative directives. It is not something you can jive your way through. You're either doing it, or you're not doing it."[2]

What Were the Management Styles of Late Twentieth-century Wardens?

Wardens' management styles of the 1970s differ greatly from those of the 1980s and those of the 1990s and today. The majority of bureaucratic wardens of the 1970s used participatory management schemes with staff and sometimes with inmates; many wardens of the 1980s chose either the control, consensual, or responsibility models to manage their institutions. In contrast, a few wardens of the 1980s, and even more in the 1990s, viewed themselves as professionals and team players dealing with institutional problems in proactive and innovative ways.

Feature 2.2: The Leadership of Richard A. McGee

According to John Conrad, Richard McGee made California corrections "a byword for decency and order, a model for emulation throughout the world, and a laboratory for change in prison and parole administration.

"It is hard to recapture the excitement of those days. We worked for a restless, perpetually dissatisfied leader who exacted superior performances from his subordinates. His intellectual curiosity swept in ideas from every point of the compass; our job was to translate these ideas into programs. It was inconceivable that a year could pass without a new experiment in the improvement of the system, a new study commissioned to find out what more could be done to make sense out of prison, or a new program to train people to do more than they had previously thought possible. Bureaucrats that we were, there was plenty of paper to shuffle, and it had to be shuffled right, but there were always task-force meetings to prepare for, and the memorandums to draw up for the refinement of an innovative plan. It is an exhilarating experience to engage in an enterprise in which all participants are convinced that they are leading the world to great improvements in the established order of things. We knew that that was the case; we could see the improvements and their effects, and we heard the acclaim from travelers who came from all over the world to see for themselves. The grumblers changed their tunes.

"In most prison systems the only excitement in humdrum routines occurs when something goes seriously wrong: an escape from maximum custody, a riot, the taking of hostages. For those of us who worked with McGee, the excitement was of a different quality—a new program that proved its worth, new legislation to solve an old problem, or a new procedure that simplified operations. There were mistakes and disappointments, but it was unthinkable that we could be allowed to subside into the management of drift . . . . Even our failures during McGee's regime had at least the benefit that something important was under trial; there was hope for a system in which optimists were in control."

Source: The foreword to Richard A. McGee. 1981. Prison and Politics. *Lexington, Massachusetts: D.C. Heath, pp. ix-x.*

Participatory Management Philosophy

Correctional administrators in the 1970s found themselves thrust into the center of shifting and volatile fields of force. They not only had to relate to the staff and inmates of their institutions but also had to interact successfully with the director, the legislature, the media, labor unions, employee organizations, law-enforcement agencies, the courts, and the various special-interest groups in the community. They knew that their negotiations within this web of relationships had to protect and maintain the institution; yet, at the same time, it was necessary to generate needed internal development and change. The corporate management model, adapted largely from the private sector, and the shared-powers model were the two styles of participatory management developed to meet the challenges of running a correctional institution.

In the corporate management model, great emphasis is placed on modern management techniques and a meaningful table of organization. This model also develops lines of authority and accountability. Management by objectives (MBO) and zero-based budgeting were two of the more widely used corporate management model strategies. Management by objectives is based on the principle that the best way to ensure success is through planning.[3] The goals of zero-based budgeting are the development of improved plans and budgets, the ability to evaluate plans and make necessary changes, and the development of functional management teams.[4]

It did not take long for these correctional administrators to discover that the new management theory did not solve the problems in American prisons. By the 1980s, most of these correctional administrators had come to realize that in spite of this private-sector management theory, most prisons had more violence, worse living conditions, and fewer programming opportunities than those under the autocrat of old.

In the 1970s, correctional administrators in some states turned to a shared-powers model to manage prisons. Inspired by a rehabilitative ideal, wardens attempted to enhance the "respect," "dignity," and "status" of both staff and inmates by granting them some power in the governance of the prison. They wished to bring inmates, as well as staff and the central office, into institutional decision making.

Tom Murton championed the inmate-participation model. He was the warden of two Arkansas prison farms between 1967 and 1968. His inmate-participation model begins with the assumption that 95 percent of the inmates will return to society.[5] The main purpose of prisons then is to help inmates learn to live in a free society. Thus, the inmate-participation model strives to make the prison society less totalitarian and more like life in a representative democracy. One means to accomplish this goal is have inmates elect their own representatives to an inmate council that operates as a legislative body.[6]

In the 1980s, nearly all correctional systems abandoned the shared-powers model. A few states, especially California, Illinois, and Washington, came close to sliding into an inmate-control model. In these states, inmate gangs wielded such power within the walls that they attempted, sometimes successfully, to dictate prison policy.[7]

Philosophies of Control, Consensus, and Responsibility

John J. DiIulio, Jr., in examining prison management during the 1980s, identified three main approaches: the Texas control model, the Michigan responsibility model, and the California consensual model.[8] In addition, functional units (and the unit management approach) began to be used in increasing number of U.S. Bureau of Prisons' institutions and represented another approach to correctional administration.[9]

The Texas control model is based on staff having total control of the institution. The Michigan responsibility model focuses on making inmates responsible for their own actions, and the California consensus model ends up with gangs running the prisons and prison administrators attempting to consult and negotiate with them.

The differences in these approaches, according to DiIulio, are rooted in differences of correctional philosophy. He adds that the importance of prison management is that it determines the quality of prison life—the order, the amenities, and the available services. Indeed, he claims that the prison disorders of the 1980s were the "simple tales of failed prison management." Bert Useem and Peter Kimball's study of prison riots support this viewpoint:

> *If one accepts our thesis that the cause of prison riots is the disorganization of the state, then it follows that maintaining a strong, coherent prison administration is the crucial ingredient in avoiding disturbances. New Mexico and the other prison systems under study "blew," not because they chose the wrong style of management, but because their efforts were so thoroughly disorganized and incoherent. In short, good administration is the key. This may be an obvious point, but if so it has been missed by other students of prison riots, such as Sykes.*[11]

DiIulio is most supportive of the control model in Texas that has been dismantled by the *Ruiz v. Estelle* court decision.[12] He recognized the defects of this control model, for he was aware that the "building tender's" system gave the inmates too much power. DiIulio and others strongly supported the order that the control model achieved, especially during the ten years (1962-1972) that George Beto was director of the department. There appeared to be less overt violence under the control model, and infractions were less frequent and less severe. This meant that prisoners were less at risk in Texas prisons than in other prisons across the nation.[13]

DiIulio is far more critical of the other two approaches to correctional management. He believes that the Michigan responsibility model maximizes inmates' responsibility for their own actions. Prisons, according to this model, are to be run by imposing minimum constraints on inmates, an approach that supposedly fosters prison community. DiIulio charges that the major internal defect of this model is the alienation and lack of support from correctional officers.[14]

The California consensus model, concludes DiIulio, is even more of a disaster. This model "is a crazy-quilt pattern of correctional principles and practices."[15] He claims that the management of California prisons eventually evolved into the question of how to manage prison gangs. He charges that former directors Raymond Procunier, the father of the consensual model, and J. J. Enomoto, his successor, consulted and negotiated with the gangs. Thus, because of California's preoccupation with gang organization and violence and the enduring instability that brings to the institution, DiIulio believes that California has "given the store away" to the inmates.[16]

In sum, with some variations, DiIulio wants a return of the Texas control model. He seems to buy into Warden Ragen's old adage that either the inmates or the staff are in control, and he believes that a paramilitary operation and unflagging discipline will recapture the prison from inmates. He adds in another place that "to punish rule violators proportionately" is the key to prison discipline and control.[17]

Disillusioned Versus Innovative Wardens

Wardens of the 1990s and early twenty-first century appear to be divided for the most part into those who are disillusioned and overwhelmed and those who are proactive and in control of their facilities. Disillusioned wardens tend to feel that they have lost their reform ideology, because they no longer have the rehabilitation ideal, human relations model, participatory management philosophy, or shared-powers model to provide the hope that the present state of imprisonment could be changed. Faced with overwhelming problems, especially in maximum-security prisons, this group would agree with those who say that the pressure is heavy duty, and that they feel numb when they leave the institution at night.

Another group of wardens are attempting to develop a new approach to correctional administration. They feel positive about their jobs, and they see themselves as proactive, rather than reactive, to the challenges of institutional leadership. These wardens are different in a number of ways from the first group. Chapter 3 expands on these differences.

What Problems Are Presented to Bureaucratic or Contemporary Wardens?

With the emergence of the bureaucratic model for state government following World War II, the administration of prisons became increasingly more difficult and complex. Prisons became crowded, institutional violence in its various forms became problematic, racial tensions and conflict became a new social phenomenon, and inmate gangs, and prisoners' rights became time-consuming and posed liability issues for wardens and superintendents. In the 1990s, a "make prisoners suffer" mood, as well as financial crises in most states, swept through American politics resulting in the withdrawal of many programs for prisoners and in the establishment of high-security units in nearly every state.

Prison Crowding

Since the mid-1970s, the dizzying rise in the prison population and incarceration rates has attracted the attention of most correctional administrators, almost to the exclusion of other problems. Indeed, between 1970 and 2002, the population of this nation's prisons increased from 196,479 to 1,367,856 and resulted in crowded conditions in nearly all state and federal institutions.[18]

This crowding has had adverse consequences in a number of ways for the Federal Bureau of Prisons and for state departments of corrections. Both staff and inmates are negatively affected by prison crowding. Crowding has particularly toxic affects in close-custody or maximum-security prisons. In these facilities, which house the more predatory inmates, multiple occupancy cells permit both inmate victimization and provide opportunity for the inmate culture to exercise authority in the confines of a cell. Intimidated inmates may feel that there is no place to go because the system cannot protect them. They can be moved to another cell, but will suffer the same consequences if the inmate leadership wants that to happen.

Staff must work in a more volatile environment, and inmates are forced to live in facilities in which they are jammed and crammed with other inmates. Furthermore, prison crowding has serious consequences for a state's economy, such as when a lawsuit leads to court-ordered changes such as the building or remodeling of correctional facilities.

Institutional Violence

Institutional violence is a serious and perplexing problem, manifesting itself in a variety of forms—riots and other major disturbances, victimization of one inmate by another, and inmate assaults on staff. In addition, staff brutality toward inmates unfortunately still takes place occasionally.

Inmate disturbances can be nonviolent or violent. Nonviolent disturbances include hunger strikes, sit-down strikes, voluntary lock-downs, work stoppages, excessive numbers of inmates reporting for sick call, and the filing of grievances by nearly everyone in a cellblock or even throughout the institution. Violent disturbances consist of crowding around correctional officers and intimidating them not to write disciplinary tickets; assaulting officers; sabotaging the plumbing, electrical, or heating systems; burning or destroying institutional property; and attempting to take control, with or without hostages, of a cellblock, a yard, or even an entire prison.

Beginning in the 1960s, riots became a threatening feature of prison life in correctional institutions in the United States. Then, on Friday, September 9, 1971, the Attica riot erupted. When assault forces retook the prison on Monday, September 13, thirty-nine individuals were killed (twenty-nine inmates and ten hostages).[19] The riot at the New Mexico State Prison in Santa Fe began shortly after midnight on Saturday, February 2, 1980. The savagery that took place eventually cost thirty-three lives and hundreds of beaten, raped, and psychologically scarred prisoners and staff.[20] During the 1980s, numerous incidents of vandalism, arson, and riots took place in men's prisons. In the 1990s, prison riots continued to be a problem as they took place in the Federal Bureau of Prisons and state prison systems in Alabama, Illinois, Ohio, Pennsylvania, Tennessee, and Texas.

In 2000, inmates committed 17,263 assaults against staff and 32,831 assaults against other inmates. Of the assaults for which medical attention was required in 2000, 1,600 of them against staff required medical attention and 7,797 against inmates required medical attention. Of the assaults referred for prosecution, 1,774 were against staff and 2,394 were against inmates.[21]

In California, inmates committed 2,813 assaults against staff and 4,397 against other inmates. Other states with large numbers of inmate assaults were Texas (2,267 on staff and 1,618 on inmates) and Missouri (1,022 on staff and 478 on inmates). The Bureau of Prisons had 1,095 inmate assaults on staff and 1,443 assaults on other inmates.[22]

Finally, severe beatings of inmates by prison staff have occurred throughout U.S. correctional history. Today, although there is less evidence of staff's inappropriate use of force on inmates, prisoners' rights organizations continue to accuse staffs of retaliating against rioting inmates after regaining control of the cellblock or prison. The most documented use of staff brutality against inmates took place in the 1990s in California's Corcoran and Pelican Bay Prisons. From 1988 to 1996, correctional officers at Corcoran Prison shot and killed seven inmates and wounded about fifty others. Lieutenant Steve Riggs, who worked at Corcoran about then charged that "of all the shootings, right off the top of my head, I'd say about 80 percent of them are [inappropriate] shootings."[23]

Racial Conflicts

In the traditional prison, African-Americans were usually docile. However, in the late 1960s and early 1970s, African-American prisoners began to incorporate the perspective of black power and saw their role as prisoners in a corrupt and oppressive state. The degradation and debasement of being an inmate still posed serious threats to self-esteem, and increasing numbers of African-American inmates began to conclude that one way to regain some sense of self-pride was to exploit and dominate whites in every conceivable way.[24]

By the 1990s, prisons were more racially polarized than ever before. Within each group there was at least one leader. Racial tension and hostility became so intense in some prisons that different racial and ethnic groups avoided each other as much as possible. Even a slight disagreement among races could quickly spark violence.[25]

Inmate Gangs

Prison gangs exist in at least forty states and in the Federal Bureau of Prisons.[26] In California, Illinois, and Texas, prison gangs are the dominant force in prison life. Prison gangs vary from loosely organized to highly organized and structured groups. The gangs that are reconstituted from the streets of cities in California and Illinois are especially highly organized. Prison gangs usually specialize in economic victimization. They generally force all independent operators out of business and either divide among themselves the spoils of drugs, gambling rackets, and prostitution rings, or they fight to the death to determine who will establish a monopoly within the prison.[27]

Prisoners' Rights

The autocratic warden ruled the prison with the assumption that the convicted felon was "civilly dead." However, from 1966 to 1976, judges did a 180-degree reversal and became extensively involved in rulings on prisoners' rights, and inmates won important rights concerning personal correspondence, their rights during disciplinary procedures, and their rights concerning the quality of medical care.[28]

Since the 1970s, prisoners have appealed to the federal courts in civil rights suits challenging every aspect of prison practices and programs. In 2000, although federal and state prisoners filed 58,257 petitions in U.S. District Courts, the Prison Litigation Reform Act (PLRA), passed by Congress and signed by President Clinton in 1996, has limited the ability of prisoners to complain about conditions of confinement and to allege violations of their constitutional rights.[29] The PLRA appears to have had the greatest impact on civil rights prisoners, from whom the number of petitions filed dropped between 1995 and 2000 from 41,679 to 25,504.[30]

Get Tough on Prisoners Mood of the 1990s

In the 1990s, a get-tough perspective advocated that society needs to "get even" with those who do social harm. This perspective argued that the longer people are incarcerated and the worse their conditions of confinement are, the less likely they will be to commit another crime. The wide acceptance of this repressive position is evident in the reinstatement of chain gangs and striped convict uniforms in some jurisdictions. In other jurisdictions, air conditioners, televisions, and weight training equipment have been removed from correctional facilities. In still other jurisdictions, incentives for good behavior have been eliminated, visiting rules revised, and educational and vocational programs have been reduced or abolished.[31]

The policy of maximizing punishments was bluntly stated by former Massachusetts Governor William Weld, who said in April 1998 that life in prison should be "akin to a walk through the fires of hell."[32] What has added to these restrictions of programs and services for inmates is the financial crisis, or budgetary shortfalls, of the early years of the twenty-first century, which have affected nearly every correctional system in the United States.

What Explains the Disillusioned Mood of the Twenty-first Century?

The mood of many correctional administrators in the early twenty-first century is one of disillusionment. In the last couple of decades of the twentieth century, resourceful correctional administrators had found ways to manage the long-standing problems, such as overpopulation, inmate gangs, violence, and racial conflict. Yet, the policy of "making prisoners' suffer" that began in the 1990s and the financial crisis, or budgetary shortfalls, which erupted in the early twenty-first century, began to affect the morale of even the most positive administrators. What was so discouraging was the elimination of positive programming that these policies had brought to prisons.

To evaluate the degree that corrections professionals might be disillusioned at the present time, individuals interviewed for this book were asked questions relating to the purpose of imprisonment, the consequences of making imprisonment a miserable experience, and whether they were encouraged or discouraged about the present.

The Purpose of Imprisonment

To ascertain how correctional administrators and other articulate spokespersons on corrections defined the purpose of imprisonment, they were asked: Should prisons function in the criminal justice system as punishment or for punishment?

Every person who was interviewed felt that individuals are sent to prison as punishment. According to these respondents, the fact that inmates have lost such freedoms as access to family and friends and employment opportunities in the community was quite sufficient punishment. This attitude contrasts with the current mood among many politicians and the publics they serve that offenders are sent to prison for punishment, and the more extreme punishments they receive, the more they will learn that crime does not pay. Feature 2.3 contains representative answers to this question.

The importance of this question is that it gets at the issue of punitiveness versus humaneness. It would be troubling for these proactive correctional administrators to support punishing inmates in a punitive way. Indeed, all of their answers, in one way or the other, suggested that the desirable purpose of imprisonment is that inmates might profit from their time of incarceration.

The Goal of Making Inmates Miserable

Not surprisingly, then, the interviewees had strong reactions to the following question: Is it possible to make the prison experience so intimidating, brutal, and miserable that offenders will fear their return to prison and become law-abiding citizens? *See* Feature 2.4. There was total

Feature 2.3: Do Prisons Functions as Punishment or for Punishment?

Orville Pung, former commissioner of corrections in Minnesota, gave this answer:

> *"I believe in the tried and true notion that you go to prison as punishment, not for punishment. In a free and democratic society, the loss of freedom is one of the most significant losses you can have. Drive by a large military cemetery and you see that people died for freedom. So, going to prison and losing all of your freedom twenty-four hours a day, seven days a week, is, in itself, all the punishment you need. To take the next step and make the condition intentionally miserable is to set up an environment in which you have nothing but retribution. Inmates, in turn, would be likely to respond in the same manner."*

James Bruton, former warden of the Minnesota Correctional Facility, Oak Park Heights, answered the question on the purpose of imprisonment in much the same way:

> *"The whole idea of the purpose of prisons is an easy one. Frank Wood always said: 'The punishment is being in prison,' and those facilities which have decided to extend the punishment beyond being in prison are making mistakes. Usually, you'll find those mistakes inherent in the way those prisons operate every day. If you look at the general public's attitudes of trying to get tough on crime and to punish offenders far beyond incarceration, I sometimes think that what they want us to do is to poke inmates with a hot stick every day and make their lives miserable. Yet, at the same time, they want us to rehabilitate people and to have them come out of prison as better persons than they when they went in. Frankly, it just doesn't work that way.*
>
> *"You have to find a way to deal with the fact that people are incarcerated. Their freedom is taken away and within this context you need to try to do everything you can to change their lives. Frank Wood put into place a concept that was 'creating an environment that is conducive to rehabilitation for those offenders who are inclined to want to make a change in their lives.' To provide an opportunity for people to make a change in their lives is critical. If somebody can't read, why wouldn't we teach them how to read? If they don't have an education, why wouldn't we teach them how to better prepare themselves for the future of employment or whatever. The fact is that 95 percent of the people who come to prison get out someday. So, the idea of locking people up and throwing away the key does not give people coming out with much of a chance."*

Sources: Interviewed in September and October of 2002.

consensus among the interviewees that this intent of making the prison experience miserable and intimidating would have serious negative repercussions. Some of the responses follow.

Are You Encouraged or Discouraged about Corrections Today?

Several of the respondents were asked to appraise how they felt about corrections in the present and to compare prisons in the early stage of their career to prisons now: Are you encouraged or discouraged? Nearly all of the answers shown in Feature 2.5 sounded some note of discouragement.

Answers differ as to why the spirit of disillusionment had such a pervasive influence on corrections. Some argue that the dark ages of

Feature 2.4: Is it Desirable to Make the Prison Experience Intimidating, Brutal, and Miserable?

Alvin J. Bronstein, former director of the American Civil Liberties Union (ACLU), responded to the question in this way:

"Absolutely not, the contrary is true. The more brutal and miserable a prison experience is, the more likely the prisoner on release will be increasingly dangerous. Charles Manson is a good example of that. He went into the juvenile system in California and was brutalized there because he was acting up. Then, he got into the adult system and was brutalized, kept in solitary and beaten, and he came out a monster. Jack Abbott in the federal system was a man that Norman Mailer arranged for the release of because he thought he was a brilliant writer, which he was. Abbott was a client of mine and had been brutalized in prison. He had been in solitary for so long at the federal penitentiary level that I wouldn't have voted to let him out if I were on the parole board. Somehow, Mailer convinced the federal folks to let him out and within weeks he killed somebody in a restaurant. I could have predicted that was going to happen. So, an intimidating, brutal prison experience does not make law-abiding citizens. It makes really dangerous people when they are released."

Chase Riveland, former secretary of corrections in Washington State, adds a similar response in his answer to the question:

"Average citizens certainly would blanch at the potential of having their freedom taken away and put in grim environmental conditions such as a prison. But I think that losing their freedom does not prevent recidivism in people who have in the past committed crimes.

"On the other hand, I think there are too many instances in this country where we placed people in our prisons in extremely onerous conditions and probably have returned them to the community in much worse shape then they were before. We now have the advent of supermax-type lockdowns where the individual is removed from human contact other than with their controllers. I suspect in the long term we are going to find out this form of confinement is extremely harmful to the individuals who have suffered through it."

Mary Leftridge Byrd, former superintendent of the State Correctional Institution at Chester, gave this response to the question of whether an intimidating and miserable prison experience would help a person avoid the experience again:

"I don't think so. If the prison experience is so miserable and brutal, I think the opposite effect will occur. I'm not a psychologist, but it seems to me that an individual would become more antisocial as a result of living in a place where there is no order, where there is no respect, and where human beings are devalued. I think that he will become more lawless if only in an effort to survive the brutality of the environment. So, in my mind, intimidation, brutality, and the intent to make a place miserable is oxymoronic to anything that looks like an environment where folks can learn to be law-abiding citizens."

Feature 2.4: Is it Desirable to Make the Prison Experience Intimidating, Brutal, and Miserable? (con't)

Burl Cain, warden of the Louisiana State Penitentiary at Angola, contributed the following response to making the prison environment so intimidating that offenders will fear their return:

"Making the prison experience so intimidating can be compared to attempting to 'scare someone straight.' These programs fail compared to being brutally honest. You can't scare someone into doing right. Criminals don't usually think that they will get caught and almost none think about the consequences of breaking the law. However, to explain the real every-day sadness that occurs from being separated from all that you know and love and to make someone realize the extreme limitations placed on what you can accomplish usually serves as a greater deterrent to people who have any desire to remain free. The cycle of violence continues with prisoners who are released after having experienced horrible prison time. They leave feeling they have been 'victimized.' It increases their negative attitude and gives them an excuse to be failures, deviants, and law breakers."

Finally, Kathleen Hawk Sawyer, former director of the Bureau of Prisons, answered this question about whether it is possible to make the prison experience so intimidating, brutal, and miserable that offenders will fear their return to prison and become law-abiding citizens:

"I believe the concept suggested in this question is misguided. The United States Constitution, along with Federal and State laws, establish minimal standards of care to which all inmates are entitled. The Federal Bureau of Prisons confines inmates in prisons and community-based facilities that are safe, humane, cost-efficient, and appropriately secure; and provides opportunities and programs to help inmates develop the skills they will need to remain crime-free after release. We have found that this approach is supported by both experience and research. For example, research documented by the Bureau of Prisons confirms significantly reduced recidivism and institution misconduct when inmates are provided with vocational and educational training and appropriate self-improvement opportunities focusing on pro-social skill development."

Sources: Interviewed September through November, 2002.

corrections in some respects have returned because of the supermax prisons and the miserable time that inmates have in these and other correctional facilities. Others explain the disillusionment because of the failure of correctional leadership to stand up to politicians and to generate excitement about the field of corrections. Still others contend that it is the struggle with the economy which make it difficult to be anything but discouraged in running a correctional system.

How Can We Move from the Spirit of Disillusionment to a New Day

One of the most serious questions today in corrections is: How can we overcome the mood of disillusionment and develop a new day in corrections? This new day must be one in which both inmates and staff are treated with dignity and respect. It must be one in which both inmates and staff are safe in correctional facilities. It must be one in which staff are motivated to come to work and feel a real sense of purpose in what they do.

Feature 2.5: Are You Encouraged or Discouraged?

Alvin J. Bronstein, former director of the American Civil Liberties Union, provides a thought-provoking answer to whether he was encouraged or discouraged:

"I would have to say both. When I started looking at prisons in the late 1960s, prisons were really pretty awful in this country. You had a lot of nineteenth century dungeons still around. You still have a few, but most of those are gone. The Los Angeles county jail is a facility that holds 7,000 people in one building. Although it was built in the 1960s, in my opinion, it is a nineteenth-century dungeon. It is as bad as the central prison or jail in Moscow today, but most of those old medieval horrible places have been closed.

"You have cleaner facilities today. You have some degree of medical care in just about every prison and jail in the country. In the 1960s and 1970s, there was no medical care in any prison in the country with a few exceptions, such as the Minnesota facilities and a couple of the California facilities.

"There are better trained staff today. In the 1960s and 1970s, there was little or no staff training. The people working as correctional officers were the dregs of the law enforcement community. People who couldn't get a job as a police officer or who had been fired as police officers wound up as prison guards. Today, both on the federal level and at the state level, there's serious training that goes on. There's also training for wardens. I know the National Institute of Corrections runs a training program for new wardens every summer. There are now professional standards for prisons: the American Correctional Association Standards and the American Public Health Association Standards. A lot of this resulted from litigation that was filed by my office and others in the 1960s and 1970s because the judges were beginning to advocate standards.

"I can remember when the statewide Alabama prison lawsuit was decided by Judge Frank Johnson. There was a lot of publicity about his decision, for he declared for the first time that these prisons were unconstitutional because they were actually making people worse and making them less able to function when they got out than when they went in. He ruled that this was a violation of the Eighth Amendment. Then, he attached to his opinion what he called minimum constitutional standards; what he really meant was court-imposed standards for the Alabama prison system, but the press caught on to this minimum-constitutional standards.

"I can remember Ken Schoen [Commissioner of Minnesota's Department of Corrections at the time] calling me the next day and asking for a copy of the standards. He wanted to make sure that Minnesota was complying with all of these things. Not every commissioner called, but as I have said, Minnesota was fairly unique.

"I should add that although in many respects we no longer have the nineteenth-century dungeons, we have twenty-first century horrible places. I'm thinking primarily of the huge prisons and the supermax prisons being built around the country, the Pelican Bay facility in California, the Oklahoma facility [McAlester Maximum Security Prison in Oklahoma City] . . . and those prisons that were built in Texas in the last few years. In many respects, they regressed to the past."

Feature 2.5: Are You Encouraged or Discouraged? (con't)

Patrick McManus, former commissioner of corrections in Kansas and corrections official in Minnesota, responded to this question of whether he is encouraged or discouraged by making this statement:

"We clearly went through a period in the 1960s and 1970s and 1980s where we did head out of the forest and the dark ages and got away from a lot of the terrible problems that had been toler-ated in prisons and jails throughout this nation.

"The political environment in which corrections is a perennial problem has emerged in the past several years with a vengeance. It is interfering with holding up corrections as a legitimate profession. I know commissioners' jobs have always been political. They are appointed by governors and so they have to be aware of their political world in which they function. But it seems that much of the leadership in corrections as a profession is disappearing. We have become more attuned to the political realities of the 1990s and the early twenty-first century, the mood of harshness and vindictiveness and the sense that we want to lock everyone up, with the notion that prisoners deserve all of our wrath and our indignation. I guess there has always been that element; prisoners have never been popular people, and they never will be, because they don't have their own constituencies. But this attitude shouldn't set the tone and agenda for corrections professionals. And I'm afraid that more and more, it does.

"What is discouraging to me is I don't see enough leadership coming from the correctional community. We have learned a lot about running prisons is the last thirty, forty, and fifty years, about what works and what doesn't work. But somehow, we don't communicate what we know very effectively to the decision makers. The discussion of correctional issues in the public has been led mostly by people who don't know very much about corrections. There was a time when corrections folks got together, had lively discussions and even some good arguments. But it was usually a vibrant and alive atmosphere, looking toward the future, where people were talking about trying new things. There was some excitement about corrections. I don't find much of that today."

Chase Riveland, former commissioner of corrections in Washington State, had this to add about whether he was encouraged or discouraged by what is taking place in corrections today:

"There is good news and bad news as I look back to when I began my career in 1964, almost forty years ago. In the correctional business in the 1960s, we were still paying attention to rehabilitative programs and treatment programming.

"Then, we moved into an era of heavily increased sentencing to prison and of finding difficulty in keeping up in building new prisons, especially in those jurisdictions where incarceration or prison sentences became a sentence of choice. The overcrowding that took place led to severe challenges to prison administrators who had to place two or more inmates in a cell that had been previously allocated for one.

"At the same time, the good news was that the corrections field was heavily challenged to improve its responses, and, for the most part, improvements did take place. I think correctional staff did a good job in responding to difficult situations, particularly in the several

Feature 2.5: Are You Encouraged or Discouraged? (con't)

years where the political rhetoric suggested 'get tough on folks' and take away all their opportunities. This was a hard dose to swallow for correctional staff who knew better.

"Yet, as I look today at the correctional future, I suspect we may be facing one of the biggest challenges that we have faced in the last fifty years. This challenge focuses on the economy being what it is: state revenues are extremely tight in at least forty-eight out of fifty state jurisdictions across the country and legislative bodies are having difficulty in balancing budgets. There really is no immediate hope for the next two, three, or four years.

"The fiscal changes are going to be enormous because during the entire period of significant growth, correctional systems in most states became one of the top two or three consumers of state revenue of all state agencies. To maintain that, of course, would be very challenging and questionable. So what I think will happen, and we are beginning to see it in some jurisdictions, is that jurisdictions are looking for ways to decrease the size of their inmate population. There will be early releases or alternatives to incarceration on the front-end, but normally those policy decisions don't come fast enough. I think we are going to find another round of severe overcrowding, which will probably be followed by intervention of the courts regarding conditions of confinement. Hopefully, policy changes can occur in most jurisdictions that will help us get back to looking at the prison as an option of last choice rather than first choice."

Sources: Interviewed in October and November of 2002.

The rest of this book is devoted to laying out a plan for the realization of this new day. Frank W. Wood, the former warden of two correctional facilities in Minnesota and the former commissioner of corrections in Minnesota, provides the principles, philosophy, and proactive leadership of this plan. He is a person who has influenced the state of corrections in Minnesota. The quality of his leadership can become a model for corrections throughout the United States and can help correctional leaders overcome their present disillusionment. Fortunately, his proactive style of leadership finds support with a number of wardens/superintendents and directors/commissioners/secretaries of corrections across the nation. What is needed now is for a critical mass of other correctional administrators to join Wood and his cohorts. Then, corrections will have an opportunity to transcend the darkness of the 1990s and to realize the possibility of the glorious light of a new day.

Summary

Changes took place following World War II. One change that had an enormous impact on corrections was the bureaucratization of corrections. State departments of corrections were established in which a director or commissioner (or a secretary in a few corrections systems) from the state capital controls what occurs in prisons throughout the state. His or her task is to make certain that individual wardens follow the rules or regulations that have been set up.

The bureaucratization of corrections was one of the reasons for the demise of the autocratic warden. The autocratic warden had no place in the new system of delegated responsibility. Yet, for the final three decades of the twentieth century, no form of prison administration seemed to be able to control the prison. The Texas Control Model was proposed in Texas and elsewhere, but the *Ruiz v. Estelle* court decision totally dismantled this system. There are also valid questions about the legitimization of this repressive and brutal system.

Others proposed models of correctional administration. Some involved the private sector management model; others had to do with staff and inmate participation in prison governance; others had to do with bringing inmate gangs into the decision-making processes that takes place within a prison. Functional units, or unit management, were proposed by the Federal Bureau of Prisons as a means to run the prison. State corrections systems have not been as willing as the federal system has been to invest resources in this means of correctional administration.[33]

The fact is that prisons were increasingly difficult to manage in the late twentieth century. They were crowded, more violent than ever before, filled with inmates who had drug and alcohol addictions and were eager to receive their drugs of choice; they dealt with racial conflicts, inmate gangs, and a decline in a rehabilitation ideology. In addition, the "make prisoners suffer" policy of the 1990s, along with financial problems in nearly every state in the early twenty-first century seemed to be totally demoralizing.

No wonder that so many wardens found that their careers posed overwhelming challenges that simply wore them down. But in the midst of those who were disillusioned, Frank Wood and a few other proactive wardens stood out. The rest of this book will examine this group and provide examples of how others can emulate their behaviors.

ENDNOTES

[1]List provided by Frank Wood.

[2]Interviewed in December 1980.

[3]Peter Drucker. 1954. *The Practice of Management.* New York: Harper; and Peter A. Pyhrr. 1973. *Zero Based Budgeting: A Practical Management Tool for Evaluating Expenses.* New York: Wiley.

[4]Pyhrr, *Zero Based Budgeting.*

[5]Tom O. Murton. 1975. *Shared Decision-Making as a Treatment Technique in Prison Management.* Minneapolis: The Murton Foundation for Criminal Justice.

[6]*Ibid.*

[7]Israel L. Barak-Glantz. 1981. Toward a Conceptual Schema of Prison Management Styles. *The Prison Journal*, p. 51.

[8]John J. DiIulio, Jr. 1987. *Governing Prisons: A Comparative Study of Correctional Management.* New York: Free Press.

[9]*See* Robert B. Levinson. 1999. *Unit Management in Prisons and Jails.* Lanham, Maryland: American Correctional Association.

[10]DiIulio, *Governing Prisons*, p. 30.

[11]Bert Useem and Peter Kimball. 1989. *Stages of Siege: U.S. Prison Riots, 1971-1986.* New York: Oxford University Press, p. 227.

[12]*Ruiz v. Estelle*, 503 F. Supp 1265 (S.D. Texas, 1980).

[13]For the development of the Texas Control Model, *see* the interview with George Beto in Clemens Bartollas. 1981. *Introduction to Corrections.* New York: Harper and Row, pp. 306-309.

[14]*Ibid.*, p. 128.

[15]*Ibid.*, pp. 128-134.

[16]*Ibid.*

[17]*Ibid.*

[18]*See* Bureau of Justice Statistics. *Prisoners in 2002.* Washington, D.C.: U.S. Department of Justice.

[19]*See* 1972. *Attica: The Official Report of the New York State Special Commission on Attica.* New York: Praeger.

[20]*See* Mark Colvin. 1990. *From Accommodation to Riot: The Penitentiary of New Mexico in Crisis.* Albany: State University of New York Press.

[21]Camille Graham Camp and George M. Camp, 2002. *The Corrections Yearbook 2001: Adult Corrections.* Middletown, Connecticut: Criminal Justice Institute, p. 53.

[22]*Ibid.*

[23]Don Knapp. 1996. California Prison at Center of Violence Accusations. CNN Interactive, November, 22. Available at http://www.cnn.com/US/9611/22/prison.shooting.

[24] *Ibid.*

[25] *See* Leo Carroll. 1974. *Hacks, Blacks, and Cons: Race Relations in a Maximum Security Prison.* Lexington, Massachusetts: Heath.

[26] American Correctional Association. 1993. *Gangs in Correctional Institutions: A National Assessment.* Lanham, Maryland: American Correctional Association, pp. 8-9.

[27] D. Orlando-Morningstar. 1997. *Prison Gangs.* Washington, D.C.: Federal Judicial Center.

[28] *See* Clemens Bartollas. 2002. *Invitation to Corrections.* Boston: Allyn and Bacon, pp. 469-475.

[29] Kathleen Maguire and Ann L. Pastore. 1999. *Bureau of Justice Statistics: Sourcebook of Criminal Justice Statistics 1998.* Washington, D.C.: U.S. Department of Justice, p. 443.

[30] John Scalia. 2002. "Prisoner Petitions Filed in U.S. District Courts, 2000, with Trends 1980-2000." *Bureau of Justice Statistics Special Report.* Washington, D.C.: U.S. Department of Justice.

[31] Stephen J. Ingley. 2000. Corrections without Correction. In John P. May, ed. *Building Violence.* Thousand Oaks, California: Sage Publications, p. 20.

[32] Governor William Weld's Keynote speech at the U.S. Attorney General's Summit on Corrections, April 27, 1998, quoted in Kenneth L. McGinnis. 2000. Make 'Em Break Rocks. In John P. May, ed. *Building Violence.* Thousand Oaks, California: Sage Publications, p. 35.

[33] Leonard Witke, ed. 2000. *Planning and Design Guide for Secure Adult and Juvenile Facilities.* Lanham, Maryland: American Correctional Association.

Chapter Three:

Reform in Minnesota Prisons: Management Trumps Architecture

David A. Ward, University of Minnesota

Trying to reform a troubled social institution calls for more than timing. It requires an executive with the right management strategy. Minnesota's Department of Corrections in the late 1960s and early 1970s had a reputation for progressive penal policy, but it also had a state penitentiary wracked by violence and disorder.

Superintendents before Wood

From 1967 to 1971, Paul W. Keve, whose background was in probation, advanced the argument that what Minnesota needed to improve the state's penal institutions were wardens with master's degrees in social work; those with degrees in other fields were advised to return to the University of Minnesota and obtain the proper credentials. Keve's administration represented the high point in the application of the medical "model" in a field that began calling itself "corrections."

According to the medical model theory, prisoners were patients suffering from various psychological ills, social disadvantages, and disabilities. These deficiencies were to be corrected by social work professionals who would diagnose, treat, and cure the prisoners of their criminal ways. Life at the state prison at Stillwater and at the St. Cloud Reformatory was not made safer by the theories of social work. The warden at Stillwater was stabbed by a prisoner, an escape attempt at Stillwater involved officers taken as hostages, a riot at Stillwater required the use of shotguns and tear gas, and there were disturbances at the reformatory. Keve was not reappointed when a new governor, Wendell Anderson, came to office. The reasons for his dismissal were not announced because negotiations were underway with a replacement—a professor of criminology from California.

The Fogel Administration

The appointment in 1971 of David Fogel ushered in three years during which his "justice model" was applied to the Department of Corrections. A due process system for prison discipline was established along with a new office for the "Ombudsman for Corrections"—an agency independent of the Department of Corrections. Fogel's dramatic entrance into the Minnesota prison scene began with his surreptitious commitment as a prisoner to Stillwater where he spent several days observing the staff and seeking inmates' views of prison life. In the months ahead, he returned to the prison to continue discussions with this group of prisoners. Warden Jack Young resigned in protest arguing that "hanging with the prisoners" cost Fogel any credibility with the staff. Bruce McManus was appointed warden, and Fogel went about the business of reform.

Stillwater was opened up to free world visitors and organizations to reduce the "damage done by the correctional experience."[1] Visiting hours were expanded from four to sixteen hours per month and barriers between the visitors and the prisoners were removed. In some weeks, the number of visitors exceeded the number of inmates—around 800. With the elimination of barriers to physical contact and so many groups meeting in various locations throughout the prison, smuggling drugs and other contraband into the prison as well as sexual activities became a problem.[2] In one highly publicized initiative, Fogel allowed the participation of several prisoners in a production at the Guthrie Theater until one of the "actors" absconded. Twelve ex-inmates were brought on staff as counselors under the theory that as "change agents" they could more easily communicate and influence prisoners than traditional employees.[3]

The custodial staff perceived Fogel as a radical reformer who brought in some of his colleagues from California to help him change the entire Department of Corrections. His extraverted personal style and what many custodial employees regarded as his disdain for their role in the correctional enterprise led to charges that some staff members were trying to sabotage his agenda by allowing prisoners to engage in activities that attracted negative press and public attention.

The real problem for Commissioner Fogel, however, was related less to objections to his penal philosophy than to the disturbing number of inmate deaths at Stillwater due to drug overdoses (three in 1971 and 1972) and suicides (seven from 1971 to 1973). Staff complained that the prison was, "out of control" and that reports of drug use, sexual activity, and other misconduct were due to the uncertainty of the custodial staff about enforcing rules in Stillwater's open, pro "inmate rights" environment. When Fogel resigned in 1973 to take a job as Commissioner of Corrections in Illinois, most Department of Corrections' employees heaved a big sigh of relief.[4]

Fogel's successor, Kenneth F. Schoen, a tall, blonde, Nordic-appearing native son made Minnesotans feel much more comfortable. Unlike the four commissioners who preceded him, Schoen had worked his way up in the Department of Corrections to the position of Superintendent of the State Training School for Girls and gained attention when he had made the institution coeducational.

The Schoen Administration

During Kenneth Schoen's tenure in Minnesota, he inherited major staff morale and inmate violence problems at Stillwater, which led to a deputy commissioner and the warden being replaced. He advanced a reform agenda that brought about fundamental changes in Minnesota's penal policy and practice. For these efforts, Schoen had the advantage of appearing to make "reasonable" the more radical changes advocated by his predecessor. His primary task still related to the dysfunctional state prison.

The open-up-the prison policy at Stillwater during the Fogel administration and the first years of the Schoen administration represented a new direction in prison management and operations. It came during an era of increasing "rights" for prisoners and a decline in belief in the efficacy of rehabilitation behind prison walls. These shifts in penal philosophy paved the way for the movement away from incarceration toward, "community corrections." The prisoners expressed increasing concern about the justice of never knowing their release date under the state's indeterminate sentencing system.

Yet, continued violence at the prison overshadowed consideration of the larger policy issues. From October 1973 to October 1975, Stillwater prison recorded fifty-six assaults on correctional officers, forty-three assaults on inmates, seventy-five cases in which prisoners possessed weapons, and three attempted escapes. The problem of suicides continued with four more, in 1974 and 1975, all by hanging, making a total of eleven in a four-year period. In addition, four inmates were murdered in 1974-1975.

The number of outside visitors and community groups coming to the prison compromised security beyond staff resources (between January and September 1975 there were 18,805 visitors). Then, in May 1975, yet another inmate murder provided the ultimate indication of the breakdown in security at the prison, as well as evidence of staff-inmate collusion.

The Segredi Case

On the morning of April 10, 1975, a lieutenant at Stillwater overheard inmate William Segredi making threats "of an extortion nature" to an officer.[5] Removed from the cell house, Segredi began naming specific employees with whom he had dealings ranging from the sale of diamond rings he obtained while in the prison, to obtaining tickets to professional hockey games which he gave to staff members, to having money orders cashed for him by a correctional officer. Segredi's attorney was called to the prison and was present when his client's statements were tape recorded; the tapes were placed in the attorney's custody with the understanding that no action would be taken pending Segredi's imminent departure on a retainer to the state of Tennessee. The lieutenant who questioned Segredi searched his cell, where he found in a notebook pages containing the names of staff members "with numbers and notations after the names."[6] Segredi's allegations against ten employees were brought to the attention of the warden, the associate warden, and the captain, and for his protection, Segredi was moved to the prison's maximum-custody unit. Over the next two weeks, he gave interviews to prison investigators and to staff of the Attorney General's Office. On May 5, Segredi informed his attorney that threats on his life had been made. Warden McManus sought to transfer him to the nearby county jail, but in the absence of approval by the sheriff who was out of town that day, the decision was made to delay the transfer until the following morning.

Also housed in the maximum-custody unit, in addition to Segredi, were six prisoners, "who had demonstrated by institution behavior that they were dangerous or potentially dangerous, [requiring that they should be] placed in a unit where they would be safe from each other, [and] segregated from the rest of the prison population." This unit had four tiers and on May 5, individual inmates were placed in cells on the second and third tiers—five prisoners, including Segredi, were placed in cells on the fourth tier. Warden McManus later reported that he "presumed the unit was operating under policies which did not permit physical contact with other occupants." A memorandum notifying staff that Segredi would be leaving the prison the next morning was left on a desk in the unit.

During the evening watch, three officers with very little experience were on duty. The officer in charge had worked at the prison for five months. The second officer had been on duty for less than three weeks, and the third for one month. Remarkably for a maximum-custody unit, a unit that in contemporary penitentiaries would be called a "control unit," a sergeant on an earlier shift had authorized the inmates to be out of their cells, free to associate with each other, until 11:00 p.m. A 10:30 p.m. entry in the log recorded that seven inmates were in the unit at that time, but none of the officers had gone to the fourth tier to physically observe the prisoners.

At 11 p.m. when two officers went up to the fourth tier, they found William Segredi dead on his bed, "a cord around his neck was attached to a cell brace above him." Suicide was ruled out the next day following an examination of the body by the county coroner. Subsequent investigation, including lie detector tests, provided no indication that any of the three officers was involved in Segredi's demise; two resigned their jobs, the third was given a temporary suspension but remained on the staff.

Four prisoners were indicted for Segredi's murder by a county grand jury. The first was tried but acquitted after another prisoner testified that he could pick the lock in the door to the maximum-security unit, meaning that up to sixty other prisoners could have had access to Segredi. At that point, the judge discharged the defendant. Two of the remaining prisoners who had been charged were transferred to prisons in other states, and the fourth was sent off to be boarded with the Federal Bureau of Prisons. No employees were indicted.

The press, the public, and legislative reaction to this event can be summed up by this headline in a local newspaper: "Segredi Slaying Laid to Prison Bungling."[7] Commissioner Schoen blamed the death on "administrative problems" at Stillwater, replaced the deputy commissioner in charge of adult male prisons, and announced that, "prison personnel are being more closely supervised, steps are being taken to bring inmate predators . . . under control . . . and hand-held metal detectors are used . . . to control the flow of weapons." Schoen told reporters, "I am convinced that the leadership and administration of the prison is in very capable hands." Warden McManus, however, expressed uncertainty as to, "whether the new policies have had any effect on drug traffic or weapons. Drug smuggling cannot be stopped. It can only be controlled."[8]

In June 1975, the Washington County Grand Jury issued a report which characterized the Segredi killing as "a tragic comedy of errors."[9] Along with a long list of recommended changes in operations at Stillwater, the grand jury called for an independent investigation of the prison. Such an investigation had already begun in the late spring of that year in response to the killings, suicides, and assaults in the prison. The Minnesota's Legislature formed a Joint Committee of the House and Senate which, in July 1975 with a staff of eleven investigators, proceeded to conduct an exhaustive investigation of Stillwater's "internal operations, programs, and administration."[10]

Despite his public expression of confidence in Warden McManus and his administration, Commissioner Schoen launched his own inquiry to be conducted by Frank W. Wood who had begun his career in the Department of Corrections in 1959 as a correctional officer at Stillwater. Two years later, he was promoted to sergeant at the Stillwater Facility; in 1963, Wood was promoted to shift supervisor at the newly opened Lino Lakes Facility where he received several additional promotions and, by 1972, he held the position of assistant to the superintendent. The following year, he took a position in the Department of Corrections' Central Office as director of inspection and enforcement. Wood and his staff were responsible for inspecting all adult county and city jails and lock-ups. They also inspected and licensed county juvenile facilities. In 1974, Wood was given the responsibility to inspect all prisons, and one year later he was asked to re-inspect Stillwater Prison. In his first report, Wood said that the tattered flag above the entrance to Stillwater seemed to symbolize conditions inside the prison.

In February 1976, the Joint House-Senate Committee released a devastating critique of the prison. In May of 1976, Schoen replaced Warden McManus with Frank Wood. Prior to his appointment, Wood persuaded Schoen that to make the changes that would be necessary at Stillwater, the prison staff and inmates had to know that the warden, not the central office, was running the prison. Three years of interventions in prison operations by central office administrators had convinced Wood that the responsibility for problems at Stillwater rested with not only the warden but with those supervising and directing the warden from the central office. Schoen agreed that Wood would run the prison with the autonomy and support he needed to bring about change.[11]

Restoring Order in Stillwater Prison

The immediate task confronting Frank Wood was to respond to the principal findings of the legislative committee report. *See* Feature 3.1.

Frank Wood's view was that "you can't have a democracy if you are running a prison, a benevolent dictatorship is required." His first steps were to replace the associate warden and the assistant to the warden; within six months all top level employees who reported directly to the warden had been replaced. He found that some employees had become intimidated and "were afraid to take things away from inmates." One administrator who was uncomfortable with the changes Wood was making told Wood "that on more than one occasion, he was throwing up in the morning while brushing his teeth before coming to work." Wood offered to locate another position for him in the department and he accepted the offer. Wood sat in on an inmate council meeting with his administrative staff to monitor the dynamics of a typical meeting. The council had been accustomed to telling the staff how things would be. Wood observed and heard inmates screaming profanities at the staff. Immediately after that meeting, he abolished the inmate council and formed a group of inmate representatives he appointed. His next move was to fire the editor of the inmate newspaper because, "He routinely incited the inmates." Wood was sued by the editor but won. For Wood, inmate editors worked for the publisher, the warden, who insisted that all articles had to be based on fact.[12]

The House-Senate Committee investigation revealed that prisoners had been allowed to accumulate large amounts of, "personal property such as television, clothing other than that

Feature 3.1: Principal Findings of the Legislative Committee Report

"The Joint Committee had concluded that the Minnesota State Prison has not provided adequate security either for its inmates or its staff, and that while there are many reasons and causes for this lack of security, the basic responsibility for the institution's inability to cope with this problem rests with the prison management.

"The Minnesota State Prison, like other prisons, has had to face new forces seeking to shape and influence the style of prison life. The courts have imposed legal standards where once they restrained their power; inmate groups asserted themselves with a new-found militancy, organizing for change and not merely conspiring to riot; community groups have said, 'open up, we want to bring the life of the community to the men in prison' and have lobbied strongly to improve prison conditions and expand opportunities for prison inmates, sometimes with unrealistic expectations; political groups have sought to radicalize those in prison and put pressure on those who run the prison; lawyers have subjected prison decisions to scrutiny they have never been exposed to before. The list could go on and on.

"These phenomena were not unique to the Minnesota State Prison. In the late 1960s, this prison began responding to their pressures. By late 1971, the changes in internal operation were taking place with precipitous speed and the prison had great difficulty coping with these changes:

- Staff were not adequately prepared to handle change, whether internal privileges of inmates or new rules for the discipline system (which did not come until late 1973).
- Staff gave up firmly enforcing the rules of the institution.
- Line staff was inadequately trained and supervised in the performance of their duties.
- The turnover rate climbed as the staff's morale declined.

The prison managers were unable to plan and implement change at a pace that maintained reasonable security while still altering the level of inmate internal freedom.

"In the end, our conviction is that improving the delivery of programs and services in the prison depends on the same factors as improving safety and security—a competent administration that is able to motivate and lead its staff in shaping ideas and making them work. This is a goal that has thus far eluded the prison and the one we hope our report will stimulate."

Source: Joint House-Senate Committee Report on the Minnesota State Prison, February 1976, pp. 7-8.

issued by the state, jewelry, books, craft supplies, and similar items. . . . Inmates are allowed to lock their cells with padlocks . . . almost every inmate had a piece of plastic or a blanket covering the complete cell door so that no one could see the contents of the cell."[13] Wood ordered the removal of all but basic items from the cells—an effort that produced thirty truckloads of items not allowed by existing rules. In the process of examining the homemade furniture that was taken to the dump, shelves and dressers with false bottoms were found to contain drugs, money, and other contraband. Some inmates protested this action by burning their mattresses, but the removal proceeded.

Only 250 of 800 inmates had work assignments; the rest wandered around the institution. A system of surprise searches and lockdowns of the entire prison not related to incidents was initiated so that according to Wood, "the inmates started wondering when the next lock up would come."[14] These searches produced large quantities of contraband and prison-made weapons. Inmates were locked up at 10 p.m. and could no longer wander about cell blocks as they had until 1 and even 2 a.m. After Wood found that Stillwater was so understaffed that some posts were not staffed, he convinced the legislature to allow the hiring of new officers until every post was occupied. He ordered a clean up of the prison which had become "filthy."

Stillwater was constructed as a traditional "fortress" prison. Cell blocks five tiers high housed hundreds of inmates. Under the previous administration, misconduct by two inmates who, for example, had a fight, resulted in extended lock-ups of large groups of prisoners—a practice Wood ended along with the ability of the physically powerful inmates to use—that is monopolize—the use of cell house telephones. "The business of running a prison is control—opportunities [for inmates] can then follow for those who want them."[15]

Shortly before Wood's appointment as warden, the previous administration had retained a food service vendor. Wood worked closely with the food service vendor to improve the sanitation, cleanliness, and the quality and content of the meals. Within six months, inmate complaints about the food were almost nonexistent. Wood introduced new rules for searching visitors and supervising visits to "stop intercourse in the visiting room" and the introduction of drugs and other contraband. A section of noncontact visiting areas was built. Those inmates violating visiting and contraband rules were assigned to noncontact visiting.

Because the prison only had thirty disciplinary segregation cells, which were always occupied, a new arrival required that someone from the unit be returned to the general population. Wood cut one of the smaller cell blocks in half and turned 120 cells into "seg" cells. When he arrived, 100 prisoners were locked up in the protective custody unit, "never to leave their cells because the staff could not protect them." A year later, the number had been reduced to twenty. Wood ended uncontrolled inmate movement and the practice of having only ten staff members on duty to release the prisoners in the morning for breakfast and their daily activities. For Wood, the staff were not proactive but reacted only after an incident or problem occurred. "They were always waiting for what the inmates would do next."[16]

Under his predecessors, there had been no system of reporting the day's events to the warden. Wood began five-mornings-a-week staff meetings during which staff reported any deviation from the routine "in detail, from plumbing that doesn't work on up." The practice of assigning the least-experienced officers to work evenings and weekends was ended. The warden told the associate warden, captain and lieutenants:

> *Before we cancel any scheduled activity because of staff shortages they would fill the posts. It is essential that we deliver*

> *to inmates what we schedule in order to maintain credibility with the inmates and our organizational integrity. In the past, inmates viewed cancellation of activities as the staff arbitrarily looking for excuses to cancel their activities. The key to getting the support of the inmates was having the warden and all department heads meet every new arrival to lay out our philosophy, principles and expectations. We treated the inmates as we'd want to be treated.*[17]

Both inmates and staff had come to assume that verbal and physical abuse was part of prison life, which led to staff intimidation. Wood's strategy was, "to reduce assault, you target verbal abuse and disrespect" and he began walking through the prison by himself—"if I'm not safe then I will lock the place up. We had lots of counts and pat-searches so the inmates would learn to submit to authority and to cut down the flow of contraband."[18]

Wood demonstrated that the staff also would be held accountable for their actions. In 1977, four prisoners succeeded in cutting through the barred windows in a cell hall and escaped. Wood demoted a sergeant and suspended him for two weeks for missing the cut bars; two lieutenants received one-week suspensions for inadequate supervision while the escapees were painting the bars. Wood fired an officer after another escape in which a prisoner hid in the industries' area and, with a homemade hook, climbed over the wall near a staffed guard tower. He also suspended six employees including the officers who had twice counted a dummy the escapee had left in his cell; eleven other officers received written reprimands. The employee's union protested, but Wood's disciplinary actions were sustained.

Given Stillwater's well-documented history of violence, suicide, drug trafficking, and the high level of staff and inmate fear from the late 1960s to the mid 1970s, the question for all parties was how successful was the managerial strategy and the specific tactics Wood employed.

Measuring Prison Reform: The Stillwater Transition Study

In 1976, the Minnesota Legislature, under the assumption that Stillwater Prison never could be properly managed within the old physical plant, appropriated $800,000 to underwrite the planning and design of a new adult-maximum security institution. Planning was completed in early 1977, and funds for construction were appropriated in June of that year. Commissioner Schoen appointed an advisory committee which included several key members of the state legislature and representatives of state law enforcement agencies and the judiciary, in addition to a number of nationally known figures in corrections; the author was a member of this committee.

The purpose of the new "facility" was to provide housing for 400 of Minnesota's most serious offenders and most disruptive and assaultive inmates—including persons convicted of crimes of violence, persons convicted of property offenses who are considered to be "professional" or "habitual" offenders in their criminal activities, and persons who proved to be escape risks, assaultive toward others inmates or staff, or were serious management problems in other correctional facilities.

Inmates in these four categories were housed in the existing state prison, the St. Cloud

Reformatory and the St. Peter Security Hospital. Given the plan advanced in 1977 to remodel Stillwater as a medium-security prison with a reduced capacity of 400 inmates, the new high-security facility was intended to provide relief to other state prisons from the problems posed by dangerous and disorderly prisoners as well as certain violent mentally disordered inmates. One of the theories behind the construction of the new prison was that not only would the programs and institutional atmosphere at the other prisons be improved by removing difficult inmates and career offenders from them, but that a high-security prison with a new physical plant, staff, and program components would have a positive effect on the in-prison and postrelease conduct of the state's most problematic inmates and serious offenders.

Milton Rector, a member of the High Security Facility Advisory Committee, and an outspoken opponent of new prison construction, participated in Minnesota's planning effort because, "if any state can bring about an improvement in its correctional system by building a new prison it is the State of Minnesota." Rector urged that a careful "before, during and after" study of the Minnesota "experiment" be undertaken by the University of Minnesota.

In response to this unusual opportunity to measure change in a prison system over time, the author proposed a collection of baseline data at Stillwater during 1978-1979. This data would then be used to compare to data gathered some twelve to eighteen months after the new high-security facility had been in operation and Stillwater converted to a medium-security prison.

This proposal, approved by Commissioner Schoen, was submitted to the National Institute of Corrections which funded the first phase of the Stillwater Transition Study in 1978. The proposed study was essentially a victim survey of Stillwater prisoners and personnel. The design called for interviews with randomly selected inmates and staff members to be followed by anonymous surveys administered to both groups. In addition to the Commissioner, this study required the approval of a warden who knew his prison so well that he could be confident of the findings, particularly for a study that would produce results of high interest to members of the state legislature and the press.

Examining Institutional Climates

The almost complete absence of research in any contemporary high-security penitentiary can be explained in part by the following difficulties:

- The tremendous problem of measuring the impact of reform in any social institution by the choice of specific measures and the perspectives of persons making the assessments
- Obtaining concrete data for these measures from populations of prisoners and staff skeptical of the value of such research
- The willingness of wardens and correctional system administrators to allow "objective" assessments of their efforts
- The reluctance of wardens and system administrators to take the risk of asking prisoners and employees to discuss their management strategies with persons outside their own agencies[19]

Administrators assume prisoners will always bad-mouth the staff and their living conditions. Administrators further assume that employees may be inclined to take advantage of the cover of an anonymous survey to criticize their bosses. Negative results in the hands of those who publish articles, read papers at criminology conferences, and make findings available to newspaper reporters, elected officials and their superiors can cost wardens more than embarrassment.

Corrections officials in this country learned the hard way that their well-intended efforts at rehabilitating prisoners turned out to be overly optimistic. Over the past two decades, as support for prisoners and their "rights" faded and fear of crime became a national political issue, high-security prisons have returned to a more traditional role. That role now calls for maintaining order while a prison system's most dangerous and repetitive offenders serve out their sentences with no expectations that the experience of incarceration—outside of the aging process—will have an impact on the prisoner's future criminal conduct.

The University of Minnesota Transition Study was intended to be a "before-after" investigation of prisons in a state not only trying to establish order in its existing penitentiary but also in the process of building a new supermax prison. The findings of the "before" phase of this project are summarized below. As the first phase began, Frank Wood took extraordinary steps to expedite the evaluation of his efforts and those of his staff. This was remarkable because his openness to research continued after the new prison at Oak Park Heights opened. By contrast, there was a paucity of research on any aspect of confinement or employment in contemporary prisons in this country.

The Stillwater Transition Study

In the first part of this project, we intended to gather data pertaining to various aspects of doing time and working at Stillwater. The focus was on problematic areas because these were features to be remedied by the Wood regime followed by the remodeling of Stillwater and the addition of the new high-security prison. The study focused particular attention toward inmate victimization—real and perceived—and staff perceptions of the dangerousness of their jobs.

Inmates were asked to report the incidence of various forms of victimization which they personally experienced, and their perceptions of the extent to which other prisoners were victimized. The survey explored the extent of illegal drug and alcohol use along with the views of inmates about the employment of women as correctional officers. The study also sought to assess the quality of relations between racial and ethnic groups and the impact of these relationships on inmate life and the work of employees.

The questionnaire for staff sought to determine their views of problem inmates, their perceptions of the "climate" of the prison, their characterization of inmate-inmate and inmate-staff relationships, their opinions of the physical plant, staffing, and programs at Stillwater, and their predictions of inmate conduct and "the climate" in the new prison.

To assure that the research identified the major issues that concerned inmates and employees before any effort was made to survey large numbers of both groups, interviews were conducted with randomly selected samples of each group. The interview guides were pretested with inmates and staff at the St. Cloud

Reformatory. Systematic interviews began at Stillwater Prison in December, 1978. By May 1979, the university research team, which included African-American male and female members and white males, had conducted interviews lasting between two and three hours with 100 inmates. Randomly selected, these inmates represented all racial and ethnic groups and included men from the general population, the disciplinary segregation unit, and those in protective custody. Only eight inmates refused the request for interviews. By August, interviews had been conducted with twenty-six members of the custodial staff, including minority and women officers, new and more experienced officers, line staff, and those at the supervisory level; two staff members refused the request for interviews.

These interviews identified major issues for inmates and employees and based on them, we added a number of items to the standardized tests, scales and items taken from studies of other prisons. In 1979, the "Inmate Opinion Survey" of twenty-nine pages was administered to fifteen former Stillwater inmates who had transferred to the Lino Lakes medium-security institution. This pretest provided an indication of the time required to fill out the form, and during the discussion that followed the inmates' completion of the survey, researchers reviewed each item with them for clarity, understanding, and relevance.

Administration of the survey occurred in June, 1979. Prior to this, Warden Wood sent inmates a memorandum assuring them that if they returned to their cells from their jobs an hour early, they would receive their pay for that time. Wood also emphasized that the study was being conducted by the University of Minnesota.

The survey was distributed and collected by the university research group aided by twenty-two inmate volunteers. The latter first filled out the form themselves, received instructions from the project director, and then, with the university staff, handed out and collected the forms from inmates throughout the prison.

The author and another senior research staff member administered the survey to inmates in the disciplinary segregation and protective custody units in an effort to seek responses from particularly important groups—a result that was largely successful. Minimum-security inmates also filled out the questionnaire. Of the 1,032 prisoners at Stillwater, researchers received usable responses from 633, or 61 percent of the population. A comparison of this group in terms of age, race and ethnicity, and type of offender with figures for the entire population provided evidence that it was representative. A high level of response was obtained for the following reasons:

- The project had been described in the prison newspaper.
- One hundred inmates knew from interviews what the study was all about.
- The members of the research team were already well identified as being from the university.

Careful pretesting provided an accurate assessment of the level of understanding of items and the time needed to complete the form.

The arrangements for the administration of this survey, as described in Frank Wood's memo, is testimony to the degree to which the warden helped in the collection of data for this project. His effort was also evident in September 1979, when a survey of staff opinions was scheduled. The lengthy questionnaire was distributed to employees on all three shifts accompanied by a memo from Warden Wood allowing them time to complete the forms on the job. Members of the university research group were present as each shift came on and off duty during a two-and-a-half-day period. Some employees took the form home with them and mailed them time back to the university. This effort produced 281 completed survey forms from 450 staff, representing all ranks and categories of personnel.

Principal Finding

This chapter presents only a brief overview of some of the key findings from a 340-page report, but the results do provide an answer to the question of whether Frank Wood's efforts, within the constraints of the old physical plant at Stillwater, succeeded in restoring law and order.

Seventy-five percent of prisoners answered, "No" to the question, "Are there any particular times of the day that you do not feel safe in this prison?" and 76 percent denied that there were places in the prison they avoided going by themselves. Eighty percent reported that they had not been sexually propositioned; 97. 5 percent said they had never been forced to have sex, and 82 percent reported that no one had taken any of their personal belongings by threat of force.

Prisoner Responses

In regards to safety, most respondents considered the prison to be fairly safe for inmates of all races. Inmates saw the prison as only slightly more dangerous for Indian and black inmates than for white or Latino inmates. Inmates reported some verbal and physical abuse of other inmates by staff; 54 percent estimated that at least 30 percent of the inmates had been verbally abused, and 39 percent estimated that at least 30 percent of the inmates had been physically abused. These figures were significantly lower however, when inmates reported their own experience; half said they had never been verbally abused, and 88 percent said they had never been physically abused by staff.

Few inmates were seen by other prisoners to be forced into sex or to be victims of physical attacks by other inmates. Some 99 percent of the respondents denied using force on another inmate to have sex; 93 percent said they did not take or give favors for sex. A somewhat higher incidence of these behaviors was reported, however, when respondents estimated the frequency of these activities in the inmate population in general, as opposed to reports of their own behavior.

Only 17.5 percent of the inmates indicated that they thought women officers should not be allowed to work at the prison. The two most frequent opinions about women officers were that they improve the prison atmosphere (37 percent); 34 percent of the respondents preferred women officers. Most respondents viewed the staff as more qualified than when they began work at the prison and, with the exception of women and staff who have worked at Stillwater for two years or less, most of the respondents said the staff had greater control over the inmates than when they first began work at the prison.

Staff Responses

Most staff did not consider their job to be extremely dangerous (the average rating was 2.90 on a scale of one to five). Younger staff and custody staff considered their jobs to be more dangerous than older staff and staff in other job classifications. Sixty-two percent said that there were places in the prison they avoided going alone (most frequently cited were the galleries in cell halls), and a third said there were certain times of the day when they did not feel safe.

Most of the staff (75 percent) reported that only a small proportion of inmates (15 percent or fewer) acted in a violent manner toward staff. Their estimates of the number of inmates who were violent toward other inmates were somewhat higher; nearly half reported that 30 percent of the inmates were violent toward other prisoners.

Most of the staff reported that over half of the inmates were not a problem for the staff, and 62 percent said they thought that fewer than 15 percent of the inmates required maximum-security confinement.

Over two-thirds of staff respondents reported that they believed that fewer than 15 percent of the inmates had been verbally abused by prison staff, and even fewer had been physically abused. Approximately three-fourths stated that 5 percent or fewer of the inmates had been physically abused by staff.

Drug use was ranked as the most serious problem by the staff, and racial antagonism among inmates was ranked as the second most serious. Violence among inmates was ranked as the third most serious problem, and minority staff considered it significantly more serious than white staff.

The majority of the s
that the staff did a fairly
ing security at the insti
supportive of the opin
important in maintai
Administrative staff co
more important for security than did custody staff.

Staff reported that they were reasonably well satisfied with their jobs, scoring around the midpoint of the job-satisfaction scale. Staff fifty years and older were the most satisfied with their jobs. Minority staff scored lowest on job satisfaction. There were no differences between male and female staff. Custody staff reported the lowest job satisfaction rating among all job classifications, with the administrative staff scoring highest.

When asked about women officers, 48 percent of the staff said that use of women officers invaded inmates' privacy. Sixty-one percent said there was no difference between male and female officers for back-ups in an emergency. Staff perceived male and female officers as getting along well but not as well as minority and white staff.

Forty-eight percent of employees stated that they had very little confidence in the general direction set by the Department's central office in the state capital.

Study Conclusions

In addition to interviews with 100 prisoners and 26 employees and surveys obtained from almost 900 staff members and inmates, all respondents had an opportunity to comment about any issue in the prison. Complaints from prisoners should be regarded as serious concerns to them, but this opportunity did not

… complaints from prisoners about the …, medical care, sanitary conditions, pro-…rams, staff "brutality," disciplinary procedures, or wages. Employees did not list complaints about the way Stillwater was being managed and operated.

Of course, these interviews and the surveys dealt with an assessment of conditions in a prison, not a hotel. Asking people who are locked up for long periods in a maximum-security prison whether they have any complaints is not likely to produce responses that "all is well," although twenty-seven inmates responded, "Nothing, adjustment is easy" when asked, "What annoys you most about doing time at Stillwater?" Our data indicated that some inmates, though not most, had concerns about safety and that staff perceived greater danger in the prison than did the inmates. The acceptance of lock-ups and shakedowns is confirmed by the survey item showing that 60 percent of the inmates reported that these features of management did not bother them.

The categories least-often selected by inmate respondents when asked what aspect of prison life they found most difficult were, not surprisingly, "custodial officers" and "rules and regulations." This finding also appeared in the Prison Preference Inventory comparisons of Stillwater prisoners to inmates in other state prison systems. Stillwater prisoners were less concerned about safety than those in other states except for Connecticut. Stillwater prisoners were less concerned than inmates in all comparison groups about the need to have activities to occupy their time and their need for environmental stability, predictability, and consistent clear-cut rules. Data from staff and inmate interviews and the surveys on the incidence and perceptions of violence clearly indicated that a significant positive improvement in safety had been achieved when compared to the findings three years earlier in the House-Senate Committee report.

In the fall of 1979, preliminary results of this survey were sent to Kenneth Schoen's successor as Commissioner of Corrections, Jack Young, the former warden at Stillwater during the early days of the Fogel administration. Young put off a decision on continuing this line of research notifying the author: "In as much as the next phase of this study could not be expected to begin until at least 1983, I have decided against making a decision or commitment concerning Phase II at this time. That decision will be reserved until the new facility is actually opened and operating." More problematic was his request that study materials be retained for future access by the Department of Corrections: "We do not at this time need to receive copies of any of the other subject data (writings, sound recordings, etc.) as long as the University of Minnesota agrees . . . to make this data available to all interested parties, including our Department."[20]

Because prisoners and employees had been clearly informed that this study was being conducted by the University of Minnesota and both groups had been given verbal and written assurances that their interview responses would be confidential, the University's Office of Research Administration denied Corrections Department personnel access to these study materials.[21] Due to these constraints, Phase II, the "after" component of the transition study, was not undertaken.

An Unusual Planning Process for a New Prison

Plans for the new prison, Oak Park Heights, proceeded on several tracks. In addition to the commissioner's advisory committee noted earlier, the Department of Corrections established sixteen planning groups to cover various elements from security to religious services. These groups had been operating under a mandate from Schoen to, "think creatively." This challenge proved to be difficult, since departmental personnel, then and now, were accustomed to policies and practices that emerged over the years and seemed to be the best way to conduct business.[22]

An international conference held in June 1978 provided further brain power and "creativity" for the planning process. Feature 3.2 presents the purpose of this gathering.

This conference brought together prominent penal policy analysts, academic researchers, prison wardens who were managing innovative high-security prisons in Sweden, Denmark, and West Germany. These presentations and discussions were intended to provide context, strategies, and caveats to Paul Silver, the architect chosen to design Oak Park Heights, and to Frank Wood, then warden-designate of the new prison along with other Department of Correction planners. More specifically, these experts intended to provide the best available knowledge on such topics as:

- Who will be the residents to be housed in last-resort prisons?
- What personality, social background, and criminal career factors might distinguish these prisoners from others?
- What are the implications of these features for staffing, programming, and managing these prisoners?
- What are the legal and constitutional issues related to maximum-security prisons including requirements for space, services, staff, and programs?
- What do the psychological and sociological studies report concerning the effects of long-term confinement?
- How does physical space and environment affect the conduct of prisoners?
- What is known about the conduct of staff and inmates living and working under conditions of maximum custody?
- How can "predators" be controlled?
- What programs can offer hope, personal satisfaction, safety, and a positive environment to these prisoners?

That Oak Park Heights evolved not into just another maximum-security penitentiary but into a "new generation" prison that brought visitors from many other states and other countries is testimony to the fact that Kenneth Schoen and Frank Wood did think, "outside the box" during the planning process.

Schoen was responsible for promoting the Community Corrections Act as it worked its way through the state legislature and for supporting the establishment of sentencing guidelines—two major new policies that changed both the number and the character of the state prison population. Schoen also deserves credit for the conception of an earth-sheltered prison, built into a hillside that looked like no other; he wanted a design that called for no walls, no guard towers, as few barred windows as possible, and housed inmates in small living

Feature 3.2: Purpose of the Conference on Planning for Oak Park Heights

"[The purpose of the conference was] to review the state of knowledge about the effects of confinement in maximum-security prisons, particularly in those states or countries where such confinement is seen as a last resort for violent, dangerous, and repetitive offenders. The proceedings were based on an established set of assumptions. The assumptions included the recognition that in every state's criminal population there is a small percentage of offenders whose criminal conduct is so violent or so persistent that at present no politically acceptable alternative exists beyond incapacitation though long-term confinement in a secure prison.

"Some American states have adopted the ultimate incapacitating sanction, capital punishment, but that sanction has not been in effect in Minnesota for almost fifty years and is not now under discussion. Because the conference was organized to help Minnesota plan its new high-security facility, the focus on viable penal sanctions therefore excluded the death penalty.

"While many, perhaps even most, criminal justice policymakers may agree that secure confinement for a small number of offenders may be necessary, maximum-security prisons are often beset by serious management problems, by violence directed toward inmates and staff, and by conditions that are described as 'inhumane.'

"Furthermore, while criminal-justice professionals may define serious criminal behavior quite specifically and classify the number of such offenders as relatively small, among the general public there is the tendency to view anyone who commits a felony as a serious offender who should be locked up in prison. . . . Many citizens seem to be convinced that if there were more people in prison, there would be less crime—a very expensive delusion, not only in terms of physical resources but in human costs.

"The set of assumptions distributed to the conference participants does not call for the expanded use of prisons, but rather presumes that use of maximum-security prisons will be limited to special populations of violent and persistent offenders. The set of assumptions is as follows:

1. Long-term imprisonment is the severest sanction available for those offenders who have committed the most serious violations of law. . . .
2. Confinement in maximum-custody prisons is intended to be punitive, to reinforce the importance of certain community norms, and to incapacitate or control individuals who have continued to violate these norms or who have not abided by the rules of more open correctional settings.
3. Long-term imprisonment is not for the purpose of rehabilitation.
4. Enlightened penal systems will have provided alternatives to incarceration in high-security facilities for the great majority of offenders. These alternatives include diversion, fines, probation, restitution, short-term jail confinement, and other community-based corrections programs.

Feature 3.2: Purpose of the Conference on Planning for Oak Park Heights (con't)

5. Confinement in or transfer to last-resort prisons will be based on due-process procedures that will have established the seriousness of the crime, the seriousness of the criminality, or clear violations of contractual agreements pertaining to alternatives to incarceration."

Source: David A. Ward and Kenneth F. Schoen, eds. 1981. Confinement in Maximum Custody: New Last Resort Prisons in the United States and Western Europe. *Lexington, Massachusetts: Lexington Books, pp. ix-x.*

groups.[22] His other more fundamental contribution was placing Frank Wood in charge of operational planning in Oak Park Heights and appointing him as warden of the new facility. Planning the staffing, security, programs, day-to-day operations, and the policies by which the new prison was to be managed was the responsibility and challenge of Frank Wood.

Oak Park Heights: A Different Type of Supermax

Oak Park Heights was conceived under the concentration model in penology; that is, the argument that a prison system's most difficult and dangerous prisoners should be concentrated in one location specifically intended to control them. This option then should allow more freedom of movement, greater privileges, and more opportunities for participation in a variety of work and remedial programs in the other prisons from which the troublemakers have been extracted.

The alternative approach, the dispersal system, is based on the argument that the influence of disruptive prisoners can be diluted by distributing them throughout a number of institutions within a penal system. Dispersal had been the option of choice in the United Kingdom, which interpreted the closing of Alcatraz in 1963 as signifying the U.S. Government's disenchantment with trying to put, "all the rotten eggs in one basket." The Bureau of Prisons, in fact, did not operate any special purpose high-security penitentiary for "management problems" from all of its prisons from 1963 until the return to concentration began with the establishment of a "control unit" at the federal penitentiary at Marion, Illinois in 1973.

The introduction of the Sentencing Guidelines System and the Community Corrections Act meant that automobile thieves, bad check writers, and the great majority of other property offenders no longer would be sent to the state prisons; they would serve time in county jails or in facilities or programs in their communities. State prisons, therefore, would house populations consisting almost entirely of persons convicted of violent crimes serving long sentences mandated under the new fixed-sentencing system. Of these, Oak Park Heights would take the most serious offenders, along with inmates who could not, or would not, adjust at other prisons.

A special feature of the new prison was the establishment of a mental health unit capable of holding thirty inmates whose mental health problems involved their acting out in a violent manner. Short-time psychiatric treatment then would be available for that group of inmates. In most penal systems, these inmates traditionally receive "bus therapy" as they are shipped between prisons and state mental hospitals while psychiatrists try to sort out those whose mental health problems require treatment and confinement as patients rather than as prisoners.

The mental health unit also was intended to provide "a change of scene" for prisoners who were serving extended periods in disciplinary segregation. Such stays, it was hoped, would give psychiatrists and psychologists an opportunity to determine whether a prisoner's violent inclinations or outbursts reflected a psychological disorder or if he (or she) was just ornery. The presence of this unit meant that unlike many other state supermax prisons, Oak Park Heights opened with on-site staff equipped to deal with the interface between psychological dysfunction, misconduct, and the prison environment.

The Physical Plant

Oak Park Heights is an earth-sheltered maximum-security prison built into a hillside overlooking the St. Croix River Valley. From a nearby road and residential area, all that is visible of the facility is a one-story brick administration building. Because it lies thirty feet or more underground, Oak Park Heights has been able to achieve significant economies in heating and cooling costs. Double parallel fences with razor ribbon between them and equipped with electronic motion-detection devices provide perimeter security, along with an armed officer in a patrol vehicle. The design does not allow prisoners to see the institution's perimeter, "so they don't know what they will encounter if they try to escape." Unlike traditional penitentiaries such as Stillwater with its thirty-foot stone walls, imposing gun towers and mammoth cell blocks with barred windows which were to carry the message of deterrence to passers by, Oak Park Heights was purposely hidden from public view.

The prison has nine units arranged in a u-shape, connected by two separate corridors, one for prisoners and one for the staff. Except for the disciplinary segregation and special housing complexes, each unit has its own eating, laundry, and indoor recreation areas and an enclosed outdoor recreation yard. In each unit, an officer in a secure control "bubble" can observe every inmate who leaves his cell and every area in which inmates interact with each other and with staff. Unit officers also can observe prisoners walking in the corridor that passes the back of each unit.

Prisoners can move from one part of the prison to another, for example from housing units to the industries or education units, without a staff escort. An inmate walking through this corridor cannot gain entrance to another unit without staff verification. There are no locations in the prison where inmates are not under visual and/or on-site staff supervision. Two officers on the floor in each unit rotate every two hours with the officer in the control bubble. (This operational feature was instituted after Wood noted that some officers assigned for their entire shift only to work in the protective environment of the control bubble tended to verbally communicate with prisoners, using more aggressive language and a different manner than did officers interacting directly with inmates on the floor in the unit.) "High intensity contact [by inmates] with staff means lots of information gets to staff."

In front of the units ranged along the hillside is a large institution yard for softball, handball, and other sports. Prisoners from no more than two units may use the yard at any one time. The nine units serve different purposes. One provides medical care, another mental health services; there is an education unit, an industries unit, and an honor unit. One disciplinary segregation unit houses short-term rule breakers and two special housing units contain prisoners who leave their cells only for solitary exercise. The ninth unit, recently activated, serves as a control unit in which prisoners leave their cells only in wrist and leg restraints and under the escort of several officers. Food carts bring meals to the kitchen in each unit; inmates may eat in their cells or the unit dining area.

Inmate cells, called rooms, range in size from 70 square feet in the living units to 153 square feet for medical and mental health rooms. Standard cells have horizontal concrete slabs which provide the base for a foam mattress and can double as a desk or table during the day; a vertical concrete configuration built into the wall contains shelves, storage space, and a flat surface for a television set. Toilets and washbasins made of stainless steel are set in concrete. Showers in all units are individually enclosed, locked stalls. Rooms have narrow, vertical windows which provide natural light and look into the large interior yard; from the second floor. Inmates can see the river valley in the distance. Oak Park Heights cannot become crowded since all cells were constructed to hold only one person. The design of the prison allowed Wood and his staff to take advantage of the strengths of both the concentration and dispersal models.

All of the Department of Corrections assaultive and disruptive prisoners could be contained in one relatively small prison at the same time: the division of the prison into nine separate, self-contained units, allowed for dispersal. As one Oak Park Heights prisoner commented, "if three or four guys get together to try to plan a protest, an escape or action against other prisoners, the next thing you know, they're living in four separate units."

Staffing

Wood was concerned that his plan to operate Oak Park Heights as a secure but humane environment for inmates and staff might be difficult to implement with a large group of veteran officers and administrators, "carrying baggage about inmates." His staff complement of 289 consisted of only 55 employees who transferred to the new prison from Stillwater and other state prisons; 234 staff members were hired "off the streets. I wanted people who would accept the concept of treating inmates as you would like a member of your family to be treated. I anticipated a high turnover rate but it didn't occur—they stayed. This staff transformed our visions into reality." Forty-five percent of the correctional officers had four-year college degrees. Thirty of the recruits were women. Wood's view was that female officers had "a calming effect on prisoners—the inmates know it's no macho thing to assault a woman."[23]

Before the prison opened, in addition to their initial training, Wood invited staff members to spend a night living in the disciplinary segregation unit cells, "so that they could get a sense of being locked up in a place where you can't get out." Staff were instructed on how to interact with prisoners, "in a nonabrasive way." As at Stillwater, inmates would be frequently "pat-searched" to condition them to submit to staff authority. Any prisoner not assigned to a job or involved in an industries, educational, or treatment program would remain locked in his cell. No protective custody unit was established; such cases would be transferred to other prisons. Only such physical force as necessary would be used to control prisoners who were acting out. "Staff who are assaulted will be allowed no pay back since they cannot preach nonviolence to prisoners and solve their own problems with violence. I told employees that I expected them and inmates to be restrained even under extreme circumstances." Prior to opening Oak Park Heights, Wood gave his security squad an unlimited number of hacksaw blades and challenged them to cut through the mullions which enclosed tool resistant steel bars and were filled with concrete. "They never made any significant headway."[24]

Policies and Programs for Prisoners

From its opening, Wood contended that the prison should not be evaluated in terms of "rehabilitation, we can't fix everything that society screwed up but the prisoners are still responsible for their actions because everyone from their circumstances did not kill, rape, or rob people. This regime is not intended to aggravate the conditions of confinement under the mistaken belief that it will make inmates averse to coming back. Our job is to maintain an environment that is conducive to change for those so inclined."[25]

When the prison opened, 93 percent of the inmates had committed crimes against persons and 43 percent had killed one or more persons. For those prisoners who wished to participate in them, Oak Park Heights offered sex-offender treatment and chemical- dependency programs. Mental health unit patients could join groups in anger management and conflict resolution. Prisoners could participate in the literacy program, earn a General Equivalency Diploma, and if they had the resources to pay for them, could take college courses. (Rather than hiring teachers, these programs were contracted out to schools, vocational-technical institutes and the University of Minnesota.) Wood established the standard religious, recreational, and legal resources.

Prisoners were allowed up to sixteen hours of contact visits each month with men in disciplinary segregation units limited to noncontact visits. All inmate telephone calls were monitored and tape recorded. Inmates were allowed out of their cells fifteen hours a day, seven days a week.

In March 1982, the proposal that Stillwater be modified to become a medium-security institution had joined the familiar myths in corrections that an old penitentiary has outlived its usefulness and should be remodeled or closed.[26] With space at Stillwater available and 400 new cells at Oak Park Heights coming on line due to the limits the new sentencing guidelines system put on state prison incarceration, the Department of Corrections found itself with empty cells. Soon prisoners from Wisconsin, Alaska, and the District of Columbia and other states, were being "boarded" in Minnesota, and Wood began a contractual agreement with the Federal Bureau of Prisons.

As a result of a series of inmate murders and the killing of two officers during the same day in October 1983, the U.S. Penitentiary at Marion Illinois—labeled by the press as "the new Alcatraz"—had moved into a lockdown mode with all congregate activity terminated. Marion held the leaders and key members of major prison gangs as well as the federal system's most accomplished escape-prone and disruptive prisoners. Director Norman A. Carlson was looking for a place to house Marion's prisoners and other federal prisoners who cooperated with federal investigators and prison authorities and thus placed their lives at risk.

These inmates had offended gang members in various ways such as not submitting to extortion, refusing to attempt to smuggle drugs into the prison through their visitors, and other demands. Most of the prisoners who came to Oak Park Heights, it should be emphasized, did not themselves seek protective custody; they were transferred because Bureau officials did not want their dead bodies to provide evidence of the consequences of informing or to admit that violence could occur in the system's most restrictive and highly controlled setting.

At Oak Park Heights, federal prisoners with the highest security rating were housed in secure accommodations under a regime in which their constitutional rights would be protected. Marion inmates began arriving soon after the prison opened. The income paid by other states and the federal government for their "boarders" provided the Department of Corrections with the funds to build a warehouse for the industry program. Wood viewed the Marion prisoners as providing a great challenge for his staff in terms of security. "Staff can never be violent enough to get these prisoners to say 'We give up, you're too violent'. This approach won't work with men who kill over a pack of cigarettes."

In the last 20 years, the more than 250 Marion and other federal prisoners who have been housed at Oak Park Heights have constituted a remarkable group of veteran convicts who had compiled many years of experience in disciplinary segregation and control units in state and federal maximum-security penitentiaries. Their perspectives on Oak Park Heights are particularly relevant because they have been so much more experienced in doing "big time" than the majority of Minnesota State prisoners. Since 1984, federal transfers have made up about 10 percent of the Oak Park Heights population; in February 2003, 35 of 360 prisoners were boarders from the federal system. Oak Park Heights has been the only state prison to house this large number of high-security federal prisoners.

Marion Prisoners View Oak Park

When they arrived, federal prisoners were surprised to be personally greeted by the warden who reviewed the contract each was required to sign. The contracts and Wood (and his successors) promised them a fresh start but also a prompt transfer back to the federal system if they abused its conditions. Over the years, about one in five of these prisoners violated their agreements, most by virtue of engaging in or threatening violence or becoming involved with drugs and other contraband.

Almost all of these federal offenders serving time for robbery, drug dealing, kidnapping, and prison murders were appalled on their arrival at Oak Park Heights at what one of them called, "the scummy quality" of the state prisoners with whom they had to live. To be housed with men who had molested children, committed incest, and raped women was beneath the dignity of the Marion prisoners whose view was that sex offenders were "perverts" who would be better off dead. Refraining from beating up sex offenders thus became one of the federal prisoners' most difficult challenges.

They also found, however, that the state prisoners were not organized in gangs. One of the principal reasons that Oak Park Heights was such a good depository for them was that the lives of many of these men had been contracted out by the Aryan Brotherhood, Mexican Mafia, and other prison gangs—none of which had a significant presence in Minnesota prisons. The comparative lack of sophistication of the state prisoners also made some of them good foils for the "wheeling and dealing" and other hustles in which the Marion convicts were so experienced. The federal prisoners learned, however, that these activities often led to transfers back to the federal system when state prisoners gave them and their activities up to the warden or other staff members.

Because the author had been conducting a study of the prison and post-release careers of Alcatraz inmates (and as an outgrowth of an assignment in 1984-85 to examine Marion under lockdown conditions for the Judiciary Committee of the U.S. House of Representatives), a proposal was submitted to the Bureau of Prisons to undertake systematic interviews with Marion prisoners to replicate the basic follow up that had been completed for the Alcatraz convicts. This proposal was approved by Director Carlson and while interviews began at Marion, the transfer of so many Marion inmates to a prison close to the University of Minnesota aided work on this study. From 1985 to 2001, the author conducted a series of interviews at Oak Park Heights with a dozen veterans from Marion's control, disciplinary, segregation, and the Director's protective custody unit. The following comments were selected from those interviews.

All of the Marion prisoners found significant differences in the privileges, programs, recreational activities, and the freedom of movement compared to the environments they had left. Most of them told the author, "When I got here [Oak Park Heights] I felt like I had been released to the free world."[27]

Two of these prisoners discussed adjustments they had to make in Minnesota:

Inmate A: Here, if I talk to somebody about Marion and tell them about the control unit and everything . . . they all said they hoped to God they didn't go.

Q: How often did you see the warden at Marion?

A: He would make the rounds up there in the control unit about once a week or every two weeks or so.

Q: Did he ever talk to you personally?

A.: Yeah, but I stopped the conversation.

Q: How often do you see Wood here?

A: Every day, he'll either make rounds up in industry or come into the unit or out on the yard.

Q: How do you feel about that?

A: I feel good about it. I mean if you've got a problem, seeing him is no problem.

Inmate B: The difference between Wood and the other wardens that I've had over me for the last half of my life is he'll do something where they didn't.

Q: With Wood you can count on something being done?

B: He'll hunt you up to let you know what it is. I never seen a guy like that, he'll come to the Unit. He come woke me up when he heard that John Paul Scott died [Former federal and Oak Park Heights prisoner].

A: He's definitely one of the best wardens I've ever seen.

B: When I first get out of the cell in the morning to go down and get my breakfast, I see him standing there. I see him at 9:30 on a Saturday morning and I'm sitting in my cell; I see him . . . just walking around...

Q: How soon did you see him after you got here?

A: Right away. He just ran down what he expected and talked about the industry and school—gave me the whole run down.

B: He made me sign a contract before I got my picture taken. He said, "Did you read the contract?" I said, "Yeah." He said, "Well I got another contract, sign right there." I think [Wood] has his balance [proportion of federal prisoners] just exactly right. Most of the federal prisoners any time they have problems, they have big problems, they're the ones they ship out. It usually involves another federal inmate. They squabble among themselves more than they do with the state inmates.

A: When I first got here, I was real paranoid for some reason. I even told "B," "Man, it looks like they are watching me." And he said, "Well, God damn it, they are supposed to, that's what they are paid for."

B: When a new inmate comes in here, it don't make no difference if he's a state or federal prisoner, when he goes into a Unit, the officer is going to see him when he comes out of his cell and he stops and looks over the tier they're looking at him. Because they're sitting there in the bubble, just glancing this way and that way, and if you're looking at him, they're looking at you. Not constantly you know, but they're gonna know just about how long you were out on the tier, you're in their eye. It took me a long time to read them. A lot of guys didn't—they shipped out three federal prisoners in one day about four months ago.

A: Here you got a lot of guys that's never been anywhere else and they think this is really a screwed up place. You hear them saying how bad it is, but to me the same things that they're complaining about—they're good to me. Like the industry here, they want more money; my God, forty cents is the most we can make in the federal system and here you start and go up to $2.20.

B: You know what? This is the first prison I've been in my life where you see no stealing at all. The guys who complain have never done any hard time; they don't know what they've missed. You can't really hold it against a person for doing something against you when he's not aware he's wrong. That's where the big adjustment comes in for us here. We come in here and guys say things that for us was automatically a killing situation.

(Inmate A was subsequently sent back to the federal system as a consequence of his involvement with a female correctional officer who lost her job due to her attachment to him.)

Inmate C had killed two prisoners and stabbed a third in three federal penitentiaries, including the Marion control unit. Because one killing involved African-American prisoners [C is white] and another situation involved the Aryan Brotherhood putting out a contract on him, he was sent to Oak Park Heights. His contract ruled out any hostile response on his part to "taunts or provocations":

It's hard to ignore threats here. It's hard to keep from killing these kids. If you have a piece on you, you're gonna kill somebody. Someday I'm going to be in a bad mood. The Minnesota prisoners won't stick together. They don't know what hard time is. They're scared of knives. I gotta knife when I got here, but I broke it up and flushed it because these guys are not armed.

But I'd rather put up with these ignorant ___ than go back to the feds and get killed. I am tired of killing and ducking and dodging. I'm a dead man looking for a place to lie down.

Several months later Inmate C was sent back to the Bureau of Prisons where he was placed in a protective custody unit.

Federal prisoner D described his reaction to Oak Park Heights:

You can't knock the security design of the Units. . . . And the people that work here had a whole different attitude than the federal correctional officers. I can sit down in the common area and talk to one of the guards for half an hour about anything and go back [to my room] and no one thinks ill of it. Whereas if I sat down and talked to a guard in the federal system for five minutes . . . that puts a stigma on you that doesn't exist in here. The physical security has a large part to do with it and everybody has their own room where they can go, close the door, and be by themselves, or paint or write, or watch TV, or study, or do any number of things they want to do alone. And, this place isn't overcrowded. Oak Park Heights is a human society even though it is restricted. But a lot of these people here are about as warped as a person can be. Like one guy in the Unit raped some little girl, and cut her breasts off and buried her in a field, and this sick stuff. You don't run into people like that in the federal system.

Q: Maybe the comparison is better to "X" federal penitentiary [X to avoid identification of this prisoner].

Inmate D: No, X is not like this at all. In X, everybody is walking around in fear of their life and everybody is armed to the teeth. It's tension filled, stress filled, who's going to attack me next? Who's going to take this away from me? I need some friends and we've got to save each other, it's just a war. Whereas here, there is hardly any tension. There's a little bit. There is a couple of people in this prison that I don't like, and they don't like me. They go around talking bad about me but they're just a handful . . . and I ignore them.

Like today, there was an argument in the library between two guys. Now at X, one of them would be dead by now. These guys just cussed each other out and walked off, and that's the end of it. . . . It's like society. It's not like X; it's not the "kill for your honor" sickness.

Q: Is the difference due to different inmates here or is it the way the prison is operated?

Inmate D: I don't think it's an either or, I think it's a blend because of the way this place is built and the fact that the guards are right on top of the unit all the time. The opportunity exists to kill people, but it's all set up to reduce tension and people don't want to get in trouble right in front of the authorities. The way the Unit is set up you got the guy right there that can see the whole Unit, but at the same time it doesn't seem to me like the prisoners are looking on the staff here as the enemy, like the federal prisons. Here, sometimes, they're even helpful. . . . it's not a vicious society. But the people here are more vicious than the federal prisoners, for what got them in here. If you had the wrong environment these people would all be at each other's throats. I think it's how they're treated and the conditions that they exist in.

If you have an argument, the main line you hear from a prisoner who's having a disagreement with one of the staff and the prisoner thinks he's right, the prisoner will say to the staff person, "I want to talk to Wood about this." And usually that makes the staff person think. "Well, am I doing the right things?" The prisoners have a button they can push and that's Warden Wood—they know that they can go talk to him, just the thought of it makes these people very responsible. These [inmates] a lot of them, look at Wood as an ally, maybe not an ally like a normal person would think, but in the federal prison the warden is the number one enemy.

The prisoners don't feel like they are being treated like trash. In the federal system, you know you are being treated like a piece of s___ whereas these people care about them still. They don't build up that big resentment toward the system even though they are locked up and even though they moan and groan and complain; it's not that deep-seeded [sic] antagonism between the federal prisoners and the staff. Like at X, it was a real hate scene. You didn't care what happened to the guard. If somebody dumped something heavy on them off the tier, you'd laugh. That was funny. Whereas there are people here, if someone jumped a guard, they'd probably fight to defend the guard. There are people here in the Unit—one guy hits another, a fight starts, and a third guy will pick up a chair and hit the aggressor over the head and stop the fight. In a federal prison, that would never happen. It's just so different here.

Not all Marion prisoners appreciated Oak Park Heights. Inmate F, another veteran convict who had made the FBI's "Most Wanted" list, was interviewed by the author at Marion after he was returned from Oak Park Heights:

There was nothing about Oak Park Heights that I liked—for long-term prisoners, it's not very good. It's sort of like a morgue. It's a nice sanitized warehouse. It's really a nerve racking place because it's got so many little rules. Every day they do a cell check. The whole setup is strictly for short-timers. You go to work and you do your job but you don't feel comfortable doing it—someone is always there looking at every piece of work you do. If you're going upstairs to get your food, you have to go through a metal detector and then two or three people are standing there looking at every piece of food you got. Someone is always telling you you're not supposed to stop or talk on the stairs or something. There's really no kind of decision you can make.

What follows is a segment from a detailed commentary by the most seasoned convict to come to Oak Park Heights, John "Buck" Logan. Logan had served time in state penitentiaries in Arkansas, Oklahoma, Texas, and Michigan, and in San Quentin, where he killed another inmate, and Folsom in California. In the federal system, he had been at Atlanta and Leavenworth. Sent to the Marion control unit after he killed another inmate at Atlanta, Logan himself was stabbed twelve times in the unit's barbershop. Because he survived this attempt on his life, Marion officials knew that Logan would have to try to kill his assailant or that the prisoner who attacked him would come back to try to finish the job. To avoid another killing, Logan was transferred to the state prison at Marquette, Michigan, then to the federal prison at Milan, Michigan and shortly after it opened, to Oak Park Heights in August 1983. During many interviews with the author, Logan brought his special perspective to the comparison of Oak Park Heights to other prisons he had experienced:

> *This makes the thirteenth prison that I have been sent to in the last thirty-five years. There are twelve prisons that I have spent at least a year or more of time in. Some of those I've been back [to] for a second and third trip. Oak Park Heights is completely different than any other prison that I've ever been in. This was really a new experience for me when I drove in here. You might as well say, the warden met me at the front door and escorted me in here. I didn't really understand it, and really didn't know what the hell was going on because out of all those prisons that I have years of time in I have seldom ever known the head warden. He certainly didn't have anything to do with me. When I got here, this well dressed, white haired gentleman showed up and stuck his hand out, introduced himself and said he was the warden and he runs Oak Park Heights. Well, I really didn't know what to think. I kinda wondered to myself who is this fool trying to impress? . . .*
>
> *He knew my record and he asked me if I understood the contract that I signed to come here, and I told him that I did. He told me that if there were any problems to come to him and he would solve them. So that's something different than I've ever seen before in any other prison. I didn't really know what to think about this. In fact, I kind of resented it because I thought maybe it looked like this guy was trying to set up me. In other words, he was gonna force me to be one of his informers because he asked me if there was anyone there that I knew and did I expect to have any problems there and I said, "No, I didn't." He knew that the person that I had been stabbed by was a Minnesota prisoner doing time in the federal system. He told me that he had a lot of friends here because he was a Minnesota native and had done a lot of time in the state. He asked me if there would be any problem with any of these guys. I told him, "No, I didn't think there'd be any problems with them," but I was definitely gonna hunt them up the first time I got an opportunity to get out on the yard—and if there was any problems I was gonna straighten them out right then.*
>
> *Wood told me, "No, you don't straighten out the problems around here, I straighten them out." When he said this, it kind of made me angry because if you have a situation with another inmate in any population that I've ever been in, if your life was in jeopardy or if his life is in jeopardy from me, there really wasn't nothing the warden could do about it but transfer me out or lock me up—or transfer him out or lock him up. The only thing the warden can do is separate us. If I have any intentions of doing time here then I'm certainly not going to run to him to lock me up and ship me back out because I might have an enemy here. . .*

Warden Wood—I really couldn't understand him. He seemed like he wanted to be your friend and was in your corner. He seemed really interested in you. . . .

I had to go through three or four days of orientation and they assigned me a job. I go upstairs to work and first day I'm up there here comes the warden and he comes directly to me and sticks his hand out and shakes hands with me and asks me how I'm doing. Called me "Mr. Logan," like I was somebody. Hell, I'd never been called Mr. by no staff or by anybody that worked in these penitentiaries in the last thirty-five years. I never had nobody treat me that way.

My first couple of years here, there was so many times that guys would get so completely out of line with their mouth and get to the point where that I had to say, "Hey asshole, you keep on, you do that anymore, and I'm done talking to you, I've talked to you twice, this is the third time—if I have to come to you again, I'm gonna cut your g______ head off." . . . The next thing you know it's all the way to the head warden and Mr. Wood himself will be breathing down your neck saying, "Mr. Logan, stop threatening the inmates—if you don't stop you are going to wake up wondering why you're on the bus back to the control unit."

John Logan did adjust to Oak Park Heights; he spent some time in disciplinary segregation as a result of "dirty" urine tests due to his proclivity to smoke marijuana in the occasional instance it found its way into his complex or work area, but he had found a much more congenial place for a man not scheduled for release from prison until the year 2030. When Logan's health deteriorated, he was sent to the Department of Correction's secure unit in a county hospital to determine the cause. After he was informed that he had terminal lung cancer, Frank Wood called the author to suggest that, since Logan had no family in Minnesota, we visit him in the hospital. Logan never got over his surprise that a penitentiary warden made such an effort on his behalf.

As Logan's health declined over the next few months, and as the end drew close, Wood wrote to the Bureau of Prisons Regional Office to seek authorization for Logan to be moved to the Family Visiting facility located on the grounds of nearby Stillwater prison. There, under supervision, he would be allowed to spend his last few days with family members who were coming from Oklahoma. The Regional Director, however, declined to approve this transfer. Logan died in his cell at Oak Park Heights, but during the last weeks of his life, he made many tape recordings to describe his history to the author. His last tape ended with an expression of gratitude that his life was ending in a prison run by a man who had shown him respect and who had done things for him that he never expected from a penitentiary warden.

Measures to Assess the Effectiveness of the Oak Park Regime

In the absence of systematic data obtained from prisoner and staff surveys, the following performance measures can help to assess the effectiveness of the management philosophy implemented by Frank Wood and the five wardens who have succeeded him during the period 1982–2003. (These are in addition to staff commentaries, included in subsequent chapters, and the inmate observations offered above.)

- No inmate or employee has been killed.
- No escapes have occurred.
- No riots, disturbances, protests, or attempts to destroy state property have involved as much as an entire unit.
- The prison received a compliance score of 100 percent the first time it applied for accreditation from the American Correctional Association.
- The Federal District Court has had no case in which the prison has been found to violate the constitutional rights of any prisoner.

These measures provide evidence that Oak Park Heights has successfully carried out its mission to contain and control the most violent offenders and the most assaultive and disruptive prisoners sent to the Minnesota Department of Corrections or received as transfers from other states and the Federal Bureau of Prisons. Oak Park Heights is a safe place for prisoners to serve their sentences and for employees to work.

Incidents at Stillwater and Oak Park Heights in Recent Decades

Lest the impression be left that nothing negative has happened at Stillwater and Oak Park Heights since 1976, the following are noted in the context of Frank Wood's statement that the task of prison administrators is to, "reduce the incidence, scope and severity of incidents that will inevitably occur in a prison environment." Stillwater and Oak Park Heights are not colleges, factories, or military bases that select their clientele and can eject those who do not follow their rules.

At Stillwater in 1982, two prisoners hid in boxes in the back of a truck and escaped when the truck passed through the sallyport. A year later, 900 windows were broken during a demonstration. In another breakout attempt, two prisoners gained access to a heavy dump truck being serviced inside the prison. The truck was rammed into two gates; the first broke but slowed the vehicle down sufficiently so that it was not able to penetrate the second set of gates. The two prisoners in the truck were wounded by gunfire from a nearby tower and later transferred to Oak Park Heights. A 1997 escape attempt that again involved prisoners trying to hide in the back of a garbage truck failed when the driver detected the men.

No escape attempts have occurred at Oak Park Heights. There was an attempt to sexually assault a female staff member, and several employees have been discharged for attempting to smuggle contraband—in one case, hacksaw blades—to prisoners. Half a dozen female employees were terminated as a result of improper relations with prisoners. (These instances of misconduct have not altered the prison's commitment to employing and promoting women: in early 2003, 40 of the 200 members of the custodial staff were female, as is the warden.)

An example of the Wood regime in action occurred in June 17, 1983, when ten officers were assaulted by inmates who were members of a biker group. Senior staff remained at the prison well into the night to be sure that the officers did not retaliate. "We went to watch meetings to remind them [line staff] that we are professionals and that violence begets violence. We worked with the officers who were assaulted, gave them time off, established a support group for them, and put more managers in the units for six weeks."

Recently, due to the state's budget deficit, the Department of Corrections has been required to cut thirty positions with the consequence that weekend out-of-cell activities for prisoners at Oak Park Heights have been cancelled.

Oak Park Heights Compared to an English Maximum-security Prison

Very few studies in the literature of penology contrast the environment of one prison to another, but such a comparison was undertaken in the 1980s by Roy D. King of the Center for Social Policy Research at the University of Wales.[28] (see the Foreword to this work). In this effort to compare Oak Park Heights to Gartree, a maximum-security "dispersal" prison in England, King spent four months at each institution. According to King, Oak Park Heights had greater control over inmate movement due to its design compared to Gartree, which housed 400 inmates in a large building that had not been constructed to serve as a maximum-security prison:

> There seems little doubt that Oak Park Heights achieved what must be one of the major objectives of any prison system—the provision of a safe custodial environment for staff and prisoners—much more effectively than did Gartree. . . . Oak Park Heights had experienced no significant control problems in its short history. . . . Gartree, on the other hand, had had a troubled and turbulent history virtually from the beginning, and staff had only recently permitted the full operation of the prison to resume. . . . A few months before field work commenced in Gartree, a sex offender was lured to another cell and murdered. . . . In both studies, prisoners were asked to rate how safe or dangerous their environment was, first for prisoners and then for staff. . . . One in three thought their environment very safe for prisoners at Oak Park Heights; one in thirty in Gartree. Conversely, fewer than one in fifty thought the prison to be very dangerous for prisoners in Oak Park Heights, compared to one in five in Gartree. In Gartree it was possible to administer a similar questionnaire to staff. . . . Nearly half the staff saw the prison as either very dangerous or quite dangerous for prisoners; and still more dramatically, almost three-quarters of them said it was dangerous for themselves and their fellow officers.[29]

King provided comparisons between the two prisons on many other issues; in most of these, Gartree did not measure up as well as Oak Park Heights. He concluded that the "new generation design contributes to the basic safety of staff and prisoners" and that "it may provide a foundation on which the other matters can be built."[30]

New Generation Prisons Need a New Generation of Managers

In the absence of any systematic comparison of Oak Park Heights to other prisons in the United States, a British Broadcasting Company radio program, *Buried Alive*, which aired in April, 1985, is worth noting for its conclusion that a prison's management is more important than its architecture. Citing the need to develop new prison designs to combat increased violence in American prisons, BBC reporters visited two "new generation prisons"—Oak Park Heights and Mecklenberg, Virginia. That new "high-tech" prisons with the latest electronic hardware can help establish safe living conditions for prisoners and working conditions for staff was said to be evident at Oak Park Heights, but the program also pointed out that Frank Wood had also achieved order at Stillwater, an old penitentiary with a traditional design.

The BBC report went on to describe how Mecklenberg, another new generation prison, had not succeeded in achieving these goals. In May 1994, six men who had committed nineteen murders between them escaped from the prison unit that housed death row. The Director of Corrections attributed the breakdown in security not to technology, but to "faults in human engineering."

Fifty officers were brought in from other prisons to shake Mecklenberg down, but three months later the prison experienced another crisis when prisoners took nine correctional officers hostage and threatened to kill them unless a list of fourteen grievances was addressed. The chief negotiator for the inmates, Alvin Bronstein, Director of the National Prison Project of the American Civil Liberties Union, stated that the prisoners' aim was to expose "old-fashioned brutality in a new generation prison."

The warden was replaced by a new warden who responded with tougher measures. He told the BBC interviewer that because his staff had become too friendly with the prisoners, he had pulled officers out of living units into hallways where, "they can observe, but not get familiar with the inmates," an approach the program noted was directly opposite to its "twin, Oak Park Heights. At Mecklenberg there is remote control from an electronic bunker, for Frank Wood, it is daily tours of the prison talking to inmates."

Wood's comments on *Buried Alive* were limited to his own prison:

> *Oak Park Heights if managed by a different style could be turned into a repressive, dungeon-like environment. It has the capacity to be dramatically abused. We talk about new generation prisons, but we need a new generation of managers. If you gave me the choice between having Oak Park Heights and an incompetent, dishonest staff, or a tent and competent and honest staff, I'll take the tent and the competent and honest staff.*

The BBC program reported that during the previous year, "teams of British architects and officials have been coming to visit Oak Park Heights, but they haven't been going to Mecklenberg," and ended by asking whether prison planners would recognize the need for new generation managers to go with new generation prisons.

Can Minnesota Sustain the Wood Management Style?

When asked what they thought would happen to the Oak Park Heights regime if Frank Wood climbed on his motorcycle and rode out of town, two former Marion prisoners replied, "It will go when he goes." This prediction has proved wrong for several reasons.

First, the Wood philosophy fits into the social and political culture of Minnesota. Second, the absence of violence, escapes, destruction of property, and federal court intervention does not provide the justification for changing what is clearly working. For these reasons, a succession of corrections commissioners appointed by Democrat and Republican governors, as well as a nontraditional governor, Jesse Ventura, have not tried to change how the state's prisons are operated. A third reason that this reform agenda did not fade away after the reformer left has to do with those who followed Frank Wood as warden at Stillwater and Oak Park Heights and then moved into senior positions in Department of Corrections as Wood himself did. When Wood left Stillwater to plan Oak Park Heights, he was succeeded by Robert Erickson, a trusted associate who had been present during Wood's reclamation of the prison.

Dennis Benson began his career as a correctional officer at Stillwater and witnessed firsthand the transition to the new regime. When Robert Erickson retired from Stillwater, Benson was named to replace him. During his tenure at Stillwater, he was responsible for major changes in the physical plant and additional improvements in operations. Benson next succeeded Wood as warden at Oak Park Heights, and in 1996, was appointed Deputy Commissioner of Corrections in charge of all institutions; he continues to serve in this position.

Fred Holbeck was associate warden of administration at Stillwater, and then moved over to become associate warden of operations at Oak Park Heights. He was appointed the first warden of a new medium-security prison at Faribault; this task involved overseeing the transition to the new facility from a former state hospital. Holbeck then served as warden at Oak Park Heights and, until his retirement, as the Department of Corrections' Director of Prison Industries.

Erik Skon transferred to Oak Park Heights from the St. Cloud Reformatory where he was a case manager. He was promoted to cell hall director at Oak Park Heights. He was later appointed warden at Oak Park Heights and then to assistant commissioner of corrections in charge of institutions.

David Crist began his career as an officer at Stillwater under Wood, moved up to the position of assistant to the warden at Oak Park Heights and then returned to Stillwater as warden, where he has overseen major changes in the physical plant and operational procedures.

James Bruton was responsible for the Office of Investigation and Internal Affair under Wood at Oak Park Heights. He was promoted to assistant to the warden at Oak Park Heights and served as deputy commissioner of corrections under Wood. After he returned to Oak Park Heights as warden, he planned the new control unit and maintained the institution's essential mission despite severe budget reductions due the state's budget deficit; he retired from this position.

Lynn Dingle held a secretarial position at Stillwater in 1976 when Wood was appointed warden. She was promoted to head of the information technology section at Oak Park Heights. She moved up to become associate warden at the Fairbault Prison, warden at the Moose Lake Prison, and superintendent of the Women's Prison at Shakopee. She currently serves as warden at Oak Park Heights, where she has opened and developed operational procedures for the new control unit.

All advocates of the Wood philosophy made their own improvements to the regimes they inherited. The influence of Frank Wood as an innovator, an agent of reform, a leader, and a mentor is described in greater detail in subsequent chapters of this book. Here, the point is that the reforms accomplished at Stillwater and then applied to the new prison at Oak Park Heights have continued for twenty-five years because Frank Wood did far more than reduce the body count and bring order out of chaos; he profoundly influenced the generation of correctional administrators who followed him.

Whether significant elements of the Wood philosophy have influenced policies and practices in other states is a question that cannot be answered with the absence of systematic study. What can be said is that the presence of so many corrections professionals and elected officials as visitors to Oak Park Heights is evidence of the high level of interest in learning about a different approach to managing high-security prisons.

The author's career in criminology has been enhanced by the opportunity to observe firsthand, and to some extent document, the application of a new direction in penal philosophy in a traditional old penitentiary and at a new type of high-security prison. Seeing Frank Wood at work has been a truly gratifying personal and professional experience.

ENDNOTES

[1] Final Report of the Joint House-Senate Committee on Minnesota State Prison, February 1976, pp 99-100.

[2] According to the legislative committee report: "While not everyone agrees as to whether the sexual behavior that was occurring in the visiting room was inappropriate, acts of sexual intercourse, masturbation, and intimate contact were confirmed by staff, visitors and inmates." *Ibid.*, p.104

[3] *Correction's Corner*, Minnesota Department of Corrections, June 30, 1972.

[4] Fogel's appointment in Illinois was not confirmed by the State Senate, and he took a faculty position at the University of Illinois, Chicago Circle.

[5] Quotations in this section are taken from "The *Segredi* Case," a report for the Joint House-Senate Committee on Minnesota State Prison, February 1976.

[6] During the course of the investigation, these pages disappeared.

[7] *St. Paul Dispatch*, July 25, 1975.

[8] *Ibid.*

[9] *Report and Recommendations by the Grand Jury*, presented to the District Court of Washington County, June 30, 1975.

[10] Final Report of the Committee, *op. cit.*, p. 4.

[11] Frank Wood, interview with the author.

[12] All of the quoted remarks, unless otherwise identified, are taken from a series of interviews with Frank Wood conducted by the author beginning in 1987 and concluding in 1999.

[13] Final Report of the Committee, *op. cit.*, pp. 26, 28.

[14] Frank Wood, interview with the author.

[15] *Ibid.*

[16] *Ibid.*

[17] *Ibid.*

[18] *Ibid.*

[19] For a review of these problems and a list of the measures that may be obtained in super max prisons, *see* David A. Ward. 1995. A Corrections Dilemma: How to Evaluate Supermax Regimes. *Corrections Today.* 57(4): 104-108. *See also* David A. Ward and Thomas G. Werlich. 2003. Alcatraz and Marion: Evaluating Super-Maximum Custody. *Punishment and Society.* 5: 53-73.

[20] Jack G. Young, Commissioner, to Professor David A. Ward, October 10, 1979.

[21] A. R. Potami, Director, Office of Research Administration, University of Minnesota to Jack G. Young, Commissioner, Minnesota Department of Corrections, December 29, 1979.

[22] Kenneth F. Schoen. 1981. New Prison Construction in Minnesota: Why a New Prison for a State Near the Bottom on the Fifty States in Prisoners per 100,000 Population. In David A. Ward and Kenneth P. Schoen, eds. *Confinement in Maximum Custody: New Last Resort Prisons in the United States and Western Europe.* Lexington, Massachusetts; Lexington Books.

[23] Fifteen percent of the Stillwater staff at that time had four-year degrees.

[24] Frank Wood, interview.

[25] *Ibid.*

[26] In California, for example, proposals to close San Quentin have been advanced since Ronald Reagan served as governor.

[27] It should be emphasized that no comparison of Oak Park Heights to Marion is being suggested here. Marion's role until 1994 when a new federal supermax penitentiary was activated at Florence, Colorado, was to take the most serious, often highly publicized federal offenders, and the most difficult and violent management cases from throughout a vast system of more than 50,000 prisoners (now 150,000) from dozens of penal institutions spread across the entire nation. Oak Park Heights has served the same purpose but for a much smaller population of prisoners—approximately 6,500 adult males in 2003 drawn from six other state prisons. At Oak Park Heights, half of the prisoners have been direct commitments, whereas only a handful of celebrity prisoners were directly committed to Marion; the others worked their way up through the disciplinary/segregation units of other federal and some state prisons. Stillwater and Oak Park Heights have boarded a small number of their prisoners with the Bureau of Prisons, for example, an inmate who was involved in twelve assaults on staff members went to Marion.

[28] Roy D. King. 1991. Maximum-Security Custody in Britain and the U.S.A.: A Study of Gartree and Oak Park Heights. *British Journal of Criminology.* 31 (Spring): 140-141.

[29] *Ibid.*, pp. 143-144.

[30] *Ibid.*, pp. 148-149.

Chapter Four:

Frank Wood: A Proactive and Principled Warden with a Humane Touch

When he retired from being commissioner of corrections in Minnesota, newspaper editorials said that Minnesota owes Frank Wood a special thanks for what he has given to the state with his correctional leadership.[1] As this chapter reveals, Frank Wood certainly shaped Minnesota—not only in the present but for years to come. He is an important figure to understand because his style of proactive and principled leadership, combined with his humane touch, could be one of the major catalysts to move corrections forward in the twenty-first century. After providing a biographical sketch of Wood's career, this chapter:

- will describe how proactive wardens are different
- will depict how they do their jobs
- will provide the characteristics of Wood's leadership, including a brief statement of his principles of proactive management
- will assess the quality of Wood's leadership, especially from the perspective of those who know him or have worked with him

The Main Events of Frank Wood's Career and Life

Francis (Frank) William Wood was born on September 24, 1938 to Leonard and Maude Wood, who lived in a small apartment on Grand Avenue in St. Paul, Minnesota. He attended Catholic grade school where he was an average student, and graduated from Johnson High School on the east side of St. Paul. During high school, Frank got his dream job at fifteen driving for a local butcher making deliveries. He also worked cutting, boning, grinding, and making meat sausage.

At eighteen, following his graduation from high school, Frank Wood and three friends joined the U.S. Army together. This was in 1956 during the Suez Canal Crisis. He completed basic training in Ft. Chafee, Arkansas and advanced military police training at Ft. Gordon, Georgia. He was stationed at Ft. Monroe, Virginia, the Continental Army Command Headquarters. He worked posts as a military policeman, patrolman, traffic controller, gate security, in the stockade, and as prisoner detail supervisor. Frank volunteered for a thirteen-month tour in Korea, where he served as a military policeman (MP) on base security, and as a security and intelligence investigator. In this position, he was assigned a jeep and a Korean interpreter. He investigated incidents involving Korean nationals in the port of Inchon. On his own time in Korea, he was invited to teach English pronunciation to Korean high school students. Invited to the homes of some of his students, he formed friendships with many of them that lasted for many years. After three years in the army as a military policeman, Wood was honorably discharged in 1959.

In 1960, Frank married Mary Elizabeth Werner. Mary's parents were one of Frank's customers on his paper route. Mary and Frank have three children. Kimberly is a police officer; Frank Matthew owns a restaurant in Woodbury, Minnesota; and Elizabeth is a cosmetologist and teaches cosmetology at Century College in White Bear Lake, Minnesota. Frank's wife Mary is retired from the Ramsey County Attorney's Officer, where she worked in the child support division.

Frank Wood's original goal was to be a Minnesota highway patrolman, but when he applied, there were no openings. He applied for a correctional officer position at the Stillwater Prison. By the time the highway patrol was ready to train a new class of highway patrolmen, Wood had been promoted to sergeant and would have had to take a pay cut. While at the Stillwater facility, he worked as a trainer teaching about riot formations, as a cell hall officer, turnkey, perimeter patrol security officer, tower officer, prisoner escort officer, and laundry supervisor. After four years at Stillwater in 1963, Frank accepted a promotion and transfer to a new juvenile and youthful offender facility at Lino Lakes. He worked as a shift supervisor, lieutenant, training director, captain, and director of secure treatment for youthful offenders and assistant to the superintendent.

In 1973, Frank Wood completed his college education while working full time. He graduated from Antioch College at the Minneapolis Campus with a bachelor's degree in law and justice administration. After ten years at Lino Lakes, he was asked to accept another promotion to the central office as the director of inspection and enforcement. The inspections division had responsibility for annually inspecting all county and city adult facilities and licensing juvenile facilities in the state of Minnesota. Inspections staff also worked with county boards and sheriffs, reviewing and approving all plans for new or remodeled jails and lockups.

In February 1976, the Minnesota Senate and House released a 267-page report extremely critical of the administration and management of the state prison. In June of 1976, Frank Wood was asked to accept the warden's position, and he returned to the Stillwater Prison as the warden, just thirteen years after his departure as a sergeant to accept a promotion at Lino Lakes. Wood and his staff made major changes in the guiding principles, philosophy, and operation of the prison. They developed and implemented the first sophisticated policies and procedures manual. It laid the foundation for accreditation of the facility. The changes reduced the frequency, scope, and seriousness of the incidents in the prison. The changes and improvements for staff and inmates resulted in very positive exposure for the institution staff.

In 1979, Wood was selected by the Minnesota Corrections Association as Corrections Person of the Year for his outstanding contributions to the field of corrections. In the same year, he was selected by the American

Correctional Association to complete the strategic management in corrections program at the University of Pennsylvania, Wharton School. He was in residence there for a few weeks.

In 1980, after four years as warden of the Stillwater facility, Frank Wood was assigned as warden of Minnesota's new high-security facility. Prior to Wood's appointment, in the early stages of planning and construction of the facility, there were a series of cost overruns. When Wood took over, he was directed to complete construction within the legislature's capital improvement appropriation, which he did. The facility accepted its first inmates in 1982, and by 1984, was experiencing national and international exposure and acclaim for not only its architecture but its operational philosophy and principles. Twenty-one years after its opening, the prison has never had an escape or an inmate or staff homicide, while confining high-risk offenders from Minnesota and other state and federal jurisdictions.

In 1985, Frank Wood accepted an appointment as a federal court evaluator and consultant related to the federal courts' intervention in Tennessee's prison system. Wood served the court and Tennessee on a part-time basis from 1985 to 1990. As a result of Wood's recommendations, along with other experts and the special master, major improvements were made in Tennessee's corrections system, and the federal court ended its oversight of the system. He received official recognition and appreciation from then Tennessee Governor, Lamar Alexander.

In 1992, Frank Wood was promoted to deputy commissioner of corrections in charge of all the Minnesota state-operated adult and juvenile institutions. In 1993, the governor appointed Wood as Minnesota's Commissioner of Corrections. He also served as a member of the States' Sentencing Guidelines Commission. As Commissioner of Corrections in Minnesota, the Commissioner has the final decision on the release of all prisoners serving life sentences.

Commissioner Wood retired in 1996 after serving thirty-seven years in the Minnesota Department of Corrections. Wood was the first warden, deputy commissioner, and commissioner to be promoted from an entry-level correctional officer through all the uniform ranks to these key leadership positions in Minnesota corrections.

Since Frank Wood's retirement in 1996, he has served as volunteer spokesman for Rebuild Resources, raising funds from foundations and individuals to build a community-based residential treatment academy for the chemically dependent. The residential facility has been in operation for more than three years. Frank also served on his parish council and as a parish administrator for two years. He further served on the board of directors and as president and chairman of the board of the Minnesota Minutemen. In 2003, Wood was selected as executive director of the Minutemen Foundation. The Minutemen raise funds to support amateur athletics in Minnesota and assisted in bringing major league baseball and football to Minnesota. Frank is a life member of the Veterans of Foreign Wars and the Disabled Veterans. He additionally is a member of the third and fourth degree Knights of Columbus.

How Do Proactive Wardens Do Their Jobs?

A proactive warden, as is true for any warden, is responsible for the security of the institution and, therefore, must maintain external control (no escapes from the prison) and internal control (no riots, disturbances, assaults, and homicides) within the walls. The proactive warden's principal responsibilities are also similar to other warden's position descriptions, except a proactive warden puts a greater emphasis on programming for inmates and development of staff. In terms of the nature and scope of the warden's job description, the proactive warden emphasizes more the importance of direct communication and rapport between the warden and staff and between the warden and the inmate body.

The proactive warden tends to see the context of the prison as a dynamic community, which has a capacity to change in a positive direction. For this to happen, it is helpful for the proactive warden to have a number of skills and expertise in several knowledge areas:

- the ability to think and conceptualize well
- the character development to know the right moral position to take
- the creativity to be a problem solver with sometimes very complex issues
- the desire and willingness to make a difference
- the willingness to take a proprietary interest in the institution

In Feature 4.1, Frank Wood develops a position description of a proactive warden who as the chief executive officer of a correctional institution is accountable for the entire scope of the operation of the prison.

How Are Proactive Wardens Different?

The author asked Frank Wood how proactive wardens differ from their disillusioned colleagues.[2] Wood identified the following ways in which he believes that proactive wardens are different.

Proactive Wardens Believe They Can Make a Difference

They believe they can have an impact and need not be limited by what others have done. This is especially true for those proactive administrators who have a strong proprietary interest in their institution and who are able to develop that same proprietary interest among staff. They believe prisons can be run in such a way that inmates and staff have hope and confidence in and respect for each other.

Proactive Wardens Have a Hands-on Approach

They spend a good deal of time walking the cellblocks, visiting inmates in their cells, touring the yard, and talking with staff at their assignments. They believe that to reduce the frequency, scope, and seriousness of the inevitable institutional problems, the top administrator must set the climate by interacting directly with inmates and all levels of staff on a regular basis. This system will provide information that is needed to avoid or defuse pending problems, as well as improve policy procedures, post orders, and job descriptions.

Proactive Wardens Realize the Importance of a Supportive Team

A major concern of these wardens is to build a team of supportive staff. This supportive team encompasses top management staff, including associate wardens and unit managers, but it also

Feature 4.1: Position Description of a Proactive Warden by Frank Wood

Principal Responsibilities, Tasks, and Performance Indicators

"Inherent in the list of responsibilities for all employees of a correctional institution, regardless of their classification, is the responsibility for institutional security; in other words, all employees are expected to be alert at all times and to report or intervene immediately in any behavior or activity which could affect our collective responsibility to protect the public, maintain security and/or control of the institution or provide for the safety of staff and residents.

"It is the responsibility of the warden to provide leadership, direction, and supervision to institution staff, and monitor the implementation of policy and procedure at the operation and service delivery level, so that the public, staff, and inmate safety and compliance with professional standards of security, control, and rehabilitation can be maintained.

"The warden is to do the following things:

- Provide thoughtful guidance and direction in the development of the organization's goals consistent with the anticipated needs of the institution and the Department of Corrections.
- Provide forums for discussion, development, and dissemination of the goals of staff at all levels to ensure that the organization's fiscal and human resources will be distributed and utilized consistent with our plan and goals.
- Provide administrative leadership in the development of the institution budget, the development of a spending plan after final appropriations are made, and monitor actual expenditures to ensure the cost-effective use of resources within the limits of legislative appropriations.
- Exercise direct supervisory authority over immediate subordinates so that applicable plans are equitably administered and employees under my jurisdiction will effectively perform assigned job duties to achieve the annual objectives of the department and institution.
- Provide opportunities for inmates to improve themselves and earn reasonable compensation by their participation in constructive programs and assignments. Eligible inmates who are inclined to learn a marketable skill, work in an institution-support assignment, complete their academic and/or vocational education, or those who express interest and meet the criteria to participate in chemical dependency, sex offender, or mental health treatment will be afforded the opportunity within the limits of the resources and space available.
- Organize, plan, and implement a full range of structured institution systems of inmate accountability and discipline consistent with established laws, policies, and regulations, and provide within this organization, the structure and resources for around-the-clock staff accountability for the total institution plant security and program.

Feature 4.1: Position Description of a Proactive Warden (con't)

- As the institution's appointing authority, provide administrative leadership in the area of labor relations to maintain a cooperative, collegial, professional, working relationship between all union, nonunion, and administrative staff.
- Coordinate the purposes and activities of each division or work section within the organizational structure to ensure that unity of objectives, internal harmony, and teamwork exists in furthering the goals and objectives of the organization.
- Participate cooperatively and compatibly with other institution heads of this department in assisting the commissioner and his deputies in fulfilling the expectations of the executive and legislative branches of government and the mission of the department of corrections.
- Continue the development of professional skills, capabilities, and competence through involvement in professional organizations, training seminars, and experiential development with colleagues in corrections and related fields of practice and study.
- Oversee the institution's Affirmative Action program and ensure compliance with federal and state laws, rules, and regulations.

Nature and Scope:

Relationships

The warden reports to the deputy commissioner of institution services. As such, the primary relationship above or at the same level of the warden are policymakers for the department. This level of authority interacts regularly with executives of the state and federal government and representatives of the legislative and judicial branches of government. In addition, it is essential that the warden develop and maintain productive and mutually beneficial relationships with union leadership, community leaders, representatives of the private sector, business, industry, and other agencies of the criminal justice system.

Within the institution, it is important that the warden maintain the trust and respect of the staff. The success of any operational program is dependent on the combined efforts of all staff working together as a team. It is imperative that the warden be accessible to all levels of staff. Regular contact with staff in formal and informal forums is essential in establishing reciprocal trust, confidence, and mutual support and respect among staff at all levels.

Institutions function only as well as the level of control and compliance of the inmate body. The warden establishes and maintains a rapport with the inmate population and sets a tone for positive interactions between staff and inmates. The levels of credibility, trust, and cooperation between staff and inmates are enhanced by informal and formal contacts with the inmate population.

Feature 4.1: Position Description of a Proactive Warden (con't)

Knowledge, Skills, and Abilities

A competent warden requires extensive knowledge and a wide range of skills and abilities. It is an administrative position at the chief executive level. A correctional institution is a dynamic community, which has the potential and capacity for drastic change to occur on a moment-by-moment basis. To adequately fulfill the responsibilities, the warden must understand all dimensions of human behavior, ranging from normal and healthy responses, to the most abnormal and deviant responses. This area of knowledge must include staff and inmate expectations, roles, needs, reactions, and formal and informal staff and inmate organizations and cultures. The warden must understand and recognize manipulations, diversions, and exploitation, staff and inmate psychological profiles, and value systems and be a judge of not only inmate and staff current skills, abilities, and limitations, but their potential as well.

The warden must understand and be conversant in many technical areas such as: law; prisoner rights; leadership; management; due process; communications; contracts; budget and finance; physical plant management; labor relations and negotiations; politics; riot control; emergency response procedures; security and principles of control; and the elements of prison programming, including work, industry, treatment, medical, educational, recreational, religious, leisure-time activities, and many others.

An effective warden must have exceptional communication skills in both writing and speaking. A warden must be an efficient manager who is able to process a high volume of accurate and quality work and have a high capacity for retention of information. The warden must be able to skillfully delegate duties and responsibilities to qualified and competent subordinates, and provide them with the support and latitude to not only utilize their talent and expertise, but encourage their development to their full personal and professional potential. The warden should be an astute listener and observer and demonstrate superior tactical and strategic skills. The warden must have good self-discipline and impulse control and ability to use and handle emotional responses with deliberation and purpose, and avoid overreacting in some situations even when there is extreme provocation. The warden must have the capacity to interact with a wide range of individuals and personalities from the inadequate, irrational inmate or the irate or uninformed citizen, to the prominent and influential leaders in government and the private sector.

The warden should have an aptitude for analysis, insight, and introspective thinking. Character strength, determination, and the tenacity to persevere under great stress and frustrating conditions are very important characteristics.

Feature 4.1: Position Description of a Proactive Warden (con't)

Understanding, managing, and controlling a prison community in a manner that continually improves the operations, requires a commitment, concern, and proprietary interest in the inmates, the staff, and the physical plant.

Problem Solving

There are numerous problem-solving opportunities inherent in the management of a prison. The warden is a key problem solver. Problems of logistics, litigation, inmate discipline, due process, inmate appeals, political and philosophical disagreement, community or special interest group criticism, service resource problems, staff discipline, and union grievances are rather common sources.

The warden establishes the philosophical tenants for problem-solving mechanisms within the organization. The warden encourages staff to solve problems at the most appropriate levels within the organization. The standards set by the warden for staff training, the involvement of staff in participatory management, organizational efficiency, and decision making at the most appropriate levels in the organization provide systems and forums for timely and efficient problem solving on an ongoing basis regardless of the warden's presence in the facility. Problems that cannot be resolved within the organizational structure are ultimately resolved by the warden.

The position of the warden is to some extent, structured by state and federal law, department of corrections' policies, and governmental agency regulations and requirements. The warden is given a broad authority and discretion to regulate and manage the institution, programs and operation consistent with his or her style, ability, personal principles and staff capabilities. The warden functions with substantial independence and minimal supervision as chief executive officer.

The warden enjoys a wide range of opportunities for creativity and substantial freedom to act and concomitantly is obligated with a high degree of accountability and responsibility to the commissioner of corrections, the legislature, the governor, and the public.

Source: The position description was developed by Frank W. Wood on August 24, 1990. On the warden's responsibilities, it does not include tasks and performance indicators.

includes captains, lieutenants, and sergeants who supervise correctional officers.

Proactive Wardens Are Receptive to Technological Innovations

This new breed of correctional administrator is quick to use the technological advantages that recently became available to corrections. Today, innovations within the prison combined with external supervision are enabling federal and some state corrections officials to shape a new prison environment based on accountability, functional integration, risk assessment, and institutional differentiation. Management information systems (MIS) have led to systemwide changes. For example, inmates are tracked more effectively throughout the system, personnel have been upgraded, and population needs can be projected. Smaller and newer prisons, better classification systems, and unit management have helped to defuse institutional violence.

Proactive Wardens Are Receptive to Improved Means of Supervising Correctional Institutions

They welcome legislative task forces that examine everything from free time (recreation) on death row to T.I.E.—Training, Industry, and Education vocational programs. They also are receptive to inmate grievance procedures. Unlike their predecessors, they do not resist court supervision of prisons, including American Civil Liberties Union attorneys, defense counsel, representatives of the attorney general, and attorneys litigating for prisoners. (It is significant, in this regard, that Frank Wood developed a unique relationship with Alvin J. Bronstein, the director of the American Civil Liberties Union, who at the time was struggling to bring prisons around the nation to a more appropriate way of managing the inmate population.)

Proactive Wardens Model the Behaviors that They Want to Elicit from Inmates and Staff

They believe that a crucial component of a human relations approach is their willingness to demonstrate to others what involvement in and understanding of others entails. They also affirm that before they can expect this response from staff, they must demonstrate to others their job commitment, trustworthiness, loyalty, and high moral integrity. Also, as part of this modeling, they attempt to show staff how to interact effectively with inmates without losing their respect and without being compromised, manipulated, or taken for a ride.

Proactive Wardens Seek American Correctional Association Accreditation

These wardens usually enthusiastically endorse the accreditation process of the American Correctional Association. An institution or a community-based program would be accredited when it meets the minimum standards proposed by the American Correctional Association (now the standards of the Commission on Accreditation for Corrections). Wardens have so widely supported the accreditation process because they feel that the standards of accreditation assured the improvement of correctional institutions, that the accreditation process provided an attainable goal, and that this process was a major step in the development of corrections.

What Characterized Frank Wood's Style of Leadership?

Frank Wood is an outstanding human being who has made valued contributions in many areas. As a correctional administrator, his approach to management of a prison will far outlast his lifetime. He has developed, more than anyone else, a philosophy and the principles of proactive management, which have the potential to transform U.S. corrections in the twenty-first century. This section will depict what characterized his management of a maximum-security prison.[4] In Feature 4.2 Alvin Bronstein explores the constitutionality of Wood's prison with that of the other prisons.

Frank Wood Knew What He Wanted to Happen in a Prison

Frank Wood had clarity in his goals and principles. A thoughtful person, he developed

Feature: 4. 2: What Was the Context of Frank Wood's Success in His Career?

Frank Wood's career was characterized by the willingness, even the drive, to continue to grow in his job and by the fact that he came into a system where there was good leadership at the top. Alvin J. Bronstein, former director of the American Civil Liberties Union, had the opportunity to observe Wood's growth and development. When he was asked to compare the constitutionally of prisons in which Wood was warden with prisons in other parts of the nation, Bronstein made these comments:

I visited two prisons that Frank Wood ran: Stillwater, the old maximum-security prison, and then Oak Park Heights, the newer and so-called "super maximum security" prison. I use that term advisedly because Oak Park Heights is not typical of the supermax facilities in this country; it wasn't when Frank was running it and to my knowledge I understand it is not typical today.

Frank was a terrific warden who continued to grow in his job. He was a better warden at Oak Park Heights than he was at Stillwater just because he was a person who learned and continued to listen to criticism and grow from it. He did come from an environment where there was a great deal of leadership above, and Frank Wood benefited from the fact that, beginning in the late 1950s and early 1960s, you had a succession of commissioners who were among the best in the nation. Starting with Paul Keve and then David Fogel. Ken Schoen came next and then Orville Pung. Frank Wood worked under these people, and then became the commissioner.

These were among the best people in the country and so with that kind of leadership, it enabled Frank to run better prisons. All of the prisons in Minnesota compare preferably to the rest of the nation. The first few times I visited the women's prison at Shakopee, I thought it was the best women's prison that I've ever seen, either in the United States or even in the most progressive countries in Europe, the Scandinavian countries. Shakopee was a superb prison. Stillwater even with an old facility was run decently. Oak Park Heights was not like most of the other supermax's where prisons were either buried underground or they're all electronically controlled.

The warden at the Oklahoma supermax facility brags about the fact that his staff never have to talk to a prisoner. That's outrageous. That's just the opposite of what Frank Wood and others did at Oak Park Heights. That prison was broken down into small units. There was a lot of programming, a lot of staff-prisoner contact. The perimeter was secure because the prison contained the so-called most dangerous of the Minnesota prisoners. The people would have problems in other facilities or would have very significant criminal records, but they were treated in a decent kind of way at Oak Park. There was an expectation that they would benefit from programming and from contact with other human beings, whereas in the other supermax prisons in this country, the expectation is that you want to treat these people like animals because they're going to behave like animals. Well, you have self-fulfilling prophecies. You treat people like animals and they do behave like animals.

That was not Frank Wood's style nor was it Minnesota's style. So, Minnesota's prisons were always from a constitutional and from a human decency point of view superior to almost all of the other prisons in this country.[3]

Source: Alvin Bronstein, interviewed October 2002.

his principles over the years, and he was continually working on how these principles could be more effectively attained or realized in a prison context. In other words, he knew what he wanted and how he could achieve these goals or principles. His basic principles of proactive management are briefly contained in Feature 4.3. These principles are more extensively developed in Chapters 5 through 9 of this volume.

Frank Wood's "Presence"

There was no question who was in charge when Wood was warden of the Minnesota Correctional Facility, Stillwater, and Minnesota Correctional Facility, Oak Park Heights. A quiet and even shy person by nature, he still had a "presence" about him. When he came into a room, his "presence" becomes apparent. When he talked to an inmate or a staff member in his office on the first day in the prison, this person instantly became aware of the "presence" of the warden. Part of the "presence" was that there was a stature about him, which set him apart from others. The fact that his mannerisms were polished and professional contributed to the feelings of this "presence," but perhaps what gave birth most of all to the "presence" was the quality of this human being. With strong beliefs and highly developed traits of honesty, sincerity, and morality, the combination of his many positive attributes communicated a beautiful spirit.

Frank Wood's Calmness

Warden Wood was a correctional administrator who had a calmness about him. This inner peace gave him the ability to maintain his composure, regardless of the circumstances taking place around him. No matter how volatile an incident may be, no matter how much he was upset by the behavior of a staff member or an inmate, and no matter how he was being challenged by a member of the legislature, he seemed to be able almost always to keep his "cool." This calmness was very reassuring to staff, because they knew that even in the worst conditions, you could count on the warden to "keep his wits around him" and to stay focused on what had to be done to resolve the situation.

Frank Wood's Charisma

There was a special quality about Warden Wood's leadership, and part of this special nature was that he had a lot of charisma. The dictionary defines charisma as "a special quality of leadership that captures the popular imagination and inspires unswerving allegiance and devotion."[5] The charismatic personality, especially the one who knows what he or she wants to accomplish, has the advantage of being believable and of being able to persuade others to become involved. Lynn Dingle, warden of Minnesota Correctional Facility at Oak Park Heights, put it this way:

> *What was different about Frank Wood? He was charismatic. Although a very quiet person, he was a very strong person and a strong leader. He was always clear how we are going to run a good institution. For instance, at the time that he took over as warden at Stillwater Prison, it was really out of control. It was a very dangerous place for everyone to work. In fact, when I started, women weren't allowed in the cellblock which changed soon after that. But after Frank Wood came in, he really took control of that facility. I am sure he paid dearly for it because now inmates were going to be held accountable for what they were doing. He literally made it a safer place to be, both for offenders and the staff.*[6]

Feature 4.3: Wood's Principles of Proactive Management

1. Proactive management begins with control. Without control of the institution, nothing positive can be accomplished.
2. An anticipatory and preventative approach is fundamental to maintaining institutional control.
3. Clear and effective communication is a requirement for proactive leadership. Being in control of the institution means that both staff and inmates clearly understand what the rules are, what is expected, and what the consequences of unacceptable behavior would be.
4. It is necessary for the warden and staff to take a proprietary interest in the institution.
5. Both staff and inmates must be treated with dignity and respect.
6. The prison must be safe for both inmates and staff.
7. The warden must be a person of integrity, credibility, and trust.
8. The warden must develop rapport with staff and inmates.
9. Cleanliness and orderliness of the institution are absolute necessities in correctional administration.
10. Staff must clearly understand the importance of accountability, attention to detail, and following the schedule.
11. A prisoner is sent to prison as punishment and, accordingly, the warden, prison staff, or politicians in the community have no right to make the process of imprisonment any more painful or miserable.
12. An inmate is to be given a safe environment conducive to rehabilitation for those who want to make a change in their lives.

Source: Jim Bruton helped develop this list in February 2003. Mr. Bruton is a former warden in the Minnesota Department of Corrections.

Frank Wood's Morality

There are those individuals with whom we come into contact at work or in the community, and we say, "Now, this is a person of integrity." Frank was admired throughout his career for being a moral person, a person of integrity, a person who would do the right thing. Steven Norris, former commissioner of corrections in Tennessee, relates a conversation he had with Frank that impressed him:

I remember once Frank and I were talking about what we had done prior to becoming involved in corrections. I think he told me at one point in his life that he owned or managed a liquor store. He got out of that when it became apparent to him that through his ownership or stewardship of a liquor store he could contribute to the public problems of society by creating an opportunity for people to buy alcohol. He knew that sometimes the alcohol led people to do stupid things and to end up in prison. He made a very simple and ethical decision that he didn't want to be involved in that. For some reason, this has always stuck with me. You don't meet many people who will make those sorts of decisions. They'll spend time rationalizing about it, but they won't do anything about it. Frank did something about it."[7]

Frank Wood's People-centeredness

In addition to having a "presence" about him, a calmness beyond the excitement of the moment, a charismatic personality, and a strong sense of morality and instinct for doing what was right, Frank Wood brought to correctional administration a people-centered focus. This focus on people was shown by the time he spent within the prison interacting with inmates and developing rapport and a relationship with staff. It was also seen in his emphasis on staff communicating with each other and developing rapport with inmates. In addition, his concern about people not being harmed in prison and being treated decently came from a basic belief that people are important and are to be valued.

Frank Wood's Fairness and Openness

You could count on being treated fairly by Warden Wood, whether you were an inmate who was involved in a disciplinary offense, a staff member who had broken the rules, or a staff member who was aspiring to a promotion or a change of assignment. As a person who was also open, he was always willing to hear others' viewpoints on how something should be done or handled. He would listen to what others had to say to him, whether they were staff, inmates, administrators from the department, or members of the legislature.

Frank Wood Outworked Everyone

Another characteristic of Wood's leadership was that he had a strong work ethic. He was greatly committed to his job, and he was always willing to pay the price of doing what he thought was the right thing to do. If that involved coming in the middle of the night to make arrangements for the search of a cellblock the next morning, he was willing to do that. If that involved developing a relationship with line staff and their supervisors on various shifts and weekends, that was what he was willing to do.

Frank Wood's Effectiveness in Working with and Empowering Others

Warden Wood was very gifted in working with and empowering others. Part of Wood's legacy is that correctional administrators who are now running the Minnesota prisons were not only trained while Wood was the presiding officer of the prison, but they looked to him as their mentor and continue to feel grateful for his guidance throughout their career. Staff found him to be supportive of their growth and development and, as a result, he maintained strong loyalty from those with whom he had worked throughout his career. In Feature 4.4, two of Wood's former staff members comment about this characteristic of teaching and empowering others.

Frank Wood's Willingness to Model Positive Behaviors

Often our actions speak much louder than our words. Leaders who propose behaviors to others that are not reflected or seen in their own lives will lose some—or perhaps a lot—of their credibility. What Warden Wood preached, he practiced. He asked staff to handle themselves with composure, even in threatening or intimidating situations, and staff could see that was how the warden handled himself. He asked for commitment from staff during the eight-

Feature 4.4: A Master Teacher

Dennis L. Benson, deputy commissioner of the Minnesota Department of Corrections, aptly expresses Frank Wood's effectiveness as a teacher in this statement:

I think the most outstanding quality that he brought to the table, besides his incredible gift of managing correctional facilities, was Wood's ability to teach and train others.

Lynn Dingle, warden of the Minnesota Correctional Facility, Oak Park Heights, said this about Frank Wood as a teacher:

I can't say enough about this man. He taught me so much. He taught a lot of us so much. I think the legacy he left behind is that our staff care so much about what they do. I hear wardens from other states talk about total apathy in their institutions. They tell me, "I'm lucky if I get them to show interest, let alone put any effort into the job." In contrast, I've been in the business twenty-eight years now, and I have found that staff are engaged because they care. They are here for the right reasons, they care about what they do, and I think that's why I have enjoyed working in this department.

Sources: Interviewed in October and November 2002.

hour shift, and staff could see that he was totally committed to doing the job.

Frank Wood's Commitment to Operating a Safe and Humane Prison

Frank Wood was absolutely committed to managing prisons that were safe and humane. He felt that the basic requirement of sending people to prison and of hiring people to work in a prison was to ensure their safety against the violation of predatory inmates. He saw a safe prison as a key ingredient to a humane facility. This meant that the facility must be humane for both staff and inmates.

Frank Wood's Commitment to Treating People with Dignity and Respect

Warden Wood continually emphasized that inmates and staff were to be treated with dignity and respect. Dennis L. Benson, deputy commissioner of the Minnesota Department of Corrections defined the principles practiced by effective wardens:

Some of the fundamental principles that guide me are to treat inmates with dignity and respect. Frank Wood used to promote the philosophy that we should treat inmates the way that we would want our son, brother, or father treated if they were incarcerated. This principle has served the Minnesota system well for many, many years. We should also create a climate where staff feel safe reporting security breaches, are able to admit mistakes, and use appropriate and acceptable discipline intervention.[8]

Frank Wood's Ability to Come Up with the Solution

Staff knew that no matter what the problem or incident, Warden Wood would somehow find a solution. It might be a budget problem, as so many correctional systems are experiencing today. It might have to do with increased tension in the facility, or with the problem of dealing with a new governor or negative members of the legislature. Whatever the problem, staff were confident that the warden would know what to do.

Frank Wood's Search for the Truth

Wood would leave no stone unturned to get to the truth. If a rumor were circulating around the facility, the warden wanted to know who started the rumor, the accuracy of the rumor, and the implications of the rumor for the security and safety of the institution.

Frank Wood's Preparation

If Warden Wood took a position, he was usually right because he researched the issues. If he had to appear before the legislature on some question relating to law and corrections, he would do the necessary homework. If he had to make a report, either as a corrections professional in Minnesota or as a federal consultant for another correctional system, his report would be well thought through and would contain all the necessary points to be made.

Frank Wood's Belief in Participatory Management

Warden Wood brought others into the decision-making process. Chapter 7 presents his approach to participatory management, but suffice it to say that Wood's operation of the prison was always characterized by the involvement of staff in decision-making. However, he did not bring inmates into the decision-making process, because he always held that this would be counterproductive to the safety and security of staff and inmates in the prison.

Frank Wood as a Confidant to Many

Warden Wood was approachable. People felt that he valued them, that he was concerned about their growth and development, and that he would do whatever he could to assist them in their correctional career. Thus, not surprisingly, staff viewed him as someone who would be a confidant, someone who you could approach about what was bothering you, someone who could be trusted not to share what you told him, and someone who would find a way to be helpful. Warden Dingle puts it this way:

> *Frank is very supportive, and there have been a few occasions where I've asked him for advice. He was probably the strongest mentor I had growing up in the Department of Corrections. [I started] at a time when women weren't even allowed in the cellblock, I never got anything but support from him. He was one that would give me options to try different jobs and to work my way up. I probably would not be sitting in his old warden's office if I had not been mentored by him. So I have been fortunate that way.*[9]

Frank Wood's Personal Stuff Did Not Get in the Way

We all have clay feet. None of us is perfect, nor is Frank Wood a perfect human being. Yet, unlike many leaders who tend to lead with an exposed ego or who are fragile because of some emotional problems they have not worked through, Frank's "stuff" did not interfere with what he brought to the table as a correctional professional.

Many individuals who knew Frank Wood admired him. Feature 4.5 contains some comments from individuals who knew and respected Frank as a human being, as a warden, as a commissioner, and as a corrections consultant for the federal courts.

Feature 4.5: The Quality of Frank Wood's Leadership

Patrick McManus, former commissioner of corrections in Kansas and a person who worked with Wood in Minnesota, gave this answer when he was asked to compare Frank Wood as a correctional administrator to others he had known through the years:

> *"Unfortunately, what Frank has done has been not typical in the profession. The thing that makes Frank so admirable, as I watched him perform over the years, is that he is a very moral man. He does not feel the need to assume a stereotypical warden's "role" when he is running his prison. The same deep principles of respect and ethical behavior emerge in his role as a warden just as they do in other parts of his life."*
>
> *"I think there is a warden role that people fall into. Typically it's the tough guy who is usually a late-night stereotype of the tough uncompromising warden. Most of the wardens who I know aren't really that kind of person in their everyday life, but some feel that they need to adopt that role when they are running their institutions."*
>
> *"Frank did not do that. As a result, his reactions were always predictable. It was basically an ethical, principled, and, therefore, predictable response to whatever was going on in the prison. It is rare to find a warden who commands the kind of respect that goes with that sort of behavior. That's what Frank did. He also communicated to his staff that he expected them to treat prisoners the way that they would want their own father, brother, or relative to be treated if they were in that situation."*
>
> *"There are a lot of good wardens, but I think few of them have been able to pull it off as well as Frank. I know there are other ethical people around, but I don't know if that is the centerpiece of their leadership style in running a prison. At least I have not encountered that with many other wardens. What Frank does gives staff permission to behave in the same way. It's not just that the warden preaches a certain type of behavior; he models a behavior based on dignity and respect that encourages staff to respond in the same way. While Frank was always very supportive of his staff, he made it not only permissible but necessary that they treat prisoners with respect and that is a situation that you don't find in many prisons."*

Alvin J. Bronstein commented:

> *"You may know the book, called* The New Red Barn, *which was edited by Bill Nagel. He was a marvelous corrections professional in this country who was part of our team. This book resulted from a Law Enforcement Assistance Administration (LEAA) study in the late 1950s and early to mid-1960s. LEAA hired this team led by Bill Nagel to review all the new prisons that had been built since 1950 to see whether the new architecture made a difference in the way the prisons were run, in their safety, in their efficiency, and in their ability to program prisoners."*
>
> *"The title of the book was called* The New Red Barn *because that was a take off of Austin McCormick's 1920s statement. He was one of the old timers in American prison history and was quoted as saying, 'Give me a few good men and an old red barn and I'll give you a good prison.'"*

Feature 4.5: The Quality of Frank Wood's Leadership (con't)

> *"Bill Nagel's study team said that these new red barns did not make a difference. What made a difference were the men and women running the prisons. You could run a good, decent, constitutional prison in an old facility as long as you had the right people. I think that sort of sums up Frank Wood's career. He is the right kind of person. He's lucky to have the right people above him, and he trained good people below him. He ran good prisons whether they were the old one in Stillwater or the new one at Oak Park Heights. The architecture had very little to do with it; it was the people involved."*

Finally, Jim Bruton, former warden in the Minnesota Department of Corrections, who had the experience of meeting with wardens all over the nation, was asked how the Minnesota prisons compared with those in other states:

> *"Well, I think that we are very different in Minnesota, and I believe that our approach is both enlightened and realistic and Minnesota owes this to the philosophy and commitment of Frank Wood. A lot of wardens used to come to Minnesota to see how it was possible to manage a maximum-security prison with the inmates out of their cell a good part of the day. They couldn't believe what they saw. We had periods of time where we went over two years without dirty urinalysis tests. We had a long period of time without finding any drugs or contraband weapons in the facility, very few assaults, and very few problems. We ran an education unit involving the most difficult-to-manage inmates where the last serious incident in the education unit was over fifteen years ago. What they found was very secure and well-managed facilities that had incentive-based programming. Inmates were given a reason to wake up every morning with good rewards for good behavior. There was a humaneness to the Minnesota's prisons in which people were treated with respect.*
>
> *"That's what Minnesota is about. I've never seen wardens who came to Minnesota, went through the facility, and didn't come out feeling positive about what they saw. I believe more than fifty [people from] foreign countries have visited Oak Park Heights, and we generally got the same kind of reaction. Usually, the first thing said was that we had a great staff, a professional staff, who believed in what we were doing. I think that is very different from a lot of states. I was always proud to be a warden in Minnesota.*
>
> *"More importantly, however, is to understand where the Minnesota philosophy of operating prisons came from and why it remains. It came from Frank Wood when he became warden at Stillwater Prison in 1976, and his legacy remains ingrained in every system today. He brought it to Stillwater and Oak Park Heights as warden and cemented it into the department as deputy commissioner and commissioner. This is a deeply committed man of heavy convictions—all centered around doing things the right way. Treating offenders with dignity and respect and providing a safe, secure, and humane environment for change was the cornerstone of his legacy. He drove the philosophy into the foundation of prison operations and to those who worked for him and with him. He was my mentor and confidant. I learned more about prisons from Frank Wood than anyone else. I consider myself very fortunate to have had the opportunity to know him as a great leader, boss, and my friend."*

Sources: Interviewed in October and November 2002.

Summary

Frank Wood was an exemplary warden whose proactive and principled philosophy was an effective means to run a prison system. There is also no question that here is a deeply moral man who treats people with dignity and respect. This author strongly believes that Wood's style of proactive and principled leadership, combined with his humane touch, could be the catalyst to move corrections forward in the twenty-first century.

However, some argue that there have been corrections giants in the past who proposed wonderful ideas, attempted to implement these ideas for a few years, and then were beaten back by the negative reaction, sometimes destroying them in the process. It is true that corrections has not been kind to giants, because as they stood alone, their innovative ideas and programs could be defeated easily by the toxic systems of which they were a part.

What seems to be different today is that there are others around the nation—chief executives of correctional institutions and heads of departments of corrections—who are proponents of this proactive approach to correctional administration.

In the final five chapters of this book, they join with Wood to form a composite understanding of what it means to be a proactive warden. Frank Wood, as it should be, is our guide through these chapters. Yet, other proactive corrections professionals join in and remind us that Wood does not stand alone.

ENDNOTES

[1]Frank Wood: He Worked to Keep People Out of Prison. 1996. *Star Tribute Editorial,* May 30.

[2]This is a revision of material in Clemens Bartollas. 2002. *Invitation to Corrections.* Boston: Allyn and Bacon, pp. 263-264.

[3]Interviewed in October 2002.

[4]Jim Bruton was extremely helpful in developing the characteristics of Frank Wood's leadership.

[5]*Webster's New Twentieth Century Dictionary—Unabridged, 2nd ed.* 1983. New York: Simon and Schuster.

[6]Interviewed in October 2002.

[7]Interviewed in October 2002.

[8]Interviewed in November 2002.

[9]Interviewed in October 2002.

Chapter Five:

Preparation for Proactive Wardens

The warden or superintendent's job in a correctional institution today is complex and requires a person of considerable resourcefulness and talent. The faint-in-heart need not apply for the position of a warden in a minimum-security prison, much less a maximum-security or high-security facility. The theme of this book, using the experiences of one former warden which are supplemented by the accounts of others, is that individuals can become proactive wardens today, operate humane facilities, and feel good about the jobs they are doing. Such proactive wardens need a period of preparation, and this chapter examines what type of preparation is necessary to become a proactive warden.

What Type of Background Would Help a Person To Be a Proactive Warden?

In a previously published book, Bartollas asked Frank Wood what type of background a person would need to be this type of warden. Wood answered with the following categories:[1]

Experience at an Entry-level Position is Helpful

This type of experience helps a person to understand from the very ground level what is going on in the institution. Starting at the bottom and working your way up gives wardens a perspective that will enhance their ability to function in the job. The warden learns to recognize the informal and formal organizations and all of the nuances of those structures.

Beginning in an entry-level position is not something that absolutely has to be done, but if a person is looking for a roadmap of how to prepare himself or herself, one ingredient is experience at the service-delivery level where an individual faces the inmate clientele on a day-to-day basis. Those who start at the managerial or administrative level have the tremendous luxury that when they are having a bad day, they can hide in their office and avoid people.

As a line officer, especially, when you drive to work for thirty minutes or an hour, there is no place to hide. If, for instance, you are working in the laundry, you know you are going to come every day Monday through Friday at 7 a.m., and you will have thirty-five inmates locked in the laundry room. Your job is to get the laundry out and keep the inmates from going after each other, to interact with them, and to conduct your business and get the job done.

Your problems at home cannot come into the prison. You may be having a good day or a bad day, had a fight with your wife, one of your kids may be in trouble, or something else is wrong at home. You have no place to go to sort that out, but the show must go on. This experience is invaluable. You gain sensitivity to some of the things that a corrections officer has to do everyday. He or she does not have the amenities and options that others do. This individual deals with threats and dangers that others do not have. He or she sometimes has to deal with verbal abuse or even the possibility of physical assault.

Involvement in the Union Movement also Can Be Helpful

Getting involved in the union movement as a line officer is also helpful for people who are planning professional careers in corrections as supervisors, managers, administrators, or wardens. This experience will help them appreciate and understand the unique aspects of organized labor. Having experience on both sides of the table is a distinct advantage. You will learn from firsthand experience that the goals and objectives of people in the union are not significantly different from what management wants to accomplish. Wood believes that honest, hardworking officers, supervisors, managers, and administrators all want the same things. When things are put out on the table for all to see, people can recognize and appreciate that we truly do want the same things.

We all want to have fair and equitable compensation for our work; to be recognized for good performance; to be supervised and led by honest competent, sensitive, and reasonable people; and to have performance standards, career advancement, and accountability applied to staff at all levels equally. Good labor/management relations are enhanced and maintained when there is clear and convincing evidence that this philosophy is practiced and not just given lip service. It must be apparent to employees at all levels that management decisions reflect these principles.

A Broad-based College Education Is Better than a Narrow-based Education

College-level academic education is important. However, Wood cautions that those planning on being correctional administrators should not get caught up in making their academic education so focused that they narrow it to social work, sociology, and the behavioral sciences and ignore some of the other essential aspects of the well-balanced academic education that they will need: business administration, fiscal management, leadership, and management techniques. Wood advocates having a broad-based and generalized college education that can be supplemented periodically in your career with specific courses that enhance your competence, effectiveness, leadership skills, and ultimately your promotability.

Staying in a Comfortable Position Is a Problem

Wood also advises people not to be tempted to stay in a comfortable position, just because the working hours and days off are good. When he looks back and sees people retiring today as correctional sergeants who started with him more than thirty years ago as correctional officers, he realizes that some of them found a comfortable spot and were unwilling to give it up. They did not try to expand their horizons by searching out and accepting real challenges in the workplace. Some people clearly focused on other aspects of their personal life and their fulfillment came from contributions to their community, church, or social organization that enhanced the quality of life for their children and community. It is very difficult to do both as you work your way up the organization from an entry-level position.

At the management level, it is a challenge to bring a healthier balance to your personal and professional life. In most of Wood's experience but not always, promotions appeared to go to those who have made and are prepared to make personal sacrifices. Wood does not know a competent long-tenured warden who did not and does not continue to make some personal sacrifices. It is also wise to be alert and look around for tough assignments, where people have failed and where there is a high staff turnover. These opportunities offer excellent challenges. Tough assignments bring recognition and exposure when wardens are able to exceed expectation and make significant contributions to improve the system.

Growing Up Poor Can Be Good Fortune

Wood does not know if he can speak for all wardens, but as he goes back and searches his memory for things that were helpful to him, he said that it would be ideal to have the good fortune of growing up poor. This ensures your exposure to good and bad people of all religions and ethnic backgrounds, because you are going to be working with those persons later in life. This helps you to understand the perspective from which these people come. When he analyzes why he had a reasonably good rapport with both staff and inmates, he attributed it to "growing up in circumstances similar to that of many of our clientele." Furthermore, coming from a local blue-collar working-class background and starting as an officer gave him an appreciation for the struggles that many of the uniformed and entry-level staff face.

The World Does not Revolve around Corrections

Wood also feels that it is important to avoid thinking that the world revolves around corrections. Many people in corrections are so narrowed in their friendships and relationships that most of their associates are corrections people. They start to think that the center of the universe is corrections, but, in reality, corrections is a very peripheral part of society's institutions.

If you maintain a wide circle of friends who are not in corrections, you will have sounding boards and can hear what is being said by other people with other perspectives on what we do in our profession. It is also important to continue your education through a broad range of reading on a wide variety of topics—history, philosophy, logic, ethics, treatment modalities, and, of equal importance, religion and theology. In addition, wardens must maintain an informed perspective on the full range of issues, local, state, and national. Wardens always will be at a disadvantage if they are not informed on how their work meshes with the changing and dynamic society in which they live.

Supervision and Managerial Experience in the Prison Is Helpful

Having supervisory and managerial experience in a prison helps individuals develop effective, unique leadership and management skills needed to be the prison chief executive officer. You need to examine how people do things, what they do right, and how you can acquire these skills and enhance your communications expertise. By being astute observers, you can learn what not to do. By watching what people do that is counterproductive or alienates staff, inmates, or others, you can learn how to avoid these pitfalls when you are in positions of authority. Also important in developing your managerial expertise is adopting your own management style rather than attempting to adopt somebody else's style whose personal characteristics and areas of strength are very different than yours. It is unlikely that his or her style will work as well for you as it does for him or her.

Wood has always believed in praising deserving staff and documenting the achievements and accomplishments of competent staff with letters of commendation with wide circulation. Only when you reach the point that you think you may have to remove that person should you start documenting negatives in written evaluations. Written evaluations are not the place to make obscure constructive suggestions. They can be verbalized.

Attention to detail is the best insurance policy against surprises and failures. Ultimately, to manage others well, you need to have a sense of commitment and purpose, a calling, and a proprietary intensity about you.

Skills in the Art of Thinking Are Important to a Warden

Critical thinking skills are important to teach both staff and inmates. Critical thinking skills can be taught by taking people through a process of helping them understand that almost every decision they are faced with has options, benefits, and consequences. If you can teach that to your staff and inmates, then when they are faced with decisions, this will allow them to go through a process of thought, analysis, or deliberation that will help them make better decisions. This occurs because they have intellectually gone through a laundry list of options, consequences, and benefits, and have come out with a more informal, practical, and usually better decision than they would have if they have not been trained in critical thinking skills. You want inmates to start doing that, too. Wood had classes for inmates on critical thinking skills.

Creativity is critical in correctional administration. Thinking creatively essentially means thinking outside the box. When you are confined to the box, you think the only way to do something is the way that it has been done for the last fifty years. It is amazing how many good creative ideas came out of just day-to-day operational things from both staff and inmates, because they were given the license, the opportunity, and the forum to suggest improved and more creative ways for doing things.

Conceptualization is also important in prison administration. For top administrators, conceptualization involves the ability to see the whole and to rise above the organizational norms. David Brierton, former warden of Stateville Correctional Center in Joliet, Illinois, used to be fond of saying that "the ability to conceptualize will happen only when the prison administrator will take time to think."[2]

Administrators who fail to conceptualize the total organization are likely to end up with crisis-centered management. This means that they will spend most of their time "putting out fires." The chances are also good that the administrator who sees only part of the problem or situation will either underreact or overreact to the problem. The chief responsibility of the administrator then is to think in terms of and to understand the total organization, while lower-level administrators are specializing in the management of their area of responsibility.

Thus, prison administrators are generalists rather than specialists. The generalist is charged with the responsibility of conceptualizing the whole organization and for developing a systemwide plan to manage it. The generalist depends on specialists to run the various units of the correctional facility. This philosophy of administration requires participatory management and input from all levels of staff. Effective generalists do not try to carry the total weight of responsibility of a correctional facility on their shoulders. Instead, they know that it is necessary to bring others into the decision-making process. The effective generalist carefully selects management staff, encourages them to become involved in staff development programs, reinforces them when they do a good job, and holds them accountable when they do not. This generalist wants to build a team that can be trusted to carry out a stated policy throughout the entire correctional facility.

Conceptualization occurs with line staff and inmates when they endeavor to understand a concept and put the concept into practice. For instance, Wood would say, let us target verbal abuse because it is important to minimize verbal abuse between inmates and staff. The reason it is important is that it will reduce the level of violence. Words are usually exchanged and tempers escalate, and the next thing you know someone gets smacked. If verbal abuse can be targeted, staff and inmates can interact with each other as human beings who have dignity and respect for each other. Targeting verbal abuse sets up another barrier to violence.

Inmates stop laughing at this concept when they see the consequences and the frequency of violence decreasing because of the reduced amount of verbal abuse in the institution. That is what Wood means by conceptualizing something, then acting on it, believing that it will work, and encouraging others to believe it will work. Hopefully, the data will prove it does work.

A final skill in the art of thinking is that of learning to administer the prison in a rational way. Correctional administration by proactive wardens can be understood as an attempt to become "rational," to be receptive to information and knowledge as the means of effecting organizational change. The purpose of rational action is to know the end to be achieved and the proper means to reach that goal. J. D. Thompson, in his book *Organizations in Action*, suggests that organizations are expected to produce results, and, therefore, their actions must be reasonable or rational.[3] Accordingly, managers must act rationally to produce the desired results.[4] One of the ways this can be done is to reduce uncertainty among inmates and staff. Another way this can be done is to draw reasonable conclusions based on the facts at hand.

For example, it became apparent to a person with knowledge of prison facilities that the Penitentiary of New Mexico at Santa Fe was in trouble in the months preceding the riot of February 2, 1980. The author toured the prison in August of 1979, and he told the staff member conducting the tour that the prison appeared to have serious problems and that it would be a miracle if it did not blow completely apart in the next six months. The staff member assured this academic that the prison was in good shape. He gave the same response to all the other corrections visitors: You may perceive problems, but we do not have a problem. The failure to see serious and deep-rooted problems was a failure of rationality, a failure to understand what was reasonable given those special circumstances.

The Importance of Trust

Tom Peters' article, "The Missing 'X-Factor': Trust," discusses the importance of trust in a correctional institution. He portrays how trust can be found in a prison by examining the administration of Warden Dennis Luther at the Federal Correctional Institution, in Bradford, Pennsylvania.[5]

In February 1989, Warden Dennis Luther opened the Federal Correctional Institution McKean in Bradford, Pennsylvania. Luther said in an interview, "I don't think prison has to be a constant negative experience for staff and inmates." He added that the prisoner's punishment is being sent to prison. Punishing inmates once they are inside is not needed.[6]

Interviewed in 1991, Luther said that he went into the profession "out of altruism" instead of joining the ministry, his second choice. In the mid-1980s, he was able to turn around the Federal Bureau of Prisons, Danbury, widely acknowledged at the time as one of the most troubled institutions in the Bureau of Prisons.[7]

Throughout his corrections career, Luther had the reputation of being a maverick and a risk-taker. He called inmates "constituents," and allowed inmates to somewhat manage themselves. At McKean, following a shakedown in an inmate's cell, correctional officers had to replace everything exactly as they found it. Luther was also respected because, as a warehouse foreman in the prison put it, "The best thing about the warden is that he never lies." Furthermore, all levels of staff and inmates felt that the warden listened to them and that their input was important for correctional change. Luther put it this way, "Line-level people have good ideas, not only about how to do their job, but about how to do your job better."[8]

Most correctional administrators, especially in maximum-security facilities, would have trouble with the degree of self-governance that Luther gave inmates. Our intent is not to argue for inmate self-government, but to point out that trust is a basic ingredient in providing order and quality of life in a prison setting. Staff must trust each other. Inmates must feel that they are safe from each other and that staff will treat them with respect and fairness. At the same time, the warden needs to be trusted by all levels of staff and by inmates.[9]

What Are the Theoretical Underpinnings of the Proactive Managerial Philosophy?

Wardens who respond to proactive and anticipatory management philosophy usually accept a learning metaphor for prison organization rather than one of the traditional metaphors. They also are strongly committed to management by power rather than by force.

The Relevance of a Learning Metaphor for Proactive Prison Managers

Correctional institutions have undergone more change in the past 30 years than they have in the previous 170 years. The change has been widely documented in a rich literature that has explored many incidents of change and the reactions of correctional administrators:

- Thomas Murton describes the scandal-reform-scandal cycle of prison change in Arkansas.[10]

- John Irwin focuses on racial consciousness and the politics of power within California prisons.[11]
- Leo Carroll describes changing race and social relations in Rhode Island.[12]
- James Jacobs examines the relationship between outside society and the administration of Stateville Penitentiary.[13]
- John DiIulio; Steve Martin and Sheldon Ekland-Olson; and Ben Crouch and James Marquart describe the impact of court decisions and administrative reaction on the management of penal institutions.[14]

In this literature, there are four metaphors for prisons as organizations:

- Prisons as machines
- Prisons as cultures
- Prisons as organisms
- Prisons as politics

Each plays a dominant role in the thinking of both the staff and administrators and in the thinking of those who analyze prison organizations.[15]

Prisons as Machines

The metaphor of the mechanistic perspective dominates the analysis of the paramilitary nature of correctional staff. The order and efficiency that should characterize prison management are achieved through the creation of a fixed division of tasks, hierarchical supervision, and detailed rules and regulations.[16]

As DiIulio and Jacobs describe the institutions they studied, it is clear that these paramilitary systems functioned more effectively prior to the early 1960s, the era of the "Big House" prison and the autocratic manager.[17] However, when the politics of race entered prisons and the "hands-off" doctrine of the courts vanished, then prison managers experienced greater difficulties in coping with their changing environment, and this metaphor did not fit as well as it had in the past.

Prisons as Cultures

The metaphor of thinking about prisons as cultures can be traced back to Donald Clemmer's *The Prison Community* and is found in nearly all sociological studies of the prison produced since. According to Clemmer, the prison, like other social groups, has a culture.[18] A cultural approach focuses attention on the ways members of an organization create, share, and transmit meanings to various aspects of organizational life.[19] For example, the inmate code, especially in past decades, provided a way for inmates to maintain solidarity and to resist institutional rules and staff. Today, the major shortcoming in applying this metaphor is that generational change among both staff and inmates has resulted in new and competing cultural meanings being imported into the prison. In other words, this metaphor is no longer as useful as it once was because "the good old days" of a unified staff and inmate culture have long passed from the prison scene.

Prisons as Organisms

Jacobs in Stateville has extensively described the relationship between prisons and their environment and has shown the transformation in metaphors from describing prisons as machines to prisons as organisms:

> *The realization of mass society as expressed in such trends as the growth of prisoners' rights and the intrusion of judicial norms into the prison has provided the impetus toward the transformation of institutional authority and administration. When the prison as an autonomous institution was located at society's periphery and beyond the reach of the courts and other core institutional systems, there was no need for the system of internal authority to become rationalized. It was only when outside interest groups began making demands on the prison and holding administrators accountable for their decisions that traditional authoritarian systems of institutional security became untenable.*[20]

Jacobs's analysis actually results in an "open system" perspective. Gareth Morgan adds that the idea of openness emphasized the key relationship between the environment and the internal functioning of the system.[21] Unquestionably, while the environmental influences on prisons are more pervasive and acknowledged today than ever before, this metaphor has limits in helping us understand the change process and the internal functioning of the prison.

Prison as Politics

The political metaphor is another that has been applied to the study and practice of understanding the prison organization. This perspective focuses on "interest, conflict, and power."[22] Different constituencies within (and external to) the prison organization have interests in how prisons organize themselves. The ability of a particular constituency to achieve its goals will be determined by its ability to exercise power. This perspective also recognizes a variety of sources of power:

- formal authority
- control over scarce resources
- organizational structure
- decision-making processes
- knowledge and information
- organizational boundaries
- control of technology

In sum, these four metaphors are inadequate in themselves to explain the prison as an organization, but each continues to influence the operation of the prison. The prison, especially the maximum-security one, remains a paramilitary organization and is likely to retain much of this structure as long as security remains the dominant concern of administrators. The unified prison culture of the past has been replaced by a number of competing groups, or subcultures, that shape the attitudes and outlooks of members. The day that the prison could keep outsiders out is long gone; indeed, one of the most widely examined research findings in recent years is that inmates are affected as much by importation from outside the prison as by the deprivations of confinement.[23] Finally, the political metaphor will always be found on all levels of prison management and inmate life, because power, authority, and conflict are likely to continue explaining the dynamics of prison life.

The proof that traditional metaphors for running a prison have failed to bring order and safety to the correctional environment, especially of maximum-security prisons, is the continual problem with riots and other major disturbances that have plagued correctional institutions in this nation for the past thirty-five years. Or, one could talk about the inmate assaults on each other or inmate assaults upon staff.

A Learning Metaphor

The problem is that the machine; culture; and political metaphors, especially, foster conservative and often reactionary agendas in the prison. These agendas are repressive and rigid. People do not think that other ways of thinking about the prison are possible. The repressiveness and rigidity of the prison is not likely to change until another metaphor begins to influence prison operations. Morgan proposes the brain metaphor, which incorporates the need to change. The brain metaphor focuses on learning. As Morgan describes it:

> *The whole process of learning hinges on an ability to remain open to changes occurring in the environment, and on an ability to challenge operating assumptions in a most fundamental way.*[24]

This ability to remain open to changes taking place in the organization provides clues of shifting patterns and trends; it allows detection of early warning signals and permits development of a strategy leading the prison in a more constructive direction. Thus, it is sometimes necessary to find new ways of seeing the organization. By seeing and thinking about the context of organizational activities and problems, managers are able to envision and create new possibilities.[25]

The capacity of "challenging operating norms and assumptions" is grounded in the belief that organizational members must be skilled in understanding the frameworks, assumptions, and norms that guide the current activities and be able to challenge and change them when necessary. What this means is that organizational members must be skilled in understanding the mind-sets or mental models that underpin how the organization operates or functions. When it is appropriate, as when a prison is on the verge of serious organizational problems, wardens must be able to develop and employ new norms and assumptions.[26]

The encouragement of an "emergent" organization suggests that contrary to traditional views of management that require imposing goals and objectives from "above" for execution "below," this brain metaphor proposes that "the behavior of intelligent systems requires a sense of the vision, norms, values, limits, or 'reference points' that are to guide behavior."[27] What this means is that organizational members, or all levels of staff, within the prison, "buy into" the vision, norms, and values of the organization.

The main strength of the brain metaphor rests on the contribution that it makes to creating a spirit of learning in an organization. A learning organization is more able to innovate, evolve, and meet the challenges of changing environments. This metaphor also offers a powerful way of thinking about the implications of new information technology and considering how this technology can be used to support the developments of learning organizations.[28]

Wardens or superintendents who accept this brain metaphor value it because it enables them to be open to new ideas, and, in turn, they are willing to expose other administrators and staff to new learning experiences. These wardens further develop a vision of organization change and find ways to gain acceptance of their vision throughout the prison. In future chapters, we will develop this metaphor for the culture of learning more completely by exploring what it means to the everyday management of the prison.

Power versus Force

In the traditional prison, there are destructive feelings of hopelessness, fear, frustration, rigid positions, and divisiveness toward everything. The response is one of force. Force leads to explosive anger that bursts forth on others, and resentment and revenge permeate everything. Sometimes, inmates are attacked and killed and, at other times, a staff member is assaulted or killed. These destructive energies lead to such characteristics of the traditional prison environment as living in a constant state of fear, being hopeless or apathetic, and pursuing whatever means of addictive escapes that are available in the prison environment.

However, using principles of power rather than force, Frank Wood and others have created an interconnected community within the prison. The proactive philosophy of prison management is full of higher-energy fields, both for staff and inmates. Accomplishment, fortitude, and determination create individual growth in spite of prison walls, bars, and the lack of freedom for inmates.

Thus, the power of the proactive model is that the level of safety, equality, inner confidence, and realistic appraisal of the problems are reflected in the lives of both management and prisoners. Staff in the proactive model then experience their jobs as stimulating, challenging, and exciting. It is not long before what takes place is that the principles underlying the proactive model implemented and lived by Frank Wood and others are mirrored within the general population of the prison and become empowering.

The majority of prisoners return to society, whereby the level of force that they learned in the community and which was reinforced in the prison context continues long after the prison experience. This force and its consequences leading to fear and distrust, hatred, robbing, hurting and killing others ripple through the inmates' lives to their families, communities, nations, and the world.

In contrast, the power of the warden in the proactive model is expressed through treating people with dignity and respect, creating a safe environment, being responsive to the needs of inmates and staff, and encouraging staff and inmates to pursue self-growth experiences. This power goes out to staff, empowering and eventually raising the energy fields of the inmates and empowering them in turn. An emotional calm and trusting environment can be realized to a far greater degree than would be thought possible in a prison environment. This is what happened in Minnesota when Frank Wood was warden, and this is what is taking place in other correctional environments which have implemented proactive management. For further discussion on this, see David R. Hawkins' fascinating book, *Power vs. Force.*[29]

What Are Critical Managerial Considerations for Proponents of Proactive Managerial Philosophy and Practice?

The author sent questions to selected respected interviewees that varied somewhat, but usually included critical considerations for persons who wish to become proponents of proactive managerial philosophy and practice. We will examine each of the following questions in the subsequent sections.

- Can you provide any insight or explain why some correctional institutions operate with rare incidents of homicide, escape, assault, and suicide while other prisons appear to struggle from crisis to crisis?
- What are the characteristics of a well-managed facility?
- What are the principles practiced by effective wardens?
- Is it important for the warden to develop and maintain a personal rapport with staff and inmates?
- How does a warden develop and maintain an organizational culture that motivates staff, develops them to their full potential while creating an environment in the prison conducive to the rehabilitation of those inmates inclined to take advantage of it?

Why Do Some Prisons Operate Well While Others Go from Crisis to Crisis?

Effective management made the difference between some prisons operating well rather than floundering from crisis to crisis, the interviewees consistently responded. Orville Pung, former commissioner of corrections in Minnesota, responded that "some institutions seem to be caught up in crisis management rather than crisis prevention. Facilities that are proactive don't react to or wait for problems to happen. Instead, they anticipate and prevent these problems and, as a result, don't have the chronic problems which others have."[30]

Dr. Reginald Wilkinson, director of corrections for Ohio's Department of Rehabilitation and Correction, added that "a well-managed facility is clear and orderly; the grounds are well kept; the officers are well groomed; the facility is well painted, and it is not cluttered. A well-managed facility also has a low level of incidence of violence, few positive drug tests, and prisoners are engaged in meaningful work experiences, vocational programs, and educational programs."[31]

Alvin J. Bronstein, former director of the American Civil Liberties Union, said that "a well-managed facility has competent staff and is a busy prison that has enough programming, space, and recreation to accommodate all of the prisoners."[32]

Jim Bruton, former Minnesota warden, gave more advice to aspiring proactive wardens: "As Frank Wood used to say, 'correctional institutions don't run safely by accident, they run well by design.' It takes a proactive approach, leaving no area of the institution without explicit detail and accountability."[33]

What Are the Characteristics of a Well-managed Facility?

Norman Carlson, former director of the Federal Bureau of Prisons and one of the most widely respected correctional administrators of the twentieth century, answered that "in a well-managed facility, staff and the inmates feel safe and secure." Carlson went on to say that "when inmates feel safe and secure, they relax; the tensions are gone, their defensive mechanisms are greatly reduced, and it's a much more harmonious institution."[34]

In addition to a safe facility, David Crist, warden of the Minnesota Correctional Facility at Stillwater, feels that a characteristic of a well-managed institution is attention to detail and effective communication "in all directions among all parties."[35] Burl Cain, warden of the Louisiana State Penitentiary at Angola warns that "a prison with unhappy inmates and staff is a dangerous, hopeless, unproductive place. It is usually noisy, filthy and depressing."[36] John Hurley, former warden in the Federal Bureau of Prisons, suggests inmates are respectful and communicative in a well-managed facility.[37] Jim Bruton adds that a well-managed facility is "clean, safe, secure, and humane."[38]

What Principles Are Practiced by Effective Managers?

William Sondervan, former director of the Maryland Division of Corrections, suggests that "if you're a good warden, you can almost smell, taste, and touch when things are going well or when things are going wrong." He contends that "a good warden has an instinctive sense of when to crack down or when to let up, when you give people a pat on the back or when to motivate to improve."[39]

Norman Carlson said that "effective wardens walk and talk. They are always out in the population." He adds that "communication skills are one of the most important factors in the making of an effective warden."[40] According to Patrick McManus, effective wardens have consistency and are persons of integrity.[41] John Hurley succinctly summarized the principles practiced by effective wardens:

- Management by walking around—see and be seen.
- Consistency—say what you mean and mean what you say.
- Sense of humor—have one.
- Integrity—doing the right thing when no one else is around.
- Compassion—life only comes once, for everyone.
- Communication—up, down, and sideways.
- Humility—being named warden is not an anointment to sainthood.[42]

In Feature 5.1, Kathleen Hawk Sawyer, former director of the Federal Bureau of Prisons, develops these answers more extensively.

Is It Important for the Warden to Develop and Maintain a Personal Rapport with Staff and Inmates?

Interviewees completely agreed that it is necessary for a warden to develop and maintain rapport with staff and inmates. Orville Pung says that it is absolutely essential for the warden "to know his or her administrative staff as well as the sergeants, lieutenants, and correctional officers."[43] Jim Bruton said that when he managed prisons, he made it a practice of getting inside the prison each day. He also indicated that he made it a practice on every Thanksgiving and Christmas to come into the prison on every shift and to go around to all staff and shake their hand and say, "Thank you for being here on a holiday."[44]

Dennis L. Benson contributes that when the warden develops and maintains rapport with staff, then staff understand his or her expectations, principles, and philosophy. "They then begin to emulate those same qualities in the workplace. With respect to inmates, it is equally important to let inmates know that you care about them, what your principles are, and what they can expect in the institution."[45]

How Does a Warden Develop and Maintain a Positive Organizational Culture?

Lynn Dingle suggests that developing and maintaining a positive organizational culture is

Feature 5.1: Principles Practiced by Effective Wardens by Kathleen Hawk Sawyer

"In observing and considering leadership styles over the years, I have noted several fundamental qualities or philosophies in effective leaders, regardless of the organizations they serve. These fundamentals for effective leadership hold true for wardens. They include:

- Having a set of values, principles, and convictions (both personal and organizational that serve as the basis for decision-making and action, combined with clear goals (or vision) and definitive plans to achieve those goals. No one will follow unless you know where you are going.
- Articulating your goals and expectations clearly, setting reasonable time lines for accomplishing those goals, and making sure staff are indeed following the path established.
- Leading by example: showing staff what you expect and remembering that your actions will be judged against your words. They should match.
- Knowing your strengths and weaknesses and being realistic in your personal assessment: if you overstate your weaknesses and underestimate your strengths, you risk being an indecisive leader; if you minimize weaknesses and exaggerate your strengths, you will not fool anyone for long and you make yourself and your institution vulnerable. Effective wardens surround themselves with staff who complement their skills and are open to feedback, criticism, and wise counsel from peers and subordinates.
- Demonstrating and earning respect: you must be someone of integrity worth following and know that respect is earned through your actions, not simply by demanding respect based solely on the position or rank you hold. You must also accord others the same respect you wish for yourself.
- Showing a commitment to mentoring and helping staff achieve their fullest potential. Staff are our most valuable asset, and their development is a win-win situation for the individual and the agency.
- Maintaining perspective and balance. Those who move into leadership roles should not lose sight of the people in their organization or let tasks assume greater importance than the people they rely upon to accomplish their mission. Additionally, it is imperative to maintain a healthy balance between work and personal aspects of life and encourage this balance in institution staff."

Source: Letter of October, 2002 in which former director Hawk Sawyer answered the interview questions.

more likely to happen when wardens are open and honest, when they encourage new ideas, when they recognize achievement, and when they emphasize training.[46] William Sondervan says that this culture is more likely to emerge when wardens practice what they preach.[47] Orville Pung adds that it is more likely to happen when there is a "we/we" rather than a "we/they" culture set up in an institution. A "we/they" culture "can only result in an environment that's hostile, negative, and difficult in which to work."[48] Norman Carlson adds that in his experience, a culture is set up when the prison first opens. "A positive culture is found when inmates feel safe and secure, where there is communication between staff and inmates, where there are opportunities for inmates to work, and where cleanliness is considered to be essential." If, however, the culture is dysfunctional, the institution will probably have problems for years, because "it is very difficult to change a culture once it is established."[49]

Summary

This chapter suggests that there are three areas of needed preparation to become a proactive warden. The first area involves the background and experiences that are helpful for a proactive warden to have. This background broadens persons and gives them a knowledge base that will equip them to be the chief executive officer of a prison. The second area is framed in theoretical language proposing that proactive wardens are able to see in ways that other wardens do not see. Their vantage point is anchored and guided by a learning metaphor and by the principle of power rather than force. The learning metaphor makes it easier for wardens to question previous assumptions, to develop a new vision of what the prison could be, and to develop operations that will enable their vision and goals to be realized. In addition, this section stated that the proactive warden is one who uses power rather than force in operating the prison. The use of power is one of calling on higher energy fields that will be healing rather than destructive to the prison environment. The final section of the chapter answers some basic questions related to management of a prison from the perspective of proactive management philosophy and practice that includes developing and maintaining personal rapport with staff and inmates and developing and maintaining a positive organizational culture.

ENDNOTES

[1]This section is updated and adapted from Clemens Bartollas and John P. Conrad. 1992. *Introduction to Corrections.* New York: Harper/Collins, pp. 20-23.

[2]Interviewed in 1977.

[3]J. D. Thompson. 1967. *Images of Organization.* New York: McGraw-Hill and J. D. Thompson. 2003. *Organizations in Action: Social Science Based Administrative Theory.* New York: McGraw-Hill

[4]*Ibid.*

[5]Tom Peters. 2002. The Missing "X-Factor": Trust. In Tara Gray, ed. *Exploring Corrections: A Book of Readings.* Boston: Allyn and Bacon, p. 175.

[6]*Ibid.*

[7]*Ibid.*

[8]*Ibid.*, p. 176.

[9]Luther, as well as many other wardens, has been able to accomplish this institution-wide trust.

[10]Thomas Murton. 1976. *The Dilemma of Prison Reform.* New York: Holt-Rinehart, and Winston.

[11]John Irwin. 1980. *Prisons in Turmoil.* Boston: Little, Brown.

[12]Leo Carroll. 1974. *Hacks, Blacks, and Cons.* Lexington, Massachusetts: Heath.

[13]James B. Jacobs. 1977. *Stateville: The Penitentiary in Mass Society.* Chicago: University of Chicago Press, p. 146.

[14]John J. DiIulio, Jr. 1987. *Governing Prisons: A Comparative Study of Correctional Management.* New York: Free Press; Ben. M. Crouch and James M. Marquart. 1989. *An Appeal to Justice: Litigated Reforms of Texas Prisons.* Austin: University of Texas Press; and Steven J. Martin and Sheldon Ekland-Olson. 1987. *Texas Prisons: The Walls Came Tumbling Down.* Austin: Texas Monthly Press.

[15]This section is adapted from Lucien X. Lombardo. 1989. Metaphors for Prison Organizations and Correctional Officer Adaptation to Change. Paper presented to the Annual Meeting of the American Society of Criminology, Reno, Nevada, November.

[16]Gareth Morgan. 1986. *Images of Organization.* Beverly Hills, California: Sage, pp. 11-31.

[17]DiIulio, *Governing Prisons*, and Jacobs, *Stateville.*

[18]Donald Clemmer. 1958. *The Prison Community.* New York: Holt, Rinehart and Winston.

[19] Morgan, *Images of Organization*, pp. 119-152.

[20] Jacobs, *Stateville*, p. 10.

[21] Morgan, *Images of Organization.*

[22] *Ibid.*, p. 160.

[23] *See* Charles W. Thomas. 1975. Prisonization or Resocialization: A Study of External Factors Associated with the Impact of Imprisonment. *Journal of Research in Crime and Delinquency.* 10(January), pp. 13-21; and Charles W. Thomas. 1970. Toward a More Inclusive Model of the Inmate Contraculture. *Criminology.* 8 (November), pp. 251-262.

[24] Morgan, *Images of Organization*, p. 91.

[25] *Ibid.*, pp. 91-94.

[26] *Ibid.*, p. 92.

[27] *Ibid.*, p. 100.

[28] *Ibid.*, p. 95.

[29] David R. Hawkins. 2002. *Power vs. Force: The Hidden Determinants of Human Behavior.* Carlsbad, California: Hay House Inc.

[30] Interviewed in October 2002.

[31] Interviewed in November 2002.

[32] Interviewed in October 2002.

[33] Interviewed in October 2002.

[34] Interviewed in October 2002.

[35] Interviewed in October 2002.

[36] Letter received on October 21, 2002 in response to the interview questions.

[37] Letter received in October of 2002 in response to the interview questions.

[38] Interviewed in October 2002.

[39] Interviewed in November 2002.

[40] Interviewed in October 2002.

[41] Interviewed in October 2002.

[42] Letter received in October of 2002 in response to the interview questions.

[43] Interviewed in October 2002.

[44] Interviewed in October 2002.

[45] Letter received on September 18, 2002 in response to the interview questions.

[46] Interviewed in November 2002.

[47] Interviewed in November 2002.

[48] Interviewed in October 2002.

[49] Interviewed in October 2002.

Chapter Six:

Standing Tall: A Person of Integrity

An essential aspect of being a proactive warden is to be a person of integrity. Those who are looked on as persons of integrity have demonstrated over a period of time that they are honest persons. They also have shown that there are no contradictions between what they say and what they do. Thus, being seen as a person of integrity, what this chapter calls "standing tall," is not something that can be earned in a day or a week. It occurs over a substantial period of time during which that integrity is tested on a regular basis. The credibility and honesty of these persons are reflected in everything they say and do.

What Is Integrity?

Stephen L. Carter's *Integrity* is a very helpful study of what integrity means in American life.[1] He believes that integrity requires three steps:

(1) discerning what is right and what is wrong

(2) acting on what you have discerned, even at personal costs

(3) saying openly that you are acting on your understanding of right from wrong

The word "integrity," derived from the same Latin root as integer, carries the sense of wholeness. A person of integrity, then, is a whole person, a person somehow undivided. "Integrity" conveys a completeness, rather than single-mindedness, and reveals a person who is confident in the knowledge that she or he is living rightly.[2] William Seymour Tyler, a former professor of Latin and Greek languages and literature at Amherst adds, "Integrity implies implicit obedience to the dictates of conscience—in other words, a heart and life habitually controlled by a sense of duty."[3]

How Does Integrity Affect the Behavior of an Enlightened Warden?

Integrity requires that wardens themselves should not exhibit negative behaviors in their management of a prison. They should not be using profanity. They should not be raising their voices and doing things contrary to what they tell staff. Even under extreme provocation, wardens cannot allow themselves to be provoked.

What this modeling positive behavior does is to deescalate negative or violent behavior, rather than to escalate it. If wardens want inmates to listen when they explain something that they do not want to hear, the wardens need to let inmates see how they handle a situation in which they are provoked. This must remain true even when inmates may swear at the warden or insult staff members. If the warden or other corrections staff respond in anger physically, they are saying to inmates: We told you not to solve your problems with violence and what we are doing is waiting for the first opportunity where you do something that justifies our laying our hands on you, getting revenge, and solving our problems with violence.

Wardens daily make decisions that have important moral, ethical, and legal implications. When their jobs are on the line, wardens sometimes resort to solutions that involve questionable tactics. A warden may make a promise without any intention of keeping it, or may resort to directing subordinates to solve a problem, and then ignore the means by which the staff accomplish the directive. Even the most enlightened wardens may lose control in the heat of an inmate disturbance or the murder of a staff member and unprofessionally retaliate against inmates. One such Midwestern warden had scantily dressed troublemakers loaded into an unheated bus on a cold winter night and transferred to an institution six hours away. Not surprisingly, some of the inmates suffered severe frostbite. This was one of the reasons why this warden lost his job!

Top-level administrative staff, who must deal directly with the problems of the prison, do more soul searching than any other institutional employee. From time to time, they must deal with such considerations as the following:

- Is the organization's influence on me so subtle that I'm not aware of it?
- How extreme will the compromises I make here have to be before I am forced to sit down and take stock of myself?
- Even if I faced up to my compromises, would I be able to do anything about them?
- Am I so conditioned to seeing things the accepted way that I've lost my objectivity?

The answers to these questions will affect the employee's level of job satisfaction and ability to function satisfactorily in the institution.[4]

In Feature 6.1, Norman C. Carlson, former director of the Federal Bureau of Prisons and recipient of the American Correctional Association's E. R. Cass Award, comments on the importance of recruiting staff who will uphold integrity in the institution and of the influence of a warden who makes ethical and moral decisions.

Integrity extends to the lives of wardens both inside and outside of the institution. Wardens cannot be in the newspaper for being a slum landlord and be good wardens. Wardens also cannot be a model of integrity if they beat their spouse and children or have problems with substance abuse. If a warden's prison is filthy, with toilets that do not work, excrement laying around, or mice infestation, nobody can make a change in that environment.

Wardens are humans, just like everyone else. They all have made mistakes, but they must have an avenue for redeeming themselves. Yet, the mistake cannot be repeated. Wardens must remember that they are not ordinary citizens. They represent a state or the Bureau of Prisons and a correctional institution. They are running a prison and ought not in any way to discredit that institution with what they do in private.

William Sondervan, former commissioner of the Maryland Division of Corrections, defines the importance of integrity to prison wardens:

> *It's an absolute must. You must have integrity in everything you do. You have to be up front, you have to be honest, and*

Feature 6.1: Interview with Norman C. Carlson

"When you recruit, you certainly attempt to find staff who have demonstrated integrity in their employment history and in their relationship with others. That is one of the reasons for the screening of employees. I think it is important to make sure that you are hiring the very best you can in terms of integrity, ethics, and personal stability. Integrity must also be re-enforced while staff are working in the institution. Wardens are the ones who are key players in emphasizing the importance of integrity.

". . . when I taught at the University of Minnesota, I cited an example of what influences a warden can have. During the 1950s, I was a case worker at the U.S. Penitentiary in Leavenworth, Kansas. A new warden came in by the name of Ches Taylor. I'll never forget the first day. While we were walking down the main corridor of the institution, the traditional telephone pole design prison, I observed and others did as well that the new warden stopped and picked up a couple of cigarette butts. That communicated to everybody the priority for cleanliness and order that he established for himself and what he expected of others. His expectations were clearly established by a very simple gesture. That resonated through the staff and again demonstrates what leadership can do in an institution simply by example."

you have to be fair. If you lack integrity, you're just simply not going to make it.[5]

Integrity Is Related to Treating Others with Dignity and Respect

One of the themes of this book is that proactive wardens treat staff and inmates with dignity and respect and ask staff to interact with inmates and each other in a way that exemplifies dignity and respect.

Treating inmates with dignity and respect has to do with how all of the staff, from warden to correctional officer, interact with inmates on a daily basis. Staff's interactions in which inmates are treated as persons are much different than when they are treated as worthless objects.

Physical abuse from staff has no place in a humane prison; inmates must be controlled, but that does not give staff the right to brutalize them in the process; nor does staff have a right to verbally abuse inmates while controlling them.

Treating inmates with dignity and respect further has to do with staff taking their requests and concerns seriously. If inmates claim that bad meat was served over the weekend, that needs to be checked, and inmates deserve an answer. Inmates are treated with dignity and respect when inmates and staff see the warden around the institution on a regular basis, and the warden listens to their concerns. When this happens, the feelings among inmates of being respected and taken seriously increase. Feature 6.2 explains what it means to treat inmates with dignity and respect.

What Is the Relationship Between Integrity and Fairness?

Fairness is a further dimension of integrity. Wardens with different rules for staff who they like than for other staff will not be perceived as persons of integrity. Similarly, wardens who practice unfairness in promotion policies will not be seen as persons of integrity. In addition, staff will raise questions about fairness for those

Feature 6.2: Treating Inmates with Dignity and Respect

Chase Riveland, former secretary of Washington State's Department of Corrections, speaks about the importance of treating individuals with respect in managing a prison:

> *"If we contrast the quality of life for staff and inmates in well-managed institutions versus those in dysfunctional ones . . . strong leadership will lead to an environment in which there is mutual respect. This mutual respect takes place among staff at all levels—among correctional officers, treatment staff, medical staff, maintenance staff—and a mutual respect between the staff and inmates. That is, of course, something that can flow both ways. Certainly, correctional staff do not have to have respect for some of the acts and behaviors that the inmates have had in the past. On the other hand, they can respect them and treat them in a humane way. Generally, most people incarcerated in a well-managed institution feel on a day-to-day basis that they are being treated respectfully."*

Mary Leftridge Byrd, former superintendent of the State Correctional Institution at Chester, Pennsylvania, believes that responding to inmates as individuals is part of being treated with dignity and respect:

> *"Inmates in this institution and other institutions that I've managed are regarded as a population of men as well as individuals. I often stand in the main hallway when the population is going to eat because it's a way to see hundreds and hundreds of people. If I can call out thirty or forty names, I think that's a good thing. Being incarcerated in prison doesn't mean that a person stops being a father, mother, brother, sister, grandfather, or grandmother."*

Sources: Interviewed in November and December 2002.

wardens who take advantage of their positions. In Feature 6.3, David Crist, warden of Minnesota Correctional Facility, Stillwater, discusses some of these relationships.

How Is Integrity Related to Empowerment of Staff?

Wardens "stand tall" when they attempt to help develop others and to advance their correctional careers. In at least three ways a proactive warden can be a person of integrity in working with other staff members.

First, the proactive warden can become a mentor to correctional staff who are new in their administrative career. Being a mentor extends from answering questions, to supporting, and intervening with staff when necessary, to modeling desired behaviors.

Second, the proactive warden can encourage staff to try new ways to accomplish goals and can give them the necessary freedom to try these innovative ways.

Third, the proactive warden can demonstrate to staff that integrity, or doing what is right, represents power rather than force in correctional administration (*see* Chapter 5). Feature 6.4 reveals interviewees' responses to the question of how wardens can empower and develop other staff.

Feature 6.3: Fairness and Integrity, Interview with David Crist

"I think that above all honesty and integrity are important principles practiced by effective wardens. Staff know when there are different rules for administrators than there are for line staff, and inmates know that. Staff and inmates know when there are different rules for middle managers than there are for line staff and inmates.

"Effective wardens are going to be persons who practice honesty and integrity and do not take advantage of their position. They also model the kind of behavior they expect from staff. They communicate well, pay attention to detail, and are out and about the facility so that they are seen frequently by staff and inmates. They are approachable by both staff and inmates when they are out and about in the facility, and they listen and follow through on suggestions or comments made by anybody whether it's staff, inmates, the community stakeholders, or members of the legislature."

Source: Interviewed in September 2002.

What Is the Importance of Wardens Having a Strong Belief System?

The stereotypical image of the warden, especially in a maximum-security prison, is that of a tough, hard, barrel-chested, cigar smoking, insensitive, sometimes limited, reactionary redneck. The reality is quite different. The proactive wardens discussed in this book are mentally and physically sharp and very competent. They are anticipatory administrators who focus on preventing problems and who have exceptional rapport with the inmates and staff because they are reasonable, sensitive, forgiving, and have very strong religious and spiritual value systems.

These wardens want their interactions with staff and inmates and the decisions they make to reflect and be a subtle testimony to their faith. They do not attempt to proselytize staff or inmates to whatever faith they may have, but they can communicate by example the relationship between them and their God. They do this in the way they interact with inmates, the way they listen, the way they respond, and the climate that they create of mutual respect and trust in the prison. Their goal is to treat inmates the way they would like to be treated, and the way they would like their father, brother, son, daughter, or close friend treated if they were in prison. They are not soft touches; they are not bleeding hearts; but they are individuals who hold to some basic truths about faith and morals.

A close relationship exits between having a strong belief system and a healthy self-esteem. Unless wardens can develop a healthy self-esteem, it is unlikely that they can help others accept themselves and develop a healthy self-esteem. We know that a lack of self-esteem breeds irresponsibility, internal conflicts, poor relationships, poor choices, confusion, loneliness, spiritual bankruptcy, and shame. Shame is the major ingredient in an individual's low self-esteem and conveys the feeling that this person is an unworthy or bad person. If prison staff are to be successful with inmates, they need to help inmates distinguish between shame and guilt. It is okay and healthy to feel some guilt when we have done something wrong. We can be a good person and make a stupid mistake for which we feel guilty.

Feature 6.4: Development of Staff Members

Pat McManus, former Commissioner of Corrections in Kansas, had this to say about the importance of the warden developing staff by modeling positive behaviors toward staff.

"I think it is important that what wardens say and what they do be consistent. The staff then knows that there is a consistency and integrity about words and directions that the warden gives. The effective warden not only interacts with staff in a respectful way, but does the same thing with prisoners.

"Frank spends a lot of time training his staff. I think a lot of wardens remove themselves too much from that function. Part of it is personality and part of it is the fact that Frank expected ethical behavior and modeled ethical behavior. Because he came up through the ranks, he did not have to prove anything as a warden. And maybe that gave him the freedom to be able to behave in a more gentle way towards prisoners than others did. He didn't have to prove he was tough. He did not have to prove that he knew what was going on. I think he felt comfortable enough that he could be gentle and firm with inmates in dealing with situations that others might have handled quite differently."

David Crist, warden of the Minnesota's Correctional Center at Stillwater, adds other ways in which the warden can motivate and develop staff:

> *"The warden can develop and motivate staff by listening, by allowing them to experiment with new approaches while you are mentoring them, by training them, and then occasionally by allowing them to make their own mistakes as long as the consequences are not going to be too dramatic. This latter approach is allowing them to make their own mistakes and then giving them a chance to learn from those mistakes.*
>
> *"Staff have to be given the opportunity at points in their careers to spread their wings to see what works for them. The warden has to understand that different staff are going to approach different issues or problems from different perspectives, and as long as they have the same goal in mind, as long as the goal is one that the warden agrees with, and as long as their personal style is professional and honest and filled with integrity, the warden should respect that there are different ways to get at different issues and allow staff the latitude within their personal styles to attain those goals.*
>
> *"The warden can't stand back and just say, "OK you guys, have a try at it." He [or she] has to monitor that process. He [or she] has to intervene when intervention is called for, but staff are ultimately more motivated and develop more when they are allowed to take on tasks and challenges that they wouldn't otherwise be given the opportunity to do."*

Dr. Reginald Wilkinson, director of the Ohio Department of Rehabilitation and Correction, also emphasizes the importance of the warden's encouragement of staff and discusses how that encouragement can improve the quality of life for staff in that facility:

> *"In a well-managed facility, when you talk to the staff—whether it is an associate warden or a person who is working in food service or laundry—they enjoy their work as if they know their little part of the prison world is the heart of the entire prison that makes the entire wheel work. This is the way the entire prison will work as a whole instead of having individuals distance*

Feature 6.4: Development of Staff Members (con't)

themselves within the facility. When staff are excited about their work, it is important that their contributions are recognized and are noticed. For example, the fact that you can fix the plumbing or repair a broken window is part of what makes everything work."

"A well-managed facility, of course, also needs leadership from the point of view of someone who knows how to call shots and to bark out orders. I am interested in our staff knowing the theory of leadership, but sometimes you need to stand back and do things to encourage staff and to maximize their potential. When you get the buy-ins from staff, then it goes along in terms of people owning the kind of things that take place. I think that has a lot to do with increased morale, with people wanting to come to work.

"I think it is important that the leadership of the prison encourages creativity and people to take some risks, even though in prison these risks must be calculated. You, especially, have to have the line staff involved. I think the days are over and done where line staff were relegated to playing subservient roles: officers just being guards and food service people just putting a ladle of food on a tray. I think it goes well beyond that.

"I also think we have to extract from the line staff the desire to do their work better. If there are dumb rules that need to be changed, they should be changed. But if we don't ask for staff's input, then we don't know what rules should be changed and how they should be changed. Then, we are missing the boat. Line staff must be allowed to affect the change process.

"But I think the most neglected group of people is the middle management. They can stop communication on the way up as well as on the way down. These are the people who think that high-ranking administrators are going to be gone in a couple of years. Some may adopt the attitude that they are going to still be here and by God, they are going to do things their way. If they aren't included, you can very easily have attitude problems from them. As a consequence, we do our best to include managers, counseling administrators, counselors, and lieutenants in the important decisions that need to be made. We do not want them to cause more problems than what might occur naturally."

Sources: Interviewed in October and November 2002.

Many professional organizations develop a code of ethics to use as a guideline to proper and acceptable behavior in medicine, law, social work, and others. These formal codes spell out official standards that the organization expects employees to meet. The American Correctional Association has a code of ethics reprinted at the end of this chapter. Wardens could adopt this and add to it. Whether proactive wardens develop a formal code of ethics or not, it is imperative that the integrity of the wardens be conveyed to other prison staff. Staff need to understand the behaviors that are expected of them as staff members. When asked about the principles practiced by effective wardens, former commissioner of corrections in Washington State, Chase Riveland spoke about the importance of wardens' values:

> *First of all, I think that it is important that effective wardens have their values clearly stated. This may or may not be in something formal like a mission statement, values statement, or a vision statement. More importantly, the values are redundantly*

stated by that individual. Those values are put into practice by the policies, procedures, and behaviors that the warden exhibits.[6]

The warden also demonstrates these values by the kinds of people he or she promotes. Staff watch those people who are promoted, and they very quickly glean the perception that there are certain qualities and characteristics that are going to make them successful in that institution. If one is promoted because of an old buddy system or because of simply loyalty, then this becomes the kind of behavior that one will see in the other staff. On the other hand, if the persons are promoted because they are competent, because they are hardworking, and because they are committed to the legitimate values of the organization, then other staff will follow in line.

For those staff members who violate what is acceptable behavior, there must be consequences that are consistent with the seriousness of the acts. Staff members who have committed illegal acts in the prison, such as bringing in drugs, must be prosecuted for their crimes.

What Is the Relationship between Integrity and Relating to Politicians?

Frank Wood advises that those aspiring to be a warden or commissioner of corrections should exercise caution in their interactions with politicians. The closer you get to politics, he warns, there is an increasing temptation and potential that you could find yourself compromising your values, principles, and integrity in an attempt to avoid telling a governor, legislator, or other politicians things he or she may not want to hear.

Many politicians appear to have focused their priorities on perpetuating themselves in office and positioning themselves for higher office. They latch on to what appears to be popular, simplistic solutions to society's problems and exploit these issues to the detriment of the nation, the state, and their constituents for personal gain. Many ignore the evidence that sound and enlightened public policy is not always popular. Advising politicians that they are wrong—when you serve at their pleasure—or telling the same thing to legislators who decide the appropriations and level of funding for the department for the next biennium, have the potential of shortening your career or of hurting your department or institution financially.

What Wood is suggesting is that wardens cannot always rely on some politicians' integrity. He advises that wardens tell politicians the truth but do not assume or expect that they will deliver. Many complex, complicated, and conflicting political strategies occur during legislative sessions, which play out in hidden agendas. Sometimes even the most perceptive political observers do not understand them all.

The important thing is just as wardens need to be astute at judging the character of inmates, they need to be that much more astute in judging the character of politicians. Some inmates want to use and exploit wardens and are looking for their vulnerability, and, unfortunately, so are some politicians. Be alert to that. Politicians, like inmates or anyone else for that matter, should have to earn the warden's respect and credibility. The only way to do that is through sustained exposure, interaction, observation in committees, on the legislative floor, and through visits in their offices.

Make certain that politicians have all the facts at their disposal as they deliberate about policy decisions they are going to make in the criminal justice field. These relationships must be cultivated. For wardens to be credible with politicians, wardens must tell them the facts even though they may not be complimentary to their position.

When wardens earn a reputation of being credible, objective, and straightforward, they will gain the respect of politicians, and the decision makers in their area are more likely to be receptive to what these wardens have to say. Hopefully, wardens will see this improved communication reflected in enlightened debate and decisions and policy in committee hearings where votes are taken. Wardens usually will see that their homework pays off, not only in what they say as they attempt to educate other people on the committee, but in the final vote when push comes to shove. Many times, wardens can bring people around to the side of good public policy that may not always be good politics.

Is It Important for Top Corrections Officials to Take a Stand on Issues about Which They Feel Strongly?

At times, proactive commissioners or directors of corrections must take a public stand when they have not received a receptive ear on the part of politicians. They need to have integrity, confidence, and conviction to tell public policy decision makers in tactful and diplomatic ways things they may not want to hear. Such stands on important issues by heads of corrections departments may be the only way in which corrections can move forward in the twenty-first century. In the past, leaders of correctional agencies have taken stands, and it was their stands that changed the face of corrections in their jurisdictions (*see* Chapter 10). In Feature 6.5, written in 1996 when Frank Wood was commissioner of corrections in Minnesota, he takes a stand on sentencing and incarceration policies that predicted accurately the toxicity of the current sentencing policy in Minnesota and elsewhere.

There is no question that this is a strong statement, one that may well incur the wrath of some politicians. Of course, there is risk in making unpopular stands. There is further no question that Minnesota and other states are where Wood said they would be today because of their sentencing policies. It would be wise to have rapport with some policy makers before criticisms are made of issues, such as the death penalty, sentencing policy, or the current policy of making prisoners suffer. Still, the fact remains that when corrections leaders in the past have been willing to make their stands known on corrections issues, corrections has moved forward to a more enlightened level.

Summary

This chapter focuses on being a person of integrity. The desired goal is that the entire staff, from the warden to the line officer, see themselves as persons of integrity. This integrity involves being honest in behavior, treating others with dignity and respect, and believing that their jobs do make a difference. Staff training and censuring or punishing staff who violate integrity are the means to communicate that integrity is what is expected from staff members in the institution.

Integrity can be taught. Integrity involves not only what takes place in the prison, but what

Feature 6.5: The Crime and Punishment Myth—"Exposed" by Frank Wood

"Over the last decade, the public has been led to believe that in order to attack the perceived increase in the crime rate, policy makers should increase prison sentences and create new felonies with long prison sentences. The demagogues and political opportunists exploited the media's appetite for sensationalizing isolated heinous, high visibility crime to enhance readership and viewership. This partnership, pursuing their own self interests, e.g., political visibility, perpetuity in elected office, aspirations for higher political office, sweeps ratings, and increased circulation, have aroused the public's prejudices and fear.

"A substantial number of the public now believe that this after-the-fact response to crime is the solution to a very complex societal crime problem. The uninformed public led by the political opportunists have embraced a love affair with prisons, and accepted the premise that our most expensive sanction is the only acceptable response to crime. This very expensive myth has been perpetrated on the public by presidential candidates, governors, congress, state legislators, state attorneys general, private sector corporate prison operators, some police and politicians at local levels of government.

"This approach to the crime problem is analogous to building more hospitals to address the AIDS problem. During the polio epidemic of the fifties and sixties, our exclusive response to polio would have focused our resources on the manufacture of iron lungs, as opposed to research into the source of the problem, which led to the Salk vaccine. [As a consequence] a lot of people would still be afflicted with polio and confined to an existence in an iron lung. We have not attacked any other complex societal problem successfully focusing on an after-the-fact response. We have now reached the point where very few politicians have the personal and political courage to stand up and question the wisdom of the dramatic, very expensive and counterproductive changes we have made in felony prison sentences. We are approaching in 1991 two million of our citizens locked up in jails and prisons in our country at an operating cost now approaching thirty billion dollars a year (which does not include prison construction costs).

"The facts are clear historically, we have always had crime and yes, even very heinous crime, bizarre gratuitous violence and multiple homicides, that deny any rational explanation. We must accept the reality that no society in history has ever eliminated crime and we will not eliminate crime in the United States. As long as humans have free will and there is a materialistic culture contrasted with millions living in poverty, that divide and separate the haves and the have nots, we will have crime. We can reduce dramatically real crime by what we do before the fact:

- mandatory parenting training
- early childhood and family support initiatives
- access for all to health care from cradle to grave

Feature 6.5: The Crime and Punishment Myth—"Exposed" (con't)

- education programs that do not write off any child even if he or she needs a one-on-one tutor
- marketable skills training and employment placement
- adult mentors for those who do not have a parent or adult in their life who models socially acceptable behavior and responsibility
- the loss of parental rights for those who are contributing to the delinquency of their children

"Spending and investing in our children today will have a dramatic impact on crime over the next two decades. This nation's decision to spend nearly 30 billion dollars a year responding after the fact to crime, commits us to even more explosive prison growth and expenditures that preclude us from attacking complex societal problems at their sources.

"Children cannot be exposed to a steady barrage of visual images filled with the most grotesque violence imaginable, on television, in video games and [then have] society expect that they will respect themselves, others, life or property. The proliferation of and access to guns by children have produced the predictable outcome. Simply put, we can have a dramatic impact on crime if we place a priority on how we raise our children.

"There are offenders who require incapacitation in prison and some are so dangerous they should never be released from prison. There are, however, thousands of people in prison who could be held accountable for their crimes, punished, sanctioned, supervised, treated, and monitored in the community. It is beyond ridiculous to have nondangerous, low-level, drug and property offenders serving long prison sentences that just a decade ago were reserved for armed robbers, rapists, and second degree murderers. The United States' exceptional economy has resulted in unprecedented employment opportunities, low unemployment, and revenue surpluses at the federal and state levels. They are the major contributing factors influencing lower crime rates, not our high incarceration rates. These same factors have made this preposterous "get tough" crime policy appear to be working and be relatively fiscally painless.

"The future is predictable. When the federal government and the states experience the inevitable economic downturn and instead of surpluses we have revenue shortfalls, the policy makers will face tough competition for very limited resources. They will be forced to revisit the self-serving wasteful and unwise crime policies of the past decade. Those in office at the time of the fiscal crunch will be forced by sheer economics to dismantle "the nations ultimate welfare state," our prisons. We could reduce our prison population by 30 percent, redirect funds to prevention, intervention, community-based punishment and sanctions, and still save billions in construction costs. Even with this reduction, the United States would not lose its current world status as the industrialized country with the highest incarceration rate. Career politicians will not risk their political futures in the current robust economic climate.

Feature 6.5: The Crime and Punishment Myth—"Exposed" (con't)

"The citizens will have to wait until the choices are narrowed between the education of our children, health care, social security, care of our elderly, highways, and others. The fierce competition of those powerful lobby interests will demand an end to funding prisons that are housing people who represent no sufficient risk to public safety at the expense of their interests and those of their constituents.

"The future holds a rude awakening for the private for-profit corporate prison industry. The corporate world is currently exploiting the naivete of governors, legislators, and other politicians who are desperately searching for a less expensive way to fund their simplistic public policy of locking every offender up and throwing the key away. It is simply the politicians' transparent attempt to delay the inevitable during their active political careers. They don't want to have to admit while they are still running for office that their politically popular, ignorant, uninformed and simplistic get-tough solution to crime was tragically flawed from its inception.

"Another plus for the politicians is the potential for campaign contributions from the private prison industry. It is becoming increasingly apparent that the corporate world does not have any mystical, secret way of running prisons less expensively than the government. Seventy to eighty percent of a secure prison's budget is staffing and staff compensation. There is very little that can be saved by cutting fixed costs, such as food, utilities, maintenance, health care, and so forth. Any substantial savings can only come from either reducing staff compensation or reducing the staff of the prison. The results have been predictable. Staff turnover will be high, and it is in most private prisons. Staff turnover is high because the staff must experience some relative degree of safety in their workplace, and they need compensation sufficient to sustain a family.

"Institutions with insufficient staff tend to regress toward creating a climate of fear, brutality, and intimidation in running the prison because they lack the staff necessary to monitor, supervise, and control the prison population. The corporate prison operation got their foot in the door by taking a predictable loss during the initial contract periods, and then increasing costs over each subsequent contract period. Privatization of our secure prisons makes as much sense as contracting with the private sector for police services in major cities across this nation. The corporate operations of secure prisons will diminish, and the corporate niche in the industry will focus on prison industry, food service, health care, minimum-security institutions, and community-based residential and day programs.

"The public should also be aware of another emerging conflict or interest. Correctional officer unions have become so large and well financed that they are now the most powerful and influential lobbyists in some states. In some states, the unions have jumped on the "get tough" bandwagon and contribute to those who can pass the "get tough" laws which will further increase their membership, revenues, and political clout.

Feature 6.5: The Crime and Punishment Myth—"Exposed" (con't)

"It is outrageous that millions of dollars that could be invested in parental training, our children's education, graduation incentives, job training, employment opportunities, prevention, intervention and community-based punishment sanctions, and offender accountability will continue to fund for-profit corporate prisons and state and federal institutions that are housing thousands of people who could be part of the nation's productive workforce and join the law-abiding community.

"The future must include a change in public attitude. The people and the policy makers will be forced to recognize how counterproductive demonizing 'ALL' offenders has been. By blocking all pathways back to the community, the offender cannot redeem himself or herself, make restitution, and join the law-abiding community as a productive citizen. We assure high recidivism and costly expansion of our prison systems when we make it almost impossible for the offender to find employment, housing, and a forum to demonstrate his/her lifestyle change.

"As a society, we must distinguish between the offenders we are mad at and those we fear. Prisons should be viewed as a finite resource. Our most expensive sanction should be reserved for those we fear, such as the murderer, the armed robber, the rapist, those who assault us, and threaten our personal safety and the safety of our children."[6]

takes place outside the prison. Wardens cannot be scoundrels in their home life, abusing their children and spouse, and expect to be looked on as exemplars of integrity in the institution. Nor can one use drugs or abuse alcohol and expect to be viewed as a person of integrity. Finally, integrity demands that corrections leaders speak out on issues that they feel are not being addressed.

ENDNOTES

[1] Stephen L. Carter. 1996. *Integrity*. New York: HarperPerennial.

[2] Ibid., p.7.

[3] Quoted in ibid., p. 8.

[4] Samuel A. Culbert. 1974. *The Organization Trap and How to Get Out of It*. New York: Basic Books, p.4.

[5] Interviewed in November 2002.

[6] Interviewed in October 2002.

AMERICAN CORRECTIONAL ASSOCIATION

CODE OF ETHICS

Preamble

The American Correctional Association expects of its members unfailing honesty, respect for the dignity and individuality of human beings and a commitment to professional and compassionate service. To this end, we subscribe to the following principles.

1. Members shall respect and protect the civil and legal rights of all individuals.

2. Members shall treat every professional situation with concern for the welfare of the individuals involved and with no intent to personal gain.

3. Members shall maintain relationships with colleagues to promote mutual respect within the profession and improve the quality of service.

4. Members shall make public criticism of their colleagues or their agencies only when warranted, verifiable, and constructive.

5. Members shall respect the importance of all disciplines within the criminal justice system and work to improve cooperation with each segment.

6. Members shall honor the public's right to information and share information with the public to the extent permitted by law subject to individuals' right to privacy.

7. Members shall respect and protect the right of the public to be safeguarded from criminal activity.

8. Members shall refrain from using their positions to secure personal privileges or advantages.

9. Members shall refrain from allowing personal interest to impair objectivity in the performance of duty while acting in an official capacity.

10. Members shall refrain from entering into any formal or informal activity or agreement which presents a conflict of interest or is inconsistent with the conscientious performance of duties.

11. Members shall refrain from accepting any gifts, services, or favors that is or appears to be improper or implies an obligation inconsistent with the free and objective exercise of professional duties.

12. Members shall clearly differentiate between personal views/statements and views/statements/positions made on behalf of the agency or Association.

13. Members shall report to appropriate authorities any corrupt or unethical behaviors in which there is sufficient evidence to justify review.

14. Members shall refrain from discriminating against any individual because of race, gender, creed, national origin, religious affiliation, age, disability, or any other type of prohibited discrimination.

15. Members shall preserve the integrity of private information; they shall refrain from seeking information on individuals beyond that which is necessary to implement responsibilities and perform their duties; members shall refrain from revealing nonpublic information unless expressly authorized to do so.

16. Members shall make all appointments, promotions, and dismissals in accordance with established civil service rules, applicable contract agreements, and individual merit, rather than furtherance of personal interests.

17. Members shall respect, promote, and contribute to a work place that is safe, healthy, and free of harassment in any form.

Adopted by the Board of Governors and Delegate Assembly in August 1994.

Chapter Seven:

Staff Development

Proactive wardens, regardless of how talented or committed they might be, will be limited unless they have the trust and support of staff throughout the institution. Those top administrative staff, who are so critical to the operation of the facility, must support the proactive style of management advocated by the warden.

Too frequently the management of correctional institutions has been characterized by conflict between line staff and the front officer and by jealousy of the power and influence of the warden by associate wardens and leading administrative staff. It is not unheard of for subordinate staff members to work at and be successful at sabotaging the work of the warden and eventually be able to have the warden replaced—sometimes by one of them. Beginning with the type of staff members that proactive wardens depicted in this book require, this chapter considers the subjects of participatory management styles and offers other suggestions for staff development. In Feature 7.1, Patrick McManus, former commissioner of corrections in Kansas, talks about the importance of staff development in changing the culture of violence in a prison.

What Type of Staff Members Are Needed for a Proactive Management Team?

Frank Wood, in a previous publication, talked about the type of staff needed for a proactive management team. "Each of us has our own strengths and limitations, and what I look for to fill the positions that answer directly to the warden are those people who can fill in the gaps where I have limitations. I also look for people who have the following characteristics:

- Who challenge me to be my very best
- Who in their own right are confident and quite capable of running the institution as well or better than I
- Who have knowledge, skills, experience, and personal characteristics that I do not exhibit as well as they do
- Who have differing perspectives and viewpoints than myself and can articulate those opposing views in a nonadversarial way, but yet are consistent with the ultimate philosophy and goals that I consider to be crucial to the pursuit of excellence in managing and operating an enlightened institution
- Who I believe will not only enhance my confidence and decision making but also will bring to the entire administrative team a higher level of review, deliberation, and consideration to ensure that we, as a team, have explored all of the possibilities and options in making tough, very complex decisions
- Who are not easily provoked and have the capacity to be restrained even under extreme provocation

Feature 7.1: Changing the Culture of Violence in a Prison by Patrick McManus

"I think that the culture of violence is probably the hallmark of turbulent present-day prisons. This culture of violence comes about for a number of reasons. One of them is that some institutions simply have poorly trained staff, poorly supervised staff, and poorly paid staff. The caliber of the people operating the facility is not particularly good because those jurisdictions do not want to provide money for the training."

"I think that the warden, director, or even the sheriff can to some extent overcome that just by standing up for what they believe with politicians and saying that adequately trained, supervised, and paid staff is the price that must be paid. Top corrections staff also must convince the remainder of the staff as well as prisoners that there is a level of respect and professionalism that can prevail in a prison. Top staff can document this level of respect and professionalism by a number of specific incidents where those principles are actually being followed. When staff is able to communicate the issue of confidence and professionalism to the prisoners, this can contribute to a peaceful and respectful prison and discourage those trends toward the turbulent or violent prison culture."

Source: Interviewed in November 2002.

- Who demonstrate and have a track record of demonstrating maturity, good judgment, insight, and wisdom
- Who, for the most part, agree with my philosophy and can communicate that they believe in it with the same sincerity and intensity that I do
- Who are honest and have integrity so that they will take stands on issues after thoughtful analysis and deliberation and not be wetting their finger and holding it up to find which way the wind is blowing on a given day
- Who are tactful and are able to articulate things well so that they can be understood by staff at all levels and by the inmate clientele
- Who have perseverance and tenacity and are in the profession for the long haul
- Who have the courage to tell the emperor that he's naked and do that appropriately, privately, and not to elevate themselves at the expense of others
- Who are not easily intimidated
- Who have the capacity to understand and relate to inmates
- Who are not arrogant, pompous, know-it-alls, offensive, condescending, caustic, abrasive, and self-righteous
- Who have the intellectual depth to know that rarely will we find simplistic solutions to society's and humankind's problems.

In sum, I look for the best and the brightest. I look for people who don't just talk the golden rule, but those who practice it—people who are loyal, and people who will be responsive to both the real and imagined concerns of inmates and staff. I look for staff who have commitment and are dedicated and able to convince other people that our profession is important and noble and that we can make a difference."[1]

This list in many ways is inspiring, but it also demands a particular type of warden to look for staff members with these qualities and for such staff members to be attracted to correctional administration.

Frank Wood is suggesting that he looks for staff who have talents and strengths in areas he does not. Such a statement conveys a person who is very confident in himself and secure in his job. He is willing to bring a person into the institution, perhaps even as an associate warden, who may have great personal talent and potential in the field of corrections.

Former Warden Wood spells out the strengths of these staff members. He wants individuals who challenge him and who keep him on his toes, who are competent and confident. Wood also wants those who have knowledge, skills, and experiences that he does not have. He wants individuals who can raise opposing viewpoints, but who are still on his team and will support his proactive policies for running an institution. Indeed, he is looking for staff who will raise the quality of the team and who will not only challenge the warden but everyone else to be his or her very best.

Wood is not looking for "hotheads" but individuals who have self-control, maturity, good judgment, insight, and wisdom. He demands integrity and honesty from staff members who, following thoughtful analysis, will take stands on controversial issues. These staff members should not be arrogant, pompous, know-it-alls, offensive, condescending, caustic, abrasive, or self-righteous. Finally, he is looking for those who have intellectual depth and are not pursuing simplistic answers. Wood summarizes what he defines as the "best and the brightest" as those who are loyal, responsive, committed, and dedicated staff members. They agree with him that corrections is an important and noble profession and that the warden and staff, working together as a team, can make a difference.

What Is the Role of Participative Management for Proactive Wardens and Their Staff?

Participatory management is, very simply put, participating in management. In other words, the functions of management are shared by all members of the organization, not just those whose job classification is described as "management."[2] See Feature 7.2 for what participatory management means.

It is very essential, however, that those who are participating in management functions clearly understand what their respective role is in this process. Each job assignment within any organization has very specific duties and responsibilities. At no time is it intended that any employee is given any liberty whatsoever to perform duties and responsibilities outside or beyond the described responsibilities of his or her job description. The exception to this is where there has been a very clear, authorized, delegated assignment given to that employee by proper authority, and even then, such an assignment is usually a temporary one and subject to being rescinded at any time.

Participative management is actually using all the collective talents and resources that exist within any organization. It provides for every employee, who has something of value to offer, to be able to contribute that ability towards the best possible informational gathering and use of that information in the decision-making process of that organization. It does not necessarily involve these people in the decision making itself, only in the issue development, informational gathering, and discussion phases of the decision-making process. Decision making must remain with those who are held accountable for decisions, through their job description and by a higher authority.

An important reason or goal of participative management is to provide the forum for the best possible decisions. In this concept lies the absolutely essential tenet that a decision is only as good as the value or quality of the information from which the decision is made. The best possible decisions will not be made and the very reason for participative management to exist will be negated if people making the decision do not have the best information at their disposal, are not the most qualified or experienced, or do not have access to the best sources of information.

In almost every case, the principal role that line staff play in the participative management process is that of providing foundation information, which will lend itself towards a better decision than what would have been possible without it. Line staff make decisions, based on their best judgment, for this is the responsibility for those who are in "management." Yet, there is no equality in participative management. Job classification remains the same; level of authority and responsibility remain the same; accountability and job descriptions remain the same.

Often employees do not understand participative management. Everyone enjoys self-enhancement, and people often tend to believe they are more qualified than what others

Feature 7.2: Frank Wood's Definition of Participative Management

Participative management means:

- Being granted the authority to carry out all the functions of management that are necessary for individuals to properly do the job they are assigned to by job description.
- Sharing in the preparatory functions such as issue development, informational gathering, and discussion which precede the decision making with those who are in higher line authority with the intention of assisting them in the eventual decision-making process.
- Being granted the personal opportunity to grow experientially and professionally by constructive delegated assignments, temporarily given to an individual for this very explicit purpose, and to accomplish the organizational goals in the most efficient manner.
- Encouraging each member of the organization to feel that he or she has a part to perform that is valuable and appreciated by the other members of the organizational staff with respect to the specific areas of job assignment given to that individual.
- Furthering a belief by higher level personnel in management that lower-level employees within the organization do have capabilities that can be depended on and should be incorporated into the activities of management at the appropriate times and at the appropriate level so that the organization's goals can be efficiently established and accomplished.

Source: Unpublished materials provided by Frank Wood.

Feature 7.3: The Importance of Developing an Organizational Culture in Which Staff Take Responsibilities for Decision Making by Dennis Benson

An effective warden needs to put together an administrative team that shares a common belief in the same principles, philosophies, and expectations. They must live and practice this belief every day. When any member of the team sees a breakdown, even at the highest level, the offending party must be called to task.

After putting together a cohesive, effective administrative team, appropriate training must be provided to middle managers. This is probably the most challenging but important group to train and convince that common principles must be adopted in order to operate a facility that treats staff and inmates fairly, consistently, and with respect. Line staff should then be trained in the agency's principles, philosophies, and expectations.

Frequent and effective training is crucial, along with appropriate intervention and discipline, using corrective disciplines whenever possible. Also important is setting up various avenues of communications—staff meetings, watch meetings, shift briefings, and so forth. These are a necessity if one is going to maintain a positive organizational culture.

Source: Interviewed in October 2002.

recognize them to be. Therefore, ego satisfaction or the desire for personal power make it natural for people to believe that what they know is all that anyone else knows and perhaps even more than what anybody else knows.

Participative management is not in any way, shape, or form, a democracy. The extent to which the participation of an employee will be permitted is limited. The intent is certainly not to catapult each subordinate member's right to participate in management up to the identical level of authority as that of a higher level management person, who is directly accountable for the results of these decisions. In Feature 7.3, Dennis L. Benson, deputy commissioner of the Minnesota Department of Corrections, talks about the importance of developing an organizational culture that brings staff into discipline-making responsibilities.

How Can Staff Be Motivated To Be Proactive?

Too many well-meaning wardens have had their best-laid plans sabotaged by staff who were resentful of the warden's authority, who were indifferent to anything but their own narrow sphere of responsibility, or who just did not like the warden and wanted to see this person fail. This sense of alienation between top administration and line staff too frequently has been the case in corrections. Line staff are quick to say that the ones in the front offices do not know what it is really like in the cellblocks.

Proactive wardens described in this book spend time in the cellblock, often without staff escort. Proactive wardens know the importance of their visibility in the prison, and they realize the importance of interacting with staff and inmates.

Proactive wardens are good at reinforcing positive behaviors. They have high expectations of staff, but are ready to train, correct, and assist when staff members are floundering. As long as staff members are honest and admit their mistakes, proactive wardens ordinarily will work with erring staff members. There are times, of course, when a staff member must be dismissed or even prosecuted for behavior that jeopardizes the security of the institution or violates the criminal law, such as bringing contraband into the prison.

Proactive wardens believe in participative management, but as the previous section spells out, they have their own slant of what participative management means in a correctional environment. Proactive wardens realize the importance of a corrections team, made up of all staff members, working together to achieve the vision of a proactive prison. The proactive prison is a humane place, and staff and even inmates can feel good about being a part of this environment.

When proactive wardens are successful in creating such a corrections team, staff members speak with pride of their involvement in this prison. Unlike line staff in prisons across the nation, who feel that they are like inmates doing time, the teamwork that can develop in proactive prison administration creates pride and ownership among the staff. The staff, then, like the warden, feel a sense of ownership in the institution. They take pride in their work and look forward to coming to work. This pride reduces the stress of prison work, improves the interaction with inmates and other staff, and increases their accountability in the job.

In Feature 7.4, Chase Riveland, former secretary of the Department of Corrections for the State of Washington, talks about the importance of staff participation in building a positive organizational culture.

Feature 7.4: Staff Participation and Organizational Culture by Chase Riveland

"The question of how a warden develops an organization culture that motivates staff and develops them to their full potential and creates a healthy environment certainly is a question that good wardens struggle with all the time. But it comes back to some basics. Leadership encompasses a whole variety of things. Some of the very pragmatic things are solid policies and procedures that are understandable to all staff in the facility. Also important is effective training, as well as ongoing training, that can bring the organization not only to the point that staff know what to do, but that they can do that in a way that contributes to the safe and healthy nature of the prison environment."

"The issue of the management team paying attention to the needs of the staff and inmates is a further one that cannot be ignored. And paying attention means caring for the personal challenges that each of the staff has whether it is on the job or, in many cases, whether it is the things that are going on in their lives that can have an impact on them both personally and professionally. The same thing happens in caring for those under our custody. Having an environment that allows inmates to wrestle with and deal with their problems is terribly critical. This will contribute to a healthy correctional environment that inmates can benefit from and feel safer in."

Source: Interviewed in October 2002.

What Processes Should Occur During the Training of New Staff Members?

Training for staff members has come a long way since a correctional officer was given a set of keys and was released to the yard. Early on, the training was extended to a day or two and usually concentrated on subjects such as riot formation. Then, training academies emerged across the nation, and staff, especially correctional officers, would spend a period of time at the academy before they arrived to begin their in-service training at the institution. Wardens varied in what type of training they offered at the prison to new staff.

Frank Wood emphasized staff development as a crucial aspect of the management of a proactive prison. New staff members received an orientation about management's expectations based on how they wanted the prison to run, what the relationship would be between staff and inmates, what their responsibilities were toward the security of the prison, what programs and services were available in the institution, and how they would handle particular problems they would face. There was training on special investigations, including gangs. Staff were taught how to avoid setups by inmates and how to use restraints in moving inmates.

Frank Wood gave special attention to the use of appropriate force. Staff were informed that they were permitted to use only the amount of force that was necessary to get an inmate under control and to move an inmate to the location where he or she was being taken. Staff training strongly emphasized that force was not to be used as an opportunity to get revenge, to get your licks in, or to retaliate because an inmate provoked an officer. Wood instituted the videotaping of incidents, so that when an inmate made an allegation of abuse or brutality, anybody who had a question about how the inmate was handled could view this. Some of the videotaped incidents were used with new staff to demonstrate appropriate and inappropriate uses of force.

He held classes on understanding the offender. This was particularly important at Oak Park Heights because 45 percent of the staff were college graduates who did not necessarily have firsthand knowledge of offenders. They did not have a good frame of reference about who was in prison, why they were there, and what some of their personal characteristics were. New staff were taught many things, including:

- the proper procedure for doing clothed and unclothed searches
- how to do a count
- key control
- incident management, including what could be learned in the future to prevent or better respond to the incident
- cardiopulmonary resuscitation (CPR) and first aid
- proper means of fire responses
- the right-to-know policy on hazardous material
- urinalysis evidence handling and other types of evidence handling
- the ways to handle escape attempts
- how to use segregation as a tool
- how to pay attention to detail

In Feature 7.5, David Crist, warden of the Minnesota Correctional Facility at Stillwater, explains why paying attention to detail is so important in the avoidance of problems and institutional crisis.

Another helpful method of training that Warden Wood employed was to assign a mentor to each new staff member. Then, for six months to a year, it was possible for a new staff member to have someone to bounce things off of in a safe place without anyone hearing about that interaction.

Warden Wood used several other unique measures for training staff. This included:

- having the staff come and spend a night sleeping in the cells
- having the staff before Oak Park Heights was opened try to cut through the tool-resistant steel bars
- developing a variety of programs in which staff could participate if they were interested

Feature 7.5: Pay Attention to Detail by David Crist

The quick and dirty answer to that question [why some institutions operate with rare incidents of serious problems] is paying attention to detail. Expanding on that, I would say training one's staff to pay attention to detail is critical. If wardens are paying attention to detail in their facilities, they are seeing things that everyday they would like improved or changed. They are likely to say, "Let's try it a little differently next time," or "What other explanations could there be for this situation?"

Tactical wardens or proactive wardens are persons who don't just rely on the way things appear to be on the surface, but will ask penetrating questions that make staff get right down to a minute level of detail. Equally important, tactical wardens allow staff to rely on them to always ask those penetrating questions. In this day and age of operating complex correctional facilities, tactical wardens train their staff to ask those questions so that when they are not there, these questions will be asked. Or, if the warden misses a relevant point, staff will raise the point. Someday, when staff get promoted, the desire is that they are willing to raise these same penetrating questions and their staff, in turn, will carry this on.

I've been a warden for five and a half years, and the longer I'm a warden, the more I realize I just don't know it all. For example, I don't know how to maintain a computer network, and there are a lot of other areas related to the prison in which I am not an expert. What I do is to hire people who have expertise in those areas.

Tactical wardens train their people in all the assignments in the prison. They teach them to pay attention to detail and to ask penetrating logical questions. They make sure that they are paying attention to the process, that they start to think that way themselves, and that they become more and more engaged in their job. Eventually, it is hoped that the warden has mentored those people so that they do their jobs at a higher level with less and less day-to-day input from the warden.

Source: Interviewed in October 2002.

In addition, Norman Carlson, director of the Federal Bureau of Prisons, began sending inmates, including very high-security federal prisoners to Oak Park Heights. These were very serious, violent, and sophisticated offenders with gang-related problems, many of whom came from Marion. Frank Wood took them in part because he understood that they were much more sophisticated in doing time, and they would represent a real challenge to his staff and staff training.[3]

Throughout this process of orientation, staff members were brought into the philosophy and principles of proactive management of the prison. They could see the involvement of other staff in the prison and the pride they had in their jobs. They learned the importance of communication with other staff members and with inmates. They soon realized that they would be treated with dignity and respect, and they were expected to treat others with dignity and respect. Thus, beyond the instruction that new staff members in the prison require, there was a process of socialization taking place, in which staff increasingly viewed themselves in terms of proactive principles and responses.

What Are Inappropriate Behaviors by Prison Managers?

Many regard management as an industrial science. A manager is someone who orchestrates the various sections of an organization with some degree of precision. Even since the early 1900s, management has been described as the process of planning, organizing, coordinating, and controlling the activities of an organization to achieve specifically identified or stated goals and objectives.

Recent examination of correctional managers has revealed that there is great folklore between what managers are supposed to do and what they actually do. The fact is that management takes place at many levels within a correctional institution. Some of the common errors that wardens and other mangers make are the following:

- Good managers must have high analytical ability to understand the complexity of problems and find innovative solutions. The truth of the matter is that too much analytical ability tends to restrict the manager's readiness to take action and get things done according to the flow and demands of the organizational requirements.
- Some managers believe that an aggressive and competitive nature contributes positively to the goals of the institution. Many managers strive to get their work done at the expense of others, compete for the available resources, strive to recruit the best staff for their unit at the expense of other units, seek to gain more support for their goals, and in so doing, cause dissension that tends to destroy the necessary objectives that are so vital to the efficient functioning of any organization.
- Many managers feel that they need a great deal of latitude to get their work done and, therefore, become very protective of their "turf." They hope that others will not understand their job well enough to interfere with their plans and ambitions, with respect to their own independent goals, which may be inconsistent with those of the total organization.
- Some managers believe that "good management" is being willing and able to make "snap" decisions and to keep things going,

rather than to take the time to research an idea, consider the options, and study the support base necessary.

- Aggressive managers tend to make decisions in areas that are not theirs to make and conceptualize the need to have their support lined up before they make these decisions.
- Some managers believe that they are to be consulted on decision making even if they know little or nothing about the topic simply because they are a member of the management team.
- Some managers believe that they can delegate their accountability along with their responsibility and authority. This is called "scapegoating," and many managers believe that if they transfer "responsibility" onto someone else, this should relieve them of any mistake or wrongdoing.
- Some managers tend to be poor in follow-up. These managers seem to believe that checking on subordinates and ensuring accountability for their actions reflects a lack of trust on their part rather than a checks and balances or proprietary interest, and in doing this, they choose to avoid one of the major areas of a manager's job.
- Some managers establish an early relationship with subordinates as a "nice" person in the hopes of being liked. Later, when things are not going well, they are forced to get tough to discipline the troops. They find out then that the troops are hostile towards the change in style.
- Some managers do not conceptualize a responsibility for the total operation of an institution and concentrate almost entirely on their own select area of responsibility. They believe that if they do their independent job well, then someone else will be responsible for coordinating this independent action with the other independent actions of other section managers.
- Some managers are convinced that they are competent to make all the decisions within their area of responsibility without input from the lower-level employees and thereby, neglect to seek counsel from subordinates before they make a decision. They believe that they have privileges with their rank that entitle them to be considered in a different light than other people within the organization, whether higher or lower.
- Some managers think that the managers' job is working at their own desk, doing their own work, demanding a conventional eight-hour day, and being insensitive to the needs of others within the organization.

These errors are found with wardens themselves; others are found with associate wardens, unit managers, and other individuals with managerial responsibilities within the prison. If wardens commit these errors, they greatly reduce the impact they can make on the institution in which they are employed. If these errors are taking place with other managers in the institution, then they reduce the ability of the management team, including all levels of institutional staff, from moving the institution to a higher plateau.

What Challenges Do Correctional Officers Face?

In some correctional systems, correctional officers have at least as many problems as the guards of yesterday. Theirs can be dangerous, dead-end, low-status jobs with confusing role expectations. Hans Toch describes how correctional officers can be imprisoned in their roles:

> *Prison guards are truly imprisoned. They are not physically confined but are locked into movie caricatures, into pejorative prophecies (sometimes self-fulfilling), into anachronistic supervision patterns, into unfair civil service definitions, into undeserved hostilities and prejudgments of their actions. Officers are imprisoned by our ignorance of who they are and what they do, which is the price they pay for working behind walls.*[4]

A study at the Stateville Correctional Center supports the opinion that the behavior of correctional officers is a product of their organizational roles and is independent of variables such as education, age, race, and political orientation. This study compared African-American and white correctional officers. Although the African-American officers were typically younger, better educated, and more liberal than the white officers, they manifested no constant differences in their attitudes toward jobs, correctional goals, other staff, and inmates.[5]

Conflicting Goals and Expectations

The skills acquired through guarding are usually transferable only to even lower-paying private security jobs. A few officers are promoted through the ranks, but these opportunities are likely to disappear early in an officer's career. Wood was promoted through the uniform ranks from officer, to sergeant, lieutenant, captain, and then warden. He did not receive his B.A. in law and justice administration until 1973 or fourteen years after he started as an officer in 1959. Still, professional training is increasingly required of prison managers, which reduces the availability of top administrative positions for officers.

The conflict of goals and expectations creates a new problem for officers. In the days of autocratic wardens, guards used to know what was expected of them, including the avoidance of undue familiarity with inmates. Today, requirements for shakedowns and counts seem to change with each new supervisor, and policies on relations with prisoners are often open to interpretation. The lack of predictability of officers' behavior, as well as the inconsistent rule-enforcement structure, has contributed to the creation of stress with inmates.[6]

In addition to the problems of low status, role confusion, and inmate defiance, correctional officers must also deal with the reality that they sometimes are treated no better than inmates. For example, they are occasionally subjected to strip searches, although many correctional officers' union chapters have become strong enough to resist this kind of control. Strip searches are necessitated by the fact that one route for illegal drugs into the prison is the officer whom inmates have identified as a willing conduit. Officers view these searches as unjust because most officers have committed no crimes.

What Are Inappropriate Behaviors by Correctional Officers?

Some correctional officers respond with inappropriate behaviors to their typically alienating roles. They take seriously the old prison saying, "The first year, a guard can't do enough for an inmate; the second year, a guard can't do enough to a convict."[7] Hans Toch and John Klofas' examination of correctional officers in the Northeast found that about a quarter of the correctional officers thought this way.[8] Some officers believe that acting tough, dominating the weak, threatening violence, and putting inmates in their place will show the captives who is in control.[9] James Marquart found that the escalating strategies used by this group moved from verbal assaults, to physically abusive "tune-ups," to overt violent "ass-whippings," and severe beatings.[10] The code of silence, which often exists in subcultures of correctional officers, serves to protect those officers, who brutalize inmates.

While Frank Wood was warden at Stillwater, there was an altercation between officers and an inmate. It was Wood's policy to have the inmates seen by medical personnel and to photograph any injuries if they were noticeable. The inmate in question had a huge set of bite marks on his back that drew blood. This inmate accused one of the officers who was restraining him of biting him. The officer denied biting the inmate for several months. On the morning of the trial, he admitted to the warden that he had bitten the inmate. During the investigation, none of the other officers involved in restraining the inmate came forward and reported what they saw. The department came very close to losing a rather expensive lawsuit, which was settled.

Unfortunately, there are a few officers who become involved in corrupt and illegal behavior that jeopardizes security and violates the law. They may agree to bring contraband into the institution because they have been set up by inmates. This violation often occurs when a correctional officers agrees to do something against the rules in order to be well liked. For example, one correctional officer agreed to mail a birthday card to an inmate's daughter on his way home from work. Although this was against policy, it meant that the card would reach the child on her birthday. Subsequently, the inmate demanded that the officer comply with other requests, threatening to report the first violation to the captain.

Some officers carry contraband for profit. Inmates who are trafficking drugs in the institution or have a large drug appetite themselves seem to be able to raise large amounts of cash. According to offenders who have spent time in federal and state institutions, inmates watch and talk with each new officer and soon figure out who can be corrupted.[11] An example is a correctional officer in a Midwestern state who was caught in a strip search with two large bags of marijuana taped across his chest. This particular individual apparently had been bringing drugs into the prison for some time and had been able to buy a Cadillac and expensive clothes with his additional tax-free income.[12]

What Can Be Done About the Code of Silence among Correctional Officers?

The code of silence has no place in a correctional institution, but the degree to which it is found in various institutions varies. It is part of an informal code that protects staff members who are violating institutional policy or sometimes violating the law. Wardens have the responsibility to communicate to staff that the staff put themselves in jeopardy every time they personally respond to somebody who is acting inconsistent with policy. That does not necessarily mean to run and ask to see the warden every time a staff person sees another deviating from policy. What it does mean is to wait for the opportune moment, take that person aside and say, "Hey, I have to work here and that's not the way we do business here."

If there is an assault on an inmate, staff members have a responsibility of doing what they have been told and of putting their action into training. They need to know that it is not in their best interest to brutalize an inmate. What you set in motion when you start trying to run an institution through intimidation, fear, and brutality is an escalating set of inevitable consequences. You are never going to intimidate or threaten inmates and get them to say that staff are tougher than they are. Even if you were to escalate to this level, which from experience, every warden knows is impossible, what you face is that you will eventually be in a courtroom or the inmate will injure or kill a staff member. You will be taken to court for brutalizing inmates, and you not only will get fired, but may end up serving time in the same prison where you were brutalizing inmates.

Staff are outnumbered every day, and what this code of silence, this informal code of protecting each other, can lead to is one of the following: You are either going to get assaulted or killed as the level of violence escalates, or you may get your throat cut before or after you are raped. If one of these happens to you, then you may be charged with a crime, because as violence escalates, you may have to hurt somebody. When you hurt somebody, you are going to court, and you will lose. Since you are outside the parameters of policy, there is no indemnification. Nobody is going to be standing up in court to defend your actions, because nobody told you to beat up an inmate, and your actions, in fact, violated institutional policy.

Intelligent staff will see that they cannot win through intimidation, fear, and violence. They will know that innocent staff can get hurt. That is why a staff member starts by confronting another officer. You must tell this staff member that he or she is putting you in jeopardy by making you a witness of this inappropriate behavior. If this goes to a courtroom, you inform the other staff member that you will not lie under oath. If this person will not listen to you, then your next response is to go to someone above you and tell this person what you observed.

Why Is Job Enrichment of Correctional Officers Such an Important Role for Proactive Wardens?

The way to make the officer's role more attractive to individuals considering a career in corrections, as well as make it more meaningful to individuals already working as officers, is to offer incentives such as career development programs to reinforce and increase the number of officers who want to provide humane services to inmates. A number of studies indicate that at least some officers enjoy providing such services. These officers see correctional work as a worthwhile endeavor.[13] In *Hard Time*, Robert Johnson strongly emphasizes this point:

> *It is by helping prisoners—by promoting secure and responsive prison regimes—that some officers rise above the limitation of their formal custodial role. They use their authority to help inmates cope with prison life; they provide human services rather than custodial repression. They do the best they can with the resources at their disposals to make the prison a better place in which to live and work.*[14]

Correctional staff, as Frank Wood has discovered in his career, can become excited about working in a humane prison in which everyone is treated with dignity and respect. The majority will be responsive in a positive way when wardens and their staff have a clear vision of what they want to accomplish with the prison, and when they see that these changes are making the prison a safer and more pleasant place in which to live and work.

Summary

The proactive warden looks for staff who are, in the words of Frank Wood, "the best and the brightest. They look for people who do not just talk the golden rule but who practice it. They want people who are loyal and people who will be responsive to both the real and imagined concerns of inmates and staff." These wardens look for staff who are committed and dedicated, who are convinced that the corrections profession is important and noble, and who believe they can make a difference.

Proactive wardens take these individuals—staff in their institutions—and provide them with the best training programs available to enhance their custodial and interpersonal skills. These wardens encourage them to be part of an important team. They reinforce positive performance whenever that is possible, and offer constructive critical feedback when that is necessary. Every staff member becomes an important part of the corrections team. Warden Wood always emphasized the importance of staff involvement in the annual review of policy procedures, post orders, job descriptions, and the accreditation documentation process. Officers grow and develop during this process, and it reinforces their identification with the organizational team because they have a forum from which to suggest policy improvements and changes.

ENDNOTES

[1] Clemens Bartollas. 2002. *Invitation to Corrections.* Boston: Allyn and Bacon, p. 265.

[2] Frank Wood wrote this section on participative management for a report he did as a consultant on the quality of prisons in Tennessee.

[3] Dr. David Ward provided this information on staff training during an interview in November 2002.

[4] Hans Toch. 1981. Foreword to Lucien X. Lombardo, *Guards Imprisoned: Correctional Officers at Work.* New York: Elsevier.

[5] James B. Jacobs and Lawrence S. Kraft. 1976. Integrating the Keepers: A Comparison of Black and White Prison Officers in Illinois. *Social Problems.* 25 (February).

[6] Lucien X, Lombardo. 1982. Alleviating Inmate Stress: Contributions from Correctional Officers. In Hans Toch and Robert Johnson, eds. *The Pains of Imprisonment.* Beverly Hills, California: Sage, p. 293.

[7] Peter Earley. 1992. *The Hot House: Life Inside Leavenworth Prison.* New York: Bantam Books, p. 221.

[8] Hans Toch and John Klofas. 1982. Alienation and Desire for Job Enrichment among Correctional Officers. *Federal Probation.* 46, pp. 35-44.

[9] Robert Johnson. 1996. *Hard Time: Understanding and Reforming the Prison.* Belmont, California: Wadsworth.

[10] J. W. Marquart. 1984. Prison Guards and the Use of Physical Coercion as a Mechanism of Prisoner Control. Paper presented at the annual meeting of the American Sociological Association, San Antonio, Texas, August.

[11] Conversations with inmates.

[12] Incident reported to Bartollas.

[13] Charles A. Linquist and John T. Whitehead. 1986. Guards Released from Prison: A Natural Experiment in Job Enrichment. *Journal of Criminal Justice.* 14, pp. 283-284.

[14] Johnson, *Hard Time*, pp. 137-138.

Chapter Eight:

The Art of Thriving in Correctional Leadership

Wardens are sometimes fired. Even good wardens at one point or another can lose their jobs. On occasion, they are called into the director or commissioner's office on a Monday morning, offered a cup of coffee, and then were given the startling news that they are terminated, effective immediately. They are informed that they are not to return to the institution. Their possessions will be boxed up and sent to them.

This scenario has taken place, but much more typically wardens know when they are in trouble. Their prisons have had a rash of incidents, riots, escapes, protests from inmates or staff, or widespread criticism from the media. Their administration may be an embarrassment to the governor or to the chief of the corrections department. The director or commissioner, as well as others, have concluded that a change of correctional leadership is needed.

Survival in the job, then, is an issue that all wardens must deal with during their career. Wardens may not be protected by civil service. Their appointment may be at the pleasure of the director or commissioner. Most wardens have seen examples of other wardens who have been terminated, and the nagging thought that this could happen to them cannot be dismissed easily.

Yet, survival is a reactive term; it is much like crisis-oriented management practices. One does not feel good and energized by the job or view the career in positive terms if survival reactions are the way in which one views the responsibility of the warden. What is far more desirable is to view what is needed for wardens to thrive in their jobs—the topic for this chapter.

Why Do Some Wardens Thrive in Their Jobs?

Wardens who thrive on the job tend to have a number of characteristics in common. Among them are the following, which we next will discuss in detail:

- They take a proprietary interest in the institution.
- They anticipate problems.
- They maintain a clean institution.
- They have a hands-on approach.
- They are predictable in their fairness and judgments.
- They have the moral and political support from politicians and the director of corrections.

Proprietary Interest in the Institution

A "proprietary interest" means that these wardens have ownership. Wardens work in a very dynamic environment, a microcosm of any small city in this nation. The warden has to be a very good observer and know about subcultures—what is going on in the inmate culture, and what is going on with the staff. Wardens who are involved directly in the day-to-day operation of the facility feel a true commitment and proprietary interest in the ownership of that facility.

A proprietary interest does not happen quickly. Wardens who are assigned on a short-term rotating basis will not develop any real proprietary interest in that institution. Instead, what you find is people who just want to get through their eighteen months, two years, or whatever time they anticipate that they will be there. However, rotating institution heads gives them another experience and expands their horizons, but they do not develop a proprietary interest in the facility, and they do not believe that they can make a difference there and move the institution to a higher plateau.

For an initial period, wardens are just getting their feet on the ground, even if they are experienced wardens. It takes time to learn the culture of the institution, to understand what is going on, and to identify the dynamics of the inmates and the staff. When wardens have had time to learn this background, culture, and socialization of the institution, they can proceed to make the changes that they anticipate are necessary.

The warden's proprietary interest in the facility will manifest itself every day in his or her interaction with staff and inmates. When staff and inmates realize the wardens have a proprietary interest, they can see that the wardens are concerned with all decisions they make—with the criteria being the best interests of the inmates and the staff.

Anticipating Problems in the Institution

Staying on top of the emerging issues and the maintenance needs of the institution is critical. Having an established organizational structure keeps information flowing to and from staff and to and from inmates. The morning meeting is a good vehicle by which staff can communicate with each other. They also can report what inmates are telling them. This will give staff some means to help control the rumors that constantly occur in prisons among staff and rumors that inmates spread. You hear that "they're gonna do this or they're gonna do that."

Wardens have a chance, as long as they are properly informed, to put information in the prison that they want staff and inmates to know. Their present and future credibility depends on that. Thus, if wardens say something is not going to happen, it should not happen. If they say to the inmates that a rumor that is going around is not accurate or based on true facts, wardens must make certain that they are telling them the truth. Every time wardens do that, they are building the credibility of the staff and the administration, and inmates can count on the warden and staff to tell the truth.

Obviously, wardens are never going to give inmates information that will provide them the opportunity to predict certain strategic and tactical things they have to do to keep the institution safe. In fact, Wood periodically would purge the institution of contraband. He would lock up the prison unannounced. Nobody knew when it was going to happen. The only person who really knew was the warden who would make a phone call at three or four in the morning and say the place is going to be locked up this morning, so start putting things in place and to serve inmates breakfast in their cells. Staff was alerted to go right into procedures developed for this type of surprise purge.

At the Stillwater Prison, Wood did surprise- or unannounced preventative-searches two-to-three times per year, but that diminished over time once staff got things under control. When things are under control, wardens do not have to do it as frequently, and they can lock up parts of the institution to be purged without engaging the entire facility.

However, wardens do not want to become predictable or do searches on any type of a schedule. When Wood was warden, he sometimes even doubled back. Inmates would complain, "Our cell block was locked up six months ago, so why is it happening again?" The answer is, "We do not want to be predictable." If you are honest with them, they will respect that. Although inmates take great joy in telling officers when a search is going to occur, they were never very accurate in speculating the time and date of when the lockdowns were going to take place.

A Clean Institution

A warden cannot have oversight or responsibility for any environment and not have control over it. If a hospital administrator allowed the hospital to be filthy and filled with anything that had the potential of compromising a patient's health, the administrator probably would lose his or her job very quickly. If a warden allows the prison to be filthy and allows things to occur within that prison that make it unsafe and insecure for staff, inmates, and the public, that warden does not have control of the environment and is likely to experience serious institutional problems. Staff and inmates never feel good about working or doing time in a dirty prison. A good institution is at least a clean institution, but it is also an institution in which staff members are in control and everyone is reasonably safe. The interviewees were clearly in agreement with the importance of a clean institution. Some of their responses are found in Feature 8.1.

A Hands-on Approach to Prison Management

A hands-on approach means that the warden keeps in regular contact with inmates and staff, visiting the cellblocks on a regular basis. It also means that wardens encourage decision making at the lowest appropriate level in the organization. A hands-on approach means that correctional officers have a certain amount of discretion in their interaction with inmates. A hands-on approach also means that the warden knows how to get things resolved. The warden does not want to be doing things that inmates should be doing for themselves, but where the warden can do something to intervene, a hands-on warden will. Thus, a hands-on approach ultimately means that involved wardens have created a climate around themselves so that both inmates and staff feel comfortable approaching them about something, but they do that at all levels in a way that does not violate the chain of command.

What wardens do not want are captains coming into a cell block, allowing inmates to bypass all the other people that they should be going through to get a decision made. The decision should be made at the lowest possible level. If the chain of command is violated, the correctional officer becomes meaningless.

Feature 8.1: The Importance of a Clean Institution

Orville Pung, former Commissioner of Corrections in Minnesota, emphasizes the importance of a clean prison:

"A well managed institution has consistent policies and procedures that are predictable and understandable. Also, a well-managed institution is clean. Now, a clean institution doesn't necessarily mean it is a good facility, but you never see a dirty institution that's a good facility. When staff and inmates are clean and the place is orderly, it's amazing how you can just simply walk through an institution and know what kind of management it is because both staff and inmates are feeling good about themselves."

John M. Hurley, former warden of the Federal Bureau of Prisons, proposes that a well-managed prison begins with a clean facility:

"A well-managed institution includes numerous characteristics. Perhaps the most visible is the cleanliness and orderliness of the facility. From the time you drive up to the facility, you observe a neat, clean, and orderly environment. This is consistent throughout the prison. Secondly, you would observe a presence of "respectfulness" between staff and inmates, staff and visitors, and perhaps more importantly, respectfulness between staff themselves. The facilities-leadership team who sets the standard by their own behavior and interactions sets this 'tone.'

"Another characteristic would be the physical plant itself. It doesn't necessarily have to be new; but rather, signage throughout is clear and visible, colors are bright and cheerful, and all incidentals are in good repair (in other words, lights actually work, pictures are hung properly, storage closets are clean, neat and orderly, and so forth). All of these and many more characteristics are choices made by the institution management about what is acceptable and expected.

"Perhaps the most important characteristic of a well-managed facility would be the evidence of strong communication—written, verbal, and visual. In other words, staff and inmates don't have to guess what's expected or required; they know because it's been communicated. Yet another characteristic would be the evidence that rules are actually enforced, for both staff and inmates. One only needs to look at the appearance of the staff and inmates to know whether any 'enforcement code' exists at the facility—for anything."

Sources: Interviewed in November 2002.

Everybody will wait to make his or her requests to administrative staff and to the warden. The same is true of the warden. If everyone can bypass the warden and go straight to the commissioner or director, the warden will be meaningless. Accordingly, wardens want to make certain staff and inmates understand how decisions ordinarily are made at the lowest appropriate level in the organization.

The warden wants all people to feel that they are involved and that they are also part of the team. To accomplish this, the warden must see that there are detailed post orders and job descriptions, which lay out that individual's latitude, discretion, and accountability.

Predictability and Thriving as a Warden

Wardens, of course, want to be predictable in some respects. They want to be predictable in the sense that staff and inmates know this person is always going to be fair and equitable in sorting out the facts, in searching for the truth, and in making a decision on something that is an issue. They want to be predictable in that they are seen as a person without radical mood swings. The warden should be someone who is calm, not mad as hell or on a terror jag disrupting the whole place because something went wrong. That erratic behavior is not good for either staff or inmates. Wardens want to be predictable in that they maintain the same principles and values they use in making decisions.

Wardens do not want to be predictable on strategic and tactical things that are necessary to make certain the institution is safe and secure. However, wardens want to make sure that policies and procedures on safety and security are available and everybody understands them. What wardens do not want to do is reveal precisely what is done in intelligence gathering. They do not want to expose people who are providing them with information that helps them to manage the institution.

Once inmates begin to realize they are not going to be identified because of some piece of information that they know will improve the environment and make it safer, they will be more willing to share information with staff, as long as the "snitch jacket" is not put on anybody. When an inmate is labeled a snitch, it is very dangerous. As an administrator, it is unforgivable to house known snitches with the general population. The riot at Santa Fe Penitentiary clearly reveals what can happen when the known snitches were housed together with the other inmates. How safe would you feel with a thousand inmates and just a few staff? How vulnerable are you going to be, especially if staff have a walk-through routine and inmates know they are not coming back for a while?

Wardens must be responsive to the real as well as the imagined concerns of inmates. Imagined concerns must be taken seriously because when individuals imagine or believe that they are being mistreated, the situation is just as real to them as a true injustice. So, unless someone comes and takes them aside and looks them directly in the eyes and explains why they should not interpret what happened to them as having been treated unfairly, those persons will believe that they have been treated unfairly.

Responding to these concerns does not mean saying yes to all of them. But there are times in which wardens are wise to say, "These are the facts, here's what happened, and we're going to make an adjustment or rectify the problem with an equitable outcome." By doing that, the warden develops credibility with the inmates. Not only that, no inmate or group of inmates can develop any issue or group of issues on which they could get broad support for a major incident in the institution. They are feeding back actual and factual information so the rumors get squelched as quickly as they emerge.

Moral and Political Support

Finally, wardens must have the moral and political support from politicians and the commissioner or director of corrections. In other words, those to whom wardens answer must provide moral and political support. When the inevitable problems occur, these supporters then are standing next to these wardens and helping them to get through that problem. What this means is that wardens are getting feedback indicating that people understand how they are attempting to run the prison and that they are receiving the fiscal and human resources to accomplish the goals that have been set to raise the institution to another plateau.

How Can Wardens Minimize Trouble in the Institution?

Anybody can get in trouble over the incidents that are going to occur in a prison. A newly appointed warden needs to understand that it is inevitable that things are going to happen in a prison. It is impossible to be able to run a humane prison where wardens can absolutely say that there will never be a problem or an incident. Wardens are dealing with hundreds and sometimes thousands of lives of people who have demonstrated a history of not solving their problems in a socially acceptable way. What wardens can do is take reasonable precautions to reduce the frequency, scope, and seriousness of those inevitable instances, but they still will occur.

When incidents do occur, they need to be addressed in a prescribed way. There are usually policies, procedures, post orders, and job descriptions that tell people what to do and how to do it. Top administrators, supervisors, and line staff have been trained to know how to respond to a problem. If the warden and staff are proactive, an incident that takes place is ordinarily not a surprise; however, it may be a surprise that it happened at this particular time. If the warden and staff knew about it, they obviously would have taken some proactive step to stop it from happening, but when it happens, they now step into the realm of responding to it in a prescribed way.

Wardens are less likely to get into trouble when a commissioner or director is competent and is familiar with the way these wardens are operating from day to day. The commissioner or director also should make periodic visits throughout the year to the institution, just stopping to chat with the warden. This top corrections official also should take a general hike around the institution with the warden. These visits should give a sense of what is happening in the institution and how much rapport the warden has with staff and inmates. See Feature 8.2 for explanations of when top corrections officials of a department know or suspect that a warden is in trouble.

Some wardens get removed for political reasons, which does not necessary mean these are legitimate reasons. It means that somebody has been identified politically as the scapegoat for whatever happened, and the warden is an easy target, much as a baseball or football coach is. When coaches do not win the playoffs, Super Bowl, or World Series, they are fired with great abandon, including good coaches. The same thing is true among wardens.

You also have incompetent wardens who are removed for good cause. This cause usually is responding to something that has happened that they have not anticipated and they have not planned how to respond to it. Or they have not been able to bring the institution together in a common purpose, common mission, common goal, and shared understanding of what everyone is trying to accomplish.

The warden's responsibility is to bring staff and inmates together to help them understand

Feature 8.2: Signs that a Warden Is in Trouble

William Sondervan, former commissioner of the Maryland Division of Corrections, says that he can identify problems in the institution when the following factors are present:

> *"Sometimes, you'll see wardens who make major blunders, errors, or mistakes, but you can also judge what's going on in the field by reviewing a variety of indexes. For example, you can look at the annual audits that are done in some of our institutions for ACA accreditation. You can evaluate how a warden manages the budget or the number of positive urinalysis results. You can look at the number of assaults on inmates and assaults on staff, as well as correctional officers' complaints. If you regularly monitor all those things, you can get a good sense of who is heading in the right direction and who is going in the wrong direction. You can identify who is in trouble and why. When you see those things, that's when you have to get involved and start turning it around the other way."*

Steven Norris, former commissioner of the Tennessee Department of Corrections, answered this way:

> *"You'll see it in a number of ways. Incidents of assault inmate to inmate and inmate to officer will go up. Escapes go up, and there is an increase in contraband, especially drug usage. I also look at whether the schedules are being maintained and adhered to. Is there adequate recreation? Is there adequate medical attention? Is there adequate access to religious ceremonies? All of those things will begin to break down if the facility is not being properly managed. If there is a problem in a correctional facility, you can walk into the facility, and you are going to be able to feel the tension."*

Orville Pung, former commissioner of the Minnesota Department of Corrections, gave this response:

> *"It is rare that you have one institution in a correctional system having problems when other ones in that system don't. I've seen systems where every institution seems to have problems—and there appear to be similar environments and institutions in most states with good systems. A commissioner knows that a warden is in trouble when an institution has chronic problems and disturbances. It is also reflected in staff and inmates' attitudes.*
>
> *"I served as president of the Association of State Correctional Administrators which got me into nearly every state in the union where I visited a lot of correctional facilities. I also had an opportunity to work in Puerto Rico for a few years after I retired. I have toured Chinese prisons, worked for the UN in Japan, and spent about a month touring the Polish prison system. Ironically, you will find that prisons are more similar than dissimilar. It's amazing because wardens face the same problems in Poland that they face in Japan that they face here. Prisons are more alike than not."*

Sources: Interviewed in October and November 2002.

that it is in their best interest to have some type of a mutual reciprocal trust and confidence in each other, and the only way that happens is by earning it on a day-to-day basis by the way in which the warden interacts with staff.

What Type of Relationships Should Staff Have with Inmates?

Thriving in correctional leadership also has to do with the type of relationships that staff have with inmates. When you talk about staff-inmate interactions or relationships, it is necessary to give some license to staff to enable them to interact on a plane that will allow them to develop some mutual and reciprocal respect between themselves and inmates. The warden can model this relationship with inmates so that the staff understand that they have permission to interact.

Chase Riveland, former secretary of Washington State's Department of Corrections, added these thoughts on the importance of staff-inmate interactions:

> *There is some question about the wisdom of staff developing and maintaining rapport with inmates. I guess the debate centers on the definition of "rapport." Certainly, leaders in order to successfully lead have to be able to communicate with those that they are leading. There are numerous ways that the communication can take place, but most effective wardens have found that showing an interest in their staff and the inmates that are under their custody is a technique that can go a long ways. I think there are successful leaders who do not do that to a great degree, but they do have to compensate in other ways in order to be able to demonstrate those leadership techniques.*[1]

There are, of course, limits on what takes place during this interaction (*see*, for example, Cornelius, 2002). As a staff member, you do not get into personal life. You do not start sharing your phone number or what is going on in your house or where you live. You can interact on a wide variety of subjects and matters without getting into your personal life, without revealing things that could compromise you, the safety of you and your family, or the security of the institution.

During staff training, staff can learn what the limits are and what lines should not be crossed in staff-inmate interaction. Another part of staff training is helping them be made aware that their job description requires them to be honest, candid, and straightforward with inmates. The problem of staff crossing the line is that it can compromise staff safety or the security of the institution.

Many inmates are seeking to compromise the integrity of the institution in some way that they can use or to exploit this information to position themselves to compromise institutional security. There is no limit to the scenarios. Unfortunately, once you have crossed the line, the inmate can compromise you by saying, "If you don't do this or that, I will have to reveal what you told me and you will lose your job."

Sam P. Garrison, former warden of Central Prison, Raleigh North Carolina, tells how inmates use personal information to set up an officer:

> *In talking with an officer over the space of a year, an inmate can learn a great deal about him. The last two officers bringing drugs into the institution were married and had a family. The whole thing was set up by inmates finding out that they went to a certain bar one night a week. All of a sudden, one officer found himself in a motel room with a prisoner's girlfriend. Then, two days later she said, "There'll be a package mailed to you that you'll take into the prison." When he resisted, she said, "Well, do you want your wife to know that you slept with me the night before*

last?" The prisoners had him in the jaws of a vice.

Wardens can tell staff members up front during their in-service training that all people make mistakes, but they need to be smart enough to recognize their mistakes. If staff members do make a mistake, it would be wise for them to run and not walk to the warden or other administrative staff. If they run and tell somebody, then perhaps the mistake can be managed. If they wait until the administrative staff finds out about some mistake they have made that has now been parlayed into something compromising the integrity, the security, and the safety of this institution, it is harder to do anything to help this staff member learn from the mistake or remain on the team.

How Does a Warden Handle the Issue of Crowding?

The warden has no control over crowding, and it is necessary to keep articulating to the policy makers what you need to do your job. This goes back to what was said earlier about having political support. Nevertheless, it is necessary to have a plan B. Of course, the best places to start if you are forced into multiple occupancy are with those inmates who are closest to heading for the street. These are the people least likely to be problematic in a prison, because they are the ones who can see the light at the end of the tunnel. If you are in a secure prison, you look for the area where you expect the least problems when you double up, and that is where you do it. Multiple occupancies ultimately come back to haunt those who are forced to do them. You can run multiple-occupancy institutions at minimum- and medium-security facilities but not in maximum. Maximum-security facilities run well when the difficult-to-manage inmates are single celled. If all the cells in a maximum-security prison are double or multiple occupancy, how does the staff send any kind of a credible message that inmates can be protected? They cannot.

Who controls the environment in a crowded prison? The inmates do. If you are calling the shots in the inmate culture and you want someone in someone else's cell, you can make that happen through intimidation and assault. An inmate will ask for a transfer and eventually will be where someone wants him. A lot of people, correctional administrators included, are bullied into a false sense of security and believe that multiple occupancy operations work because of the lower reported incidents. The reason incidents are not reported as frequently is they do not need to settle problems out in the yard or the kitchen or corridor; they can settle them right in the cell. Somebody can tell somebody else they have a problem with their cellmate and let that person take care of it. So, you might see people coming through the food line or on the yard with black eyes and split lips, and nobody says anything. The level of violence and incidents has not diminished; they just are not getting reported anymore because the inmates know it is almost impossible for the warden and staff to protect vulnerable inmates.

What about Being Disillusioned?

Being disillusioned has many facets and we will discuss each of the following ones:

- How do effective wardens differ from disillusioned ones?
- How tough is it to hang on when you are disillusioned?

- Do inmates know if staff are disillusioned?
- How does one avoid becoming disillusioned in repressive systems?

How Do Effective Wardens Differ from Disillusioned Ones?

Effective wardens create a forum where they can get positive and critical feedback, and it is not threatening to persons to give it. A climate is established where information is shared-even information that is not complimentary. The disillusioned warden is more likely to be somebody who is holding on and trying to maintain the status quo, as opposed to trying to find creative ways to improve the institution and to move it to another plateau. That is immediately visible and obvious to staff and inmates.

When staff and inmates became aware that the warden is disillusioned, it increases the likelihood of their being disillusioned. When the warden and other staff become disillusioned, the institution is on a pathway to disaster. In other words, the institution ultimately will not be able to respond to some major crisis or incident, nor will the institution be able to avoid crisis or incidents in the future because the warden has not put in place anything that is anticipatory, preventative, and proactive.

One of the ways that the competent warden puts preventative and strategic plans in place is that staff are told that these plans reduce the potential for an incident to occur that must be dealt with at a time when it is not advantageous to staff. The following dialog shows how Frank Wood communicated to staff that putting in a solid eight hours would benefit them in the long run.

The warden can say to the staff, "Do you like to be called up in the middle of the night because we have got one thousand inmates that will not go back into their cells? We're calling all the staff back to the institution to deal with this." The warden then can say, "If you don't like that, give us a solid eight hours while you are here where we are all focused on the preventative things and proactive things that are going to reduce the likelihood of that happening. Now, your weekends will be your own, your evenings will be your own, because we have the institution under control. So there's an advantage to you to be engaged in this way."

How Tough Is It to Hang on When You Are Disillusioned?

Some disillusioned wardens just try to maintain the status quo to survive. They know that if they can just hang on for another year or two, their transfer, promotion, or retirement will be better. Everyone can identify this hanging-on process at any level of the organization.

Some wardens get to the point of disillusionment when they begin to see that they do not have the moral, political, and resource support to do their jobs. That is not always the case, but sometimes it is. You can imagine how hopeless you feel if you know what needs to be done and how to do it, and you cannot get the political and moral support and/or the fiscal and human resources to proceed to do it. Sometimes, a disillusioned warden is also an incompetent warden or somebody who does not know how to make the changes or what changes to make to bring the institution under control.

Other consequences of being disillusioned make it tougher to just hang on. When you are demoralized, you begin to demoralize your managerial staff around you and, in turn, to demoralize the rest of the institution. Problems begin to emerge with poor labor relations, low morale among staff, and an increased frequency of incidents among inmates and between inmates and staff. Staff are not functioning and acting as a team, and the inmates immediately see the vulnerabilities in the system. The frequency, scope, and seriousness of incidents increase as a result of all of the staff not being on the same wave length and on the same team, committed and believing in what they can do and what they can accomplish. Then, departures occur. People choose to get out of there because they see what is happening, and they do not want to be a part of the chaos that is present in the prison. Also, at the upper and lower levels, the turnover among staff becomes alarmingly high.

Wardens can survive six, eight, or ten years while there are problems in their institution. The only reason that this takes place is because they may be operating an institution in some remote area where there is very little oversight. When walking through the institution, it is obvious that it is not clean; the food is not good; there is a we/they mentality between inmates and staff, but it survives because of its remoteness, its lack of oversight, and its lack of any media exposure. Other wardens have survived for five to ten years where the politics are such that what the public really wants out of its prison system is they do not want to hear about it. So, if the institution stays out of the media, the governor, the commissioner, or the director, and the public is happy.

Do Inmates Know If Staff Are Disillusioned?

Some inmates may not be analytical enough to be able to articulate the dynamics of what is going on in the organization, but they know things are changing and not working well. They are aware that the organization is in disarray, but they may not be able to explain why. Other inmates are astute analysts who can figure out what is going on, what the dynamics are, and what is happening in the staff culture.

There may not be a real consensus, but inmates have a general sense of how well the warden is doing. The majority of inmates know when they have a good warden and staff. They know when the warden has earned their trust and respect. They may not articulate it; they may not espouse it, or may not pass it on to other inmates, but they appreciate the quality of life they enjoy in that institution. Nevertheless, very few, if any, are going to praise a warden publicly.

In Feature 8.3, an exception is the letter to Frank Wood when he was appointed commissioner of corrections from Harvy L. Carignan, a long-term inmate.

How Does One Avoid Becoming Disillusioned in Repressive Systems?

Wardens must keep reinforcing the things they can and should be doing right because they do not always get what they want. Wardens with a proprietary interest continue to build up what they can build up: the relationships, the interactions, and the communications. They keep struggling with it. They try to deal with the frustration of the inmate, explain to them, and stay in contact with them, and help them understand that the political arena is dictating this and not the intelligent informed corrections professional. They let inmates know that this is not their idea; rather it is the demagogues and the political opportunists forcing this down the throats of the corrections professionals. As wardens communicate that they do

Feature 8.3: Letter to Frank W. Wood

Dear Mr. Wood:

"The new warden's in the hallway! You guys up there on the galley either get in your cells or go to the yard!" the "B" Cellblock duty sergeant yelled. To a man, we ran down the stairs and into the hallway leading to the yard-we wanted to see the new warden!

I cannot remember the date, not the year even, but it was either 1977 or 1978.

My first impression was that you were much older than you turned out to be: I guessed middle fifties-you were thirty-seven. You were wearing a grey tweed blazer-like jacket with leather reinforced elbows. I thought it may be your "smoking" jacket, something you found comfort in. In those days there was very little of it for any of us at Stillwater. Neither the guards nor the inmates were comfortable with their situation. Even at this late date it seems you yourself was [sic] not overjoyed with what you saw or must have been contemplating doing. I erroneously assumed you were enjoying yourself and reacted accordingly. I had never met anyone who could hide his feelings so masterfully. Guess what: I still do not know what you are thinking, but I have learned a lot about you in the interim.

For the first four or five years I did not understand you and I cannot truthfully say I wanted to. I had just read a book by Dr. Edgar Schein in which he espoused building prisons such as you had described to the press and others and using them to brainwash inmates. I can still remember what he wrote: "I would like you to think of brainwashing, not in terms of politics, ethics and morals, but in terms of the deliberate changing of human behavior and attitudes by a group of men who have relatively complete control over the environment in which the captive population lives." Consequently, I fully expected Oak Park Heights to be a pseudo-scientific experimental laboratory-like place operating under the guise of a long-term penal facility. Most erroneously I deemed you a protagonist of the practice of human experimentation and brainwashing who justified his views on the basis that such treatment would be beneficial to society. Little did I suspect that your basic principles to satisfy moral, ethical, and legal concepts would not allow for such acts. I was convinced that the mission of Oak Park Heights was to silence in-prison critics, inmate leaders, and all assumed troublemakers of every political belief and religious persuasion. I believed only the thinnest veneer of civilization would exist in this microcosm in which you would be the not-too-benevolent dictator!

Although the above assessment with minor variations still exists in the minds of many of the inmates, I long ago changed my thinking and was won over to yours and your way of getting things accomplished. After eleven years of living in your brain-child I could not help but change my mind and neither can any other intelligent and discerning person. Stillwater had been a rudderless ship and I had to see the wake at Oak Park Heights to know the difference.

Feature 8.3: Letter to Frank W. Wood (con't)

Within my peer group, it is often said you are a philosopher-warden. From a group as unknowing and unpractical as this is may not seem like such high praise. However, there are some few of us who are aware of these philosophical implications and the need for them. To the extent that such changes have occurred between the two prisons it would be impossible to over-emphasize either the ground-breaking or the results derived from your innovations.

Connotations can vary according to context, but I mean only to convey a fully positive image of you and your accomplishments. To some, usually the old heads amongst the inmates and guards, it is still unrealistic idealism, but I know better because I am aware of and have discerned the hard realities of which you are the creator and originator. You had the guts to say to hell with the historical aspects of prison and to create a new workable philosophy and to put it in to work in place of the old. And although I have carefully considered all the characteristics of your creation I am aware that I am vastly understating it. I have neither the intelligence to comprehend it completely nor the education to fully appreciate it. Consequently, I am not the best interpreter nor the most able commentator, but you can be assured I am most sincere. I am not a scholar, only an inmate who has served some fourteen years of a life sentence under the aegis of your wardenship who is doing his best to say a great deal by means of a very small ability. For that reason I have not dwelled upon the creations and innovations. I need not because they are a matter of public record. A lot of water has gone under the bridge between that day at Stillwater when I first saw you. Between then and now you have touched a lot of lives and I know most of us are the better for it. Fair play and innate honesty is always acceptable, no matter when or where it is employed.

Lastly, I am not trying to memorialize what you have done—time will take of that—but to congratulate you and to wish you every success in your new position of Commissioner of Corrections for the State of Minnesota. You looked good at the top, Mr. Wood, and all the better because you damned well deserved it.

Source: Letter to Frank Wood on August 3, 1993 from the Minnesota Correctional Facility, Stillwater.

not necessarily agree with what they are forced to do, they still have to do it. In this way, the warden can keep reciprocal trust and communication going with the staff and inmates. They do not just assume that they will catch on because they will tend to see you as part of the problem and maybe even perceive that your staff and you are glad this is happening.

Can Proactive Wardens Make a Difference?

Proactive wardens not only believe they can make a difference, but they also can help other people in their organization believe that they can make a difference as well. They can make a difference in terms of improving the quality of life in the institution, which creates a climate where it is possible for people to change. If you open your cell door in the morning at 6 a.m. and you are preoccupied with your survival that day, you are not likely to be interested in change. In too many prisons, what survival for the day means is whether another inmate is going to try to threaten you or whether an officer is going to somehow demonize, demean, or brutalize you. If that is what you face every morning when you step out of your cell, you are not likely to make any life-sustaining changes in your way of looking at life. It is unlikely that the inmates are going to be law-abiding citizens on the street if every day in prison they must face the choice between survival and change.

In contrast, inmates feel much different about the institution and about the possibility of doing something positive about their lives in a prison with a proactive warden. When the cell door opens in the morning, they know that a good nutritious breakfast is there waiting for them. They are confident that staff is going to treat them with dignity and respect even when they are out of line and have done something that is unacceptable. They are aware that if an injustice does inadvertently occur, someone will be there they can talk to who will make every attempt to resolve the problem and isolate the predator.

A proactive warden's philosophy of treating others with dignity and respect and of being a person of integrity also will affect the involvement of staff. Instead of being a solitary force for trying to do good, staff members are led by a proactive warden and are joined by similarly committed staff. The whole becomes much greater than the parts. The quality of life for staff has improved in such a prison, and staff, in turn, are affected in how they treat each other and inmates.

Furthermore, these types of wardens make a difference because they focus on growth, self-development, a higher plateau, and improved structure and operations. In other words, they are always looking to see if anything is applicable to improve the way they do business. They, in effect, are attempting to stay ahead of the curve and to be out front and proactive. These wardens perceive that this is the logical and intelligent thing to do in any business, not just in prisons. But what is happening is that these wardens in their dynamic, process model are demanding the best from themselves and others; likewise, staff and inmates tend to respond with improved responses.

Summary

To thrive as a warden, one has to be secure in the job, which means to work in a secure environment in which staff are in control. This chapter considered a number of topics concerned with feeling positive, thriving, and governing a secure institution. Not surprisingly, the improved quality of life for inmates and staff promised by this proactive approach to correctional administration will reduce institutional problems and incidents. When persons are handled with respect, which some prisoners are not used to, it is not surprising that they respond in more cooperative and supportive ways to this organizational structure and philosophy. When officers, who in some prisons feel that they are treated worse than inmates, are treated with dignity and respect, it is also not surprising that they become valued and contributing members of a "team."

There is nothing about this proactive model that promotes victimization of others, that suggests there are not consequences for negative behavior, and that holds to naïve notions about what prisoners will or will not do. Following in the footsteps of the other proactive wardens, they expect the institution to be clean, safe, productive, and secure. They are not interested in giving their power away to inmates, nor are they interested in violating inmates in any way. They concur that inmates come to prison as punishment for their violations of the law, but they do not come "to make them suffer," as some politicians were clambering in the 1990s. If an inmate wants to profit from imprisonment, proactive wardens are committed to giving them opportunities to do that.

ENDNOTES

[1]Interviewed in November 2002.

[2]Interviewed in August 1980.

Chapter Nine:

The Humane Prison

One of the major challenges of wardens is to do what they can to achieve a secure and humane prison. A warden learns very quickly that the first priority of a warden is the protection of society, and this protection depends on a secure prison. If there is too much internal disorder (in other words, collective disturbances or riots, assaults, or murders) or there is a rash of external disorder (escapes), wardens are aware that their days on the job are numbered. But, in addition to a secure prison that protects society, a prison must achieve other necessary qualities to be a humane place. The task of this chapter is to examine what it means for a prison to be humane and to show how that can be accomplished in today's correctional climate.

Is the Creation of a Humane Correctional Facility Beyond the Hope of Corrections?

It is a strange story. It began with a small cast of characters, men who were certain that Captain Lynds' model of prison management had to be abandoned in favor of innovations unprecedented in the United States. These idealists brought together the tough-minded wardens and keepers of America's prisons and induced them to sign off on a radical new Declaration of Principles to guide the reformation of the nation's prisons.

Eloquent American reformers denounced repression and urged that prisoners have educational opportunities and religious instruction. No one was prepared to speak up for the traditions of the Auburn Silent System or the Pennsylvania's Eastern State Penitentiary. Delegates gave powerful support to the meeting's presiding officer, Ohio Governor Rutherford B. Hayes, who later became the nineteenth president of the United States.[1]

Blake McKelvey, a historian of American corrections, described the meeting further:

> *[It was a] mountain-top experience, more of a religious revival than a professional conference. Because the reformers knew exactly what they wanted and more important, what they did not want, a memorable document emerged from their exalted deliberations. Practical prison men [and women] from twenty-two states, Canada, and Latin American nations enthusiastically rose above the monotony of four gray walls, men in stripes shuffling in lock-step, sullen faces staring through the bars, coarse mush and coffee made of bread crusts, armed sentries stalking the walls. They forgot it all and voted for their remarkable declaration of principles.*[2]

There were thirty-seven principles in all. Ever since their resounding acceptance in 1870, they have been admired, respectfully quoted, and often ruefully dismissed as visionary. In actuality, most of them have had a profound impact on the practice of corrections.

Yet, the 1870 zealots were disappointed by attempts to put their principles into daily practice. The American prison system was still modeled after the Auburn silent system with small and dreary cells and the dehumanization of the prison population. In 1870, with a great deal of fanfare, Zebulon Brockway introduced his reformatory system at Elmira, but he himself had to agree at the end of his long career that the prison at Elmira was not a lot different from those that used the Auburn system.

In many ways, as the next section suggests, corrections in the United States has escaped from the dark ages. Still, the prisons in this nation are not usually looked to as a model and humane facility worthy of replication in other nations. Alvin J. Bronstein, former director of the American Civil Liberties Union (ACLU) defined a humane prison:

> *There aren't any. The definition in my dictionary of humane is having the best quality of human beings, kind, tender, merciful, sympathetic, civilizing, and humanizing. There are no prisons in the world that have those qualities. I have visited some marvelous prisons, one in particular in Denmark.*
>
> *In fact the warden or governor of that prison, the late Eric Anderson, was part of the committee that advised Ken Schoen on the configuration of Oak Park Heights before it was built. I should also mention that I was on that committee as well. We had a series of meetings, then one long conference in Minnesota. There were three people from Europe, and there were a bunch of American experts. I was there sort of giving the prisoners' point of view, which was fairly indicative of the sensitivity of the Minnesota Department of Corrections when they had the leading prison critic in the country sitting in on the planning of their new prison. I think their strategy made a lot of sense, and I found it a really useful and fascinating experience.*
>
> *Eric Anderson's prison in Ringe, Denmark has been written up in many national and international publications and was the subject of a program on Sixty Minutes. It was one of the most interesting and thoughtful and decent prisons I have ever been to. I have visited it about six times, because Anderson was a friend. Each time I would leave the prison I would say, "Eric this is just a marvelous institution you're running." He would always say, "Yes, Al, but remember all prisons damage people and this prison as good as it is may also damage people."*
>
> *The answer to this question is that when you look at a prison, it must be inhumane because it is totally different from being in a free society. You are not free to make decisions about most things that go on in the day. When you get up, what you eat, and what you're going to do, those decisions are made for you. Accordingly, it is a dehumanizing experience, but that can be minimized. My idea of a good prison is one that does not make persons worse when they leave than when they came in, that doesn't make them less able to function in the real world and most prisons do that.*[3]

What Are Some Horror Stories of Corrections in the Past?

During the "dark ages of corrections," discipline in American prisons was rough and physical, and public flogging was not unusual. One famous warden allowed himself to be photographed in the art of flogging a misbehaving prisoner, explaining to the watching press that "men aren't here for playing hooky from Sunday school."[4] Connecticut actually had a flogging post at a prison until the 1960s. Until 1966, when the federal courts outlawed the practice, the strap was used to punish prisoners in Mississippi and Arkansas. This strap was made of leather, three-and-a-half to five-and-a-half feet in length, about four inches wide, with a wooden handle eight-to-twelve inches long. Arkansas had an informal requirement that strapping be limited to ten blows on the buttocks at a time for any single offense. Sometimes, though not always, the prisoner's posterior might be bare.[5]

Prison industry traditionally involved any miserable and punitive work. Pay, if any, was in pennies. Some states had coal mines in which prisoners were required to labor regardless of their skill or experience in mining. The danger of work in such conditions was great, but concern for the safety of convicts was not a priority. Depending on demand, most prisons had some sort of hard labor for convicts to do. If no hard labor was available, then prison officials simply made up such labor, such as to move rocks from one pile to another. *See* Feature 9.1 for the account of the San Quentin Jute Mill.

Until the late 1990s, all prisoners in Texas did their first six months of imprisonment "on the line," breaking soil, planting cotton, hoeing weeds, and gathering cotton. The state's prison system was endowed with 100,000 acres of arable land, nearly all of which was farmable. For anyone who viewed these prisoners dressed in clean white uniforms each day working in the hard Texas sun, sometimes from dawn to dusk, there was no question that this was a brutal and inhumane system.

Then, until recently, there were the dark, dingy, deteriorating, and depressive dungeons that characterized large maximum-security prisons. Nearly every state had one or more of these facilities, with small cages, stone walls, and multitiered cellblocks that made them seem oppressive and unfit for human habitation. But in the 1980s and 1990s, more and more of the facilities were torn down or adapted to other functions. The new prisons that were built are much different than these dungeons of the past. It is significant in this regard that half or more of current prisons were built since 1980.

It is easy to take these and other categories and show how imprisonment is so much better than it was in the past. With isolated examples, staff brutality is largely a thing of the past. Inmates have much better living conditions than they did in the Big House prisons. Prison employment pays more, the work day is shorter, and prison employment is usually less undesirable than before. The food is dramatically better than formerly, so are medical and dental services. Staff are better trained and, as a rule, are more professional than the guards of the past.

Yet, it cannot be denied that when a person is incarcerated in a long-term institution, he or she has lost much. The task in a free and democratic society is to see that prisons damage individuals as little as possible and that for those who are interested, they have opportunities to make improvements in their lives. Ultimately, then, our responsibility is to make the prison experience as humane as possible.

Feature 9.1: The San Quentin Jute Mill

At San Quentin, all able-bodied prisoners were required to work for a year in an antiquated jute mill, making burlap sacks for sale to California farmers, whose demand for burlap always exceeded the productive capacity of the mill. The looms and spinners were so old that replacements for worn-out parts had to be fabricated at the prison. The mill was dark and crowded. The noise from spinners and looms was deafening. The air was thick with dust and jute fiber. The danger from the rickety machinery was considerable. In this gloomy atmosphere, it was easy for a convict to hurl objects at an adversary, or sometimes at a guard, without detection.

Assignment to the mill was for a year. During that time, prisoners had to complete a daily task—so many spools of yarn, so many yards of burlap sacking—to the satisfaction of the foreman; otherwise, the day did not count toward the fulfillment of the required year. With heavy irony, the assignment lieutenant would explain to prisoners that it was for their benefit to learn to work in an industry in which measured performance would qualify them for the demands of industrial employment in a free society. At the end of the mandatory year, convicts could be assigned to more constructive activities, to school, to vocational training, or to less miserable work such as the manufacture of spare parts for the looms. Return to the mill was a dreaded sanction for prisoners who had been found guilty of serious disciplinary infractions.

In 1953, after the mill had been in service for eighty years, a fire of mysterious origin destroyed the plant. Arson was thought to be the cause, but no arsonist was ever found. The wonder was that it took so many years for the demolition of this firetrap to be accomplished. It was replaced by a cotton mill with modern machinery with which fabrics were produced to manufacture clothing for inmates in all California institutions. Employment there was not the most prized assignment for San Quentin prisoners, but veterans of the jute mill saw little reason to complain.

Source: Lore reported by correctional personnel at San Quentin to John P. Conrad.

What Are the Ingredients of a Humane Prison?

John Conrad and Simon Dinitz's ingredients of a humane prison have been widely circulated. They claim that a worthwhile goal is to create institutions that simulate as closely as possible the conditions of the real world. The simulation of the real can be accomplished when prisons are lawful, safe, industrious, and hopeful.[6]

The Lawful Prison

The lawful prison is one that prevents proscribed actions and provides inmates with all the rights granted by federal and state law. Violators within the prison are punished appropriately under conditions in which due-process procedures prevail. If prison administrators tolerate unlawful conduct by staff or inmates, such as freely flowing drugs, thriving gambling rackets, brutality, and prostitution rings, nothing that they attempt will succeed.

The Safe Prison

Both inmates and staff must be assured of their safety in prison. Physical attacks on staff and inmates do take place in minimum-security institutions, but medium- and maximum-security prisons are the most likely settings for physical and sexual victimization, stabbings, and homicides. Correctional officers across the United States express a common complaint: They have neither the control nor the respect they used to have, nor do inmates feel any safer. The new breed of inmates brings with it criminal expertise and street gang sophistication, the mechanics of narcotics distribution, and an inclination to mayhem at a level previously unknown in U.S. prisons.

The physical design of the prison and its operations must ensure that adequately trained correctional officers are in close contact with inmates in living quarters and at work assignments. Officers can best serve the interests of order and safety when they are competent in human relations, so that information can flow freely between inmates and officers without fear that it will be misused, without expectation of special favor, and under conditions of respect and responsibility.

The Industrious Prison

Idleness is one of the real problems of prison life today. What work there is to be done in crowded facilities is spread so thin that it is no longer work. The yards and cellblocks are full of bored inmates. Some inmates engage in physical fitness activities, but too many inmates scheme during idle hours about drug drop offs, prostitution rings, and "hitting" (stabbing) inmates in competing gangs.

In the 1980s and 1990s, prison industries revived. This trend has emerged as a result of the pioneering involvement of a few private corporations and the driving force of former Supreme Court Chief Justice Warren E. Burger. Burger formulated the "factories with fences" concept and began promoting it with great energy. One of Burger's widely quoted observations is "To put people behind walls and bars and do little or nothing to change them is to win a battle but lose a war. It is wrong. It is expensive. It is stupid."[7]

The Hopeful Prison

Prisons should renew hope. Loss of hope is one of the consequences of a criminal career. To renew hope, prisons should offer inmates programs such as remedial elementary education, vocational training, individual and group therapy, and self-help techniques. No penalty should be levied against an inmate for failure to participate in a program, but there must be some incentive to engage in treatment. In the hopeful prison, inmates would feel that they have some say about their own lives. There is strong evidence that the freedom to make some decisions is needed to build a sense of responsibility. Finally, in the hopeful prison, inmates would feel that they will receive acceptance in the outside community. Otherwise, the only reality for the inmate is the cellblock, the yard, and the prison industrial plant.[8]

What Is the Relationship Between Quality of Life and a Humane Prison?

In a report that Frank Wood wrote on selected adult correctional facilities in the Tennessee Department of Corrections, he defined quality of life. Although admitting that the term "quality of life" is nebulous, vague, and lacks definite form or limits, he goes on to define it. Feature 9.2 is an excerpt from the "quality of life" section of the report.

Feature 9.2: Quality of Life in a Correctional Institution by Frank Wood

"To define the term and to more sharply focus on what conditions and variables make up the criteria for evaluating the 'quality of life' in correctional institutions, some background is necessary. Before defining and/or evaluating the 'quality of life' in a correctional institution setting, it is essential that we establish some very basic and fundamental concepts:

1. The mission of the institution and staff is to create and maintain an environment conducive to the rehabilitation of those individuals confined to the institution, who are inclined to change and/or rehabilitate themselves.
2. It is also necessary to accept the premise that institutions are not designed to punish those who reside in them, nor are the staff employed to punish or in any way, aggravate the conditions of confinement for the purpose of punishing the inmate population. There is no question that society confines people to prisons for a variety of reasons—incapacitation, deterrence, rehabilitation and yes, retribution (punishment).
3. It is important that punishment be understood and restricted to the individual's loss of personal freedom and the access to and limited isolation from family, friends, and community.

"With that background, 'quality of life,' as it applies to a correctional institution setting can be defined. The term, quality of life, in correctional institutions represents a broad range of social and environmental conditions, which impact on an inmate's and/or staff's physical, emotional, and mental health. For the inmate, quality of life requires a climate that permits, encourages, and facilitates self-evaluation and improvement, including personal growth, awareness, and change, all of which have the potential of improving the predictability of an inmate's successful return to the community as a productive member of society, should he/she be so inclined.

"For the staff it begins with recruitment of honest, intelligent, sensitive individuals who are able to relate to people and provide those selected, with relevant training, which will equip them to work in the correctional environment. Compensation that is competitive and commensurate with their classification, assignment, and level of responsibility is essential. Employees must be provided with leadership, supervision, guidance, policy, procedures, post orders, and a clear picture of what is expected of them. All employees in a correctional environment can reasonably expect that they and the administration must take every reasonable and prudent precaution to reduce the frequency, scope, and dangerousness of inevitable incidents in the institution environment.

"The working environment should provide training, experience, and opportunities for employees to be promoted to their full potential. They should also be provided with a fringe benefits package and afforded the opportunities to responsibly utilize all aspects of the fringe benefit package, and have reasonable working hours in an environment that is clean and healthy."

Source: Frank W. Wood, Report on Conditions at Selected Adult Correctional Facilities in the Tennessee Department of Corrections. *This report was submitted to officials of the Tennessee Department of Corrections and the Assistant Attorney General in June 1985.*

This report contains a number of issues that are related to creating a humane form of confinement for inmates and a humane facility in which staff and other personnel can work. As previously stated, a major hope for corrections that has been frequently overlooked is that more than half of all correctional institutions are less than twenty years old. What this means is that so many of the dungeons of the past, the nineteenth-century fortresses, have been torn down or have been converted to other uses or purposes.

Reduce double celling. Another step to be pursued is to reduce double celling or the use of large dormitories. The problem with double celling is that inmates cannot be protected from other inmates. Gangs within the prison are sometimes able to influence the celling of inmates; it is not unusual for a sexually passive inmate to be placed with a sexual predator. Sexual predators are one of the groups who need to be single celled.

Restrict lockdowns. Locking an institution down for extended periods should be done only on an emergency basis and, when that happens, rapid steps must be taken to resolve the problem that led to this emergency status. There are inmates who cannot be trusted to live in a peaceful way with other inmates. These inmates must be isolated from the rest of the inmate population. For other inmates, keeping inmates locked down for extended periods without good cause is both inhumane policy and crisis-centered management that is likely to increase problems in the long run.

Ensure privacy. Inmates have the right in a decent correctional system to have some privacy in their cells. They do not have a right to keep contraband in their cells or to engage in illegal acts while in their cells, and for that reason correctional staff must conduct unannounced cell searches. Yet, there is a big difference in correctional officers coming in, tearing up a cell, needlessly destroying personal property (such as pictures), and leaving the cell all torn up. Privacy means that inmates' personal property is respected; it needs to be searched but not destroyed. Privacy also includes the respect of restoring the cell to the shape it was before the search.

Treat inmates with decency and respect. Inmates have a right to be treated with decency and respect. Correctional institutions of the past certainly can be faulted for their tendency to punish inmates as severely as possible. Part of punishing inmates and making prisons undesirable was to take away any dignity from inmates. They were known by a number; were dressed in a drab uniform, that often had stripes; were sometimes tortured as a means of punishing inappropriate behaviors, such as speaking to another inmate; and frequently were treated with contempt by their "keepers." Prison administrators were further known to forbid civil conversations between correctional officers and inmates. The attempt was made not only to deny the individuality of inmates but to destroy their dignity as human beings.

Keep inmates safe. The safety of inmates must always be a top concern in a humane prison. Many inmates have a history of being predators and will continue this behavior in a prison context if given the opportunity. Weaker inmates or those without organizations to provide support for them find themselves thrust into institutions in which they feel that they are unable to protect themselves. No matter what else takes place, a prison cannot claim to be humane if inmates are being raped, assaulted, and murdered by others inmates on a regular basis. Too many inmates in the past have done their time in constant dread of being attacked; fear begets fear and the consequence will always be a more disruptive prison. The argument can be made that all inmates cannot be protected, because there are so many areas of indefensible space in which the weak can be victimized. The fact is that prison administrators must adopt policy, which is translated into practice by all staff, which will more likely ensure the protection of inmates.

Classify inmates properly. The classification of inmates is important in a humane prison. Proper classification can do much to provide a secure and safe facility. Classification also can be helpful in dealing with troublesome inmates, such as moving them to a different institution or to a more secure unit within that facility.

Protect safety of staff. Staff also have a right to be protected in a humane and decent correctional system. Officers know that at any given day they may be assaulted by inmates. Staff assaults are always possible, because regardless of how well a prison is run, incidents are sometimes inevitable. Nevertheless, the warden and associate wardens must make very clear to inmates that assaults against staff are totally unacceptable and the consequences will be very severe. The inmates need to know that the warden's position is very simple: If you touch or if you lay your hands on my staff, I will do everything possible to make certain that you pay for this for a long time. If you assault my staff, the warden is reminding inmates, there is a substantial penalty for doing that. Inmates will be prosecuted by the prison internal disciplinary system, and if they violated any state law or federal law, they will be prosecuted in the courts for that and given additional time.

Control gang activities. In a humane prison, the quality of life issue mandates that one group of inmates, such as a prison gang, does not control the inmate population. This is not accomplished so easily. The correctional climate is such today that in at least forty states and the Federal Bureau of Prisons, there are inmate gangs, and some of these gangs have enormous influence in the prison.[9] In a society where gangs flourish and intimidation is a way of life, the gangs have influence over other inmates. For the last ten years, Bartollas has studied the influence of gangs on prison life. He has gotten to know the leaders of some of the largest gangs in the United States. They have claimed that they have at times "kept the lid" on the prison by defusing violent situations, that they have influenced the reduction of rapes and assaults that have taken place in some correctional systems, and that they have intervened with other gang leaders to seek peaceful solutions.

Perhaps some of these claims are true, but the fact is that gangs have no place in a humane prison. Fortunately, wardens seem to have gotten beyond seeing the need to negotiate with gangs, but it would appear that the only way to operate a prison is to deny the recognition of gangs. They are given no privileges. They have no rights. This nonrecognition of gangs extends to gang leaders who may be high-profile inmates and some of whom may have become legends.

Deflect racial tensions. Nor do humane prisons have any place for racial tensions to control prison life and contribute to conflicts and violence. A casual visitor to a prison setting instantly sees the importance of race. Those who work within a prison can document even more how race influences much of the interaction among inmates. It does not take much to spark a violent reaction over race. A slight bump, a hard look or stare, or the rumor that inmates from another race have interfered with an upcoming drug deal may be all it takes to fuel a race riot. Inmates tend to isolate themselves racially, and in many prisons friendships with members of other racial groups are frowned upon by members of their own racial groups.

There is no simple solution to racial conflict within a prison. As one of the many problems that have been imported to the prison from the larger social setting, it seems that the conditions of prison life seem to worsen racial relations and tensions. It is not uncommon to hear the comment from inmates, "I wasn't a racist until I came to prison." What proactive wardens know is that this conflict among inmates, like others, must be managed by anticipating problems and using preventative approaches. In a sense, the approach is communicated that you do not have to like each other, but it is necessary that you get along. What this means is that there will be no intimidation and exploitation of other racial groups. This also means that name calling and other forms of "put-downs" will not be tolerated.

Provide opportunities for individual growth. An important aspect of the quality of life in a humane prison is to provide opportunities for individuals who want to grow and profit from their confinement. Bedford Hills, New York State's only maximum-security facility for women, is known throughout the nation for its innovative programs. Elaine A. Lord, superintendent of this facility since 1984, has encouraged inmates to get involved in the development of their own programs, usually with some outside help. These programs have dealt with issues such as helping teens cope with prison life, dealing with parenting from a distance, providing AIDS counseling and education, bringing college back into the facility, understanding family violence, furnishing peer-tutoring for ABE and GED, and providing pre- and postnatal workshops. This facility, even though it is located in one of the most affluent towns in the United States, has found that it is able to connect with the facility through the inmates' children. Superintendent Lord and her staff developed the summer host family program in which people from the community open their homes to the inmates' children for a week or two. They bring them to the facility each morning and pick them up each afternoon. Thus, the children get to visit their mothers every day for a week or two, providing an opportunity for mother/child relationships to grow stronger, and to supplement the occasional visits that occur throughout the year.[10]

Humane facilities for men also may include programs for inmates and their families. During the time Wood was a warden at the Minnesota State Prison at Stillwater, he and his staff instituted a family counseling and private visitation program. A contract was secured with Family Service of St. Paul for a counselor to work with married couples and their families (restricted to couples married prior to the inmates' incarceration period). This counseling was a precondition for using the old staff residence on the grounds of the minimum-security unit where an individual could go with his family and spend a weekend. Inmates who were within 120 days of the end of their stay in minimum security were eligible for this program, which was part of a phased transition back into the community. After inmates went through counseling and family visitation, in the next phase—the furlough process—they spent a weekend at home prior to their release.

Mary Leftridge Byrd tells of a similar program at the State Correctional Institution at Chester:

> *I should also say that working with women offenders has really been very helpful to me in innumerable ways in terms of dealing with men. My experience with women has taught me that they require attention when they are locked up. Men like it, but women require it. A lot of things we did with the women at FCI Muncy I have been able to do here at SCI Chester, including having a baby program. We use computerized baby dolls that look just like real babies. They cry and soil their diapers. You may have seen these babies, for this product is used in high schools, junior high schools, and other classrooms.*
>
> *So, if you hear there are babies in the prison that is not a figment of someone's imagination. You have to imagine an inmate walking down the main corridor in a state prison with a baby in his arms and the baby is crying. His peers are saying, "Oh man, can't you do something about that baby?" It is really funny. The "dads" keep the babies five nights.*
>
> *We have an annual children's day here, and I'm sure we're the only men's prison where that happens. We have structured activities, reading circles, and that kind of thing. They have a little acting class that takes place, and the children have a great choice of activities for that day.*
>
> *The caregivers last year felt disconnected because they bring the kids in and put then in a visiting room. Then, the dads come out and spend the entire day with them, but the caregivers felt that they didn't know what was going on with the child. We created a simultaneous program for caregivers upstairs in our training room, and last year TV monitors were added so the caregivers, while they were interacting with our staff, could look at the monitors and see what the kids were doing in the visiting room. That was well received. The inmates really embrace and take good care of this program. It's only annual, but next year, I'm going to try and do it twice, once around Father's Day, and then in January because it's right after Christmas and everybody's pretty much got the post holiday blues. Whatever happens to the rest of us it happens to inmates in a more magnified way.*[11]

Create opportunities for inmates to learn a marketable skill. A high priority of programs in a humane prison is to create opportunities for inmates to learn a marketable skill. Too many inmates come to prison without a marketable skill. One of the challenges of vocational programs in prison is to get out of obsolete training for nonexistent jobs. For example, prisons need to get out of twine production and move into areas such as data processing, school bus repair, tire recapping, and auto body work.

Offer inmates educational opportunities. Educational opportunities are also an important area in a quality-based humane prison. It is almost a necessity that a high number of inmates attain at least a GED (general equivalency diploma) certificates while they are in prison. Higher educational opportunities need to be available for those who want to pursue them.

Offer substance abuse treatment and education programs. Chemical dependency programs are necessary, because a large percentage of inmates today have chemical abuse in their history, and a large percentage were under the influence at the time of the commission of the crime for which they are imprisoned.

Provide adequate medical and dental services for inmates. In addition, a humane prison has adequate medical and dental services. Prisoners always have been critical of medical care within the prison. They typically have claimed that the medical care was inadequate and physicians were incompetent, that requested treatment was denied, that special diets were not provided, and that medical treatment and drugs were forced on them. Medical services have become one of the most important and troubling issues because of infectious diseases (HIV, AIDs, hepatitis B, hepatitis C, tuberculosis), female health issues, mental health problems, and elderly prisoners' medical concerns. The increased lengths of sentences, because of the recently revised criminal codes in most states, have added to the problem. Prisoners are staying longer and more of them are there for the duration of their natural lives. All of this places enormous demands on medical services that have become increasingly costly.

Offer recreational services for inmates. Finally, recreational services are a vital part of the programming of a humane prison. It was some of these services that were under heavy criticism by "make them suffer" advocates in the 1990s. Recreational services, according to these misled individuals, made "doing time" too easy and softened the punishment of what inmates were supposed to have received in prison. This misguided policy experienced success in some states and in the Federal Bureau of Prisons.

Can Management Make a Difference in Creating Humane Prisons?

Some claim that crowded prisons, the "make prisoners suffer" mood of the 1990s, the expanding number of inmates with long or life sentences, the number of inmate gangs, and the violence of today's inmates make it literally impossible to have a humane prison. One of the themes of this book is that a well-managed prison has much more of an improved quality of life than a dysfunctional facility. When interviewees were asked to contrast the quality of life for staff and inmates in well-managed institutions versus the quality of life for staff and inmates in dysfunctional facilities, they gave the responses in Feature 9.3.

How Is It Possible to Have a Humane Prison in the Present "Make Prisoners Suffer" Mood?

Our position is that people are sent to prison as punishment. Nothing in prison should be done to aggravate the conditions of confinement under the mistaken belief that you somehow are going to make people change their attitude, behavior, or criminality by making life so miserable for them in prison. The consequence of this inhumane behavior is that you will be returning very angry and potentially dangerous people to live among us in society.

This is the sad story of what is taking place in prisons today. Perhaps, it would be more accurate to say that is what politicians are creating. The "make prisoners suffer" mood has resulted in taking away the privileges, the cigarettes, the exercise equipment, and the programs of inmates. In some respect, this punitive

Figure 9.3: The Quality of Life in Well-managed Prisons

Alvin J. Bronstein, former director of the American Civil Libertes Union compared both types of institutions:

"Well, you know, I've seen both of those kinds of facilities. I can remember the old maximum-security prison in Rhode Island when I first went there in 1974. That's a facility that was built about 1890 and was full of blind spots and dead ends, and the prison was totally in the control of prisoners. Prisoners had a union there, and the guards had abdicated responsibility thinking it was a terribly dangerous prison. There were stabbings and assaults on a daily basis.

"We reviewed eight years of newspaper clippings in preparation for filing in federal court and found an unbelievable volume of assaults and stabbing incidents. In fact, the former Minnesota corrections commissioner, Dave Fogel, was one of our expert witnesses, and in reviewing the data, he said that it was an extraordinary amount of dangerousness and assaults.

"The reason that this institution was out of control was that there was a lack of management, a badly trained staff who were dominated by an unprofessional union. The prisoners were running the facility, which is not a good thing to happen. Even though I'm a prisoner's advocate, I think that professional staff rather than inmates ought to be running prisons.

"I go back there now, and I see some of the same officers who reminisce about how they used to fear going to work in the morning, and [recall how] they came home every day in the evening with a terrible headache because of the stress they were under. Whereas now, though the prison is slightly crowded, it's well run and managed, is busy, and staff know what they are doing. The prisoners have a lot of programs. You know it's not a peaceful place, no prisons are, but it's a busy place without a lot of anxiety, practically no suicides, no escapes and no assaults. So again, it is lack of crowding, good management by the staff, and lots of programs that make a well-managed institution."

Continued on page 161

attitude is attempting to make imprisonment the worst hell that humans can create.

What is interesting is that inmates are taking it. Perhaps, and we say this somewhat with tongue in cheek, we have the wrong people in prison. We seem to have a great many docile people who are in prison who do not need to be there, because if we had the right people in prison, they would not take it. If their numbers were large enough, at some point the cumulative effect of this would manifest itself in something that we would not like to see.

Historically, we have seen this cyclical thing where politicians and prison staffs get enlightened and prisons operate for a long time, with relative calm. Prison officials, staff, and politicians then slip into complacency, until someone gets the idea to make it miserable for inmates, poking sticks at them, demonizing them, and making them suffer. All of a sudden, not surprisingly, prison riots and disturbances occur. Staff and inmates get hurt and killed.

A major challenge in a regressive system is to avoid becoming disillusioned. This will happen unless wardens keep reinforcing the things they can and should be doing. The fact is that

Figure 9.3: The Quality of Life in Well-managed Prisons (con't)

David Crist, warden of the Minnesota Correctional Facility, Stillwater, characterized the quality of life in a well-managed facility this way:

"I guess the main differences I see in a well-managed institution versus dysfunctional institutions have to do with the amount of communication that goes on between management and labor and management and the offenders. In a facility where there's lots of communication going in both directions, not just downwards from the top, then there's a lot of discussion. That discussion leads to better management of the facility. The quality of life then for staff and inmates that results through this process is a more predictable routine on a day-to-day basis. [There are] fewer surprises, fewer incidents of major scope, and overall a better, more routine and quieter quality of life where staff and inmates cooperate with one another to keep the place on a day-to-day basis on an even keel."

Dennis L. Benson, deputy commissioner of the Minnesota Department of Corrections, has this to say about the quality of life in a well-managed facility:

> *"The quality of life for both staff and inmates in a well-managed institution is identifiable almost as one walks through the facility. In this setting, staff like to come to work; don't quit their jobs; don't abuse sick leave; and act, dress, and respond in a professional manner. In a dysfunctional setting, the opposite is true. I can attest to this because I have worked in both settings. Very early in my career the Stillwater correctional facility was incredibly dysfunctional. Turnover rates were excessively high; staff were poorly dressed, poorly groomed, poorly trained, and responded abhorrently to issues regarding each other and the inmates under their care."*

Sources: Interviewed in September and October 2002.

wardens do not always get what they want. Yet, because proactive wardens have a proprietary interest in the institution, they continue to build up what they can build up, including the relationships and positive interactions between staff and inmates.

It is very important that enlightened wardens not abandon their operational philosophy and principles during periods of misguided policy changes. Wardens and staff, of course, must obey state and federal laws. However, they know that aggravating the conditions of confinement by making life miserable for those in prison will not serve as a deterrent to criminal behavior or reduce recidivism as some politicians would have the public believe. Historically, hanging pickpockets did not work in Europe and, in fact, pickpockets practiced their trade at public hangings. There are no studies or empirical evidence to support the conclusion that making life miserable for inmates reduces crime or recidivism. The fact is that 80 to 90 percent of those in prison will be released someday. If they are returned to society as angry illiterates without marketable skills, society will reap the logical consequences of these politically misguided policies.

Periods of repression and reform are cyclical. But during the repressive period, inmates must know their wardens have not abandoned their philosophy, beliefs, principles, and practices. Wardens lose leadership and credibility with the public, the staff, and the inmates when they abandon their long-held professional beliefs and principles because those exploiting the crime issue have led the public to accept poor public policy that cannot be supported by any empirical research.

In some cases, it would be tactically and strategically unwise to openly and publicly challenge a misguided governor. The result could be that this enlightened warden would be replaced with someone who actually believes the political rhetoric. This would not be good for the public, the staff, or the institution. The survival in the system of enlightened criminal justice professionals is critical to the future of sound correction and criminal justice policy. A measure of hope can be added here in that the current cycle of making prisoners suffer will likely pass. It has come and gone in the past, and cooler minds will likely prevail in the near future in correctional policymaking.

Summary

Prisons are no longer in the "dark ages," and significant positive change has taken place in correctional environments in recent decades. The classic definition of the ingredients of a humane prison, taken from the work of Conrad and Dinitz, is that a humane prison be lawful, safe, industrious, and hopeful. This chapter probed a number of issues relating to the relationship between quality of life and a humane prison. A well-managed prison is the connective link between quality of life and a humane prison. A major challenge today is how a humane prison can become a reality or remain a reality in the very repressive correctional environment that was created in the 1990s. It is possible to create and operate a humane facility, even in a time of repression, providing that wardens are proactive and courageous in their leadership.

ENDNOTES

[1]Hayes' interest was much more than nominal. When he retired from the White House, he accepted the presidency of the National Prison Association (the forerunner of the American Correctional Association) and continued in that role for ten years—the rest of his life.

[2]Blake McKelvey. 1936. *American Prisons: A Study in American Social History*. Chicago: University of Chicago Press, p. 71.

[3]Interviewed in October 2002.

[4]Elam Lynds is frequently quoted for making this comment.

[5]*See Jackson v. Bishop*, 404 F.2d 571 (8th Cir. 1968).

[6]This section on the humane prison is adapted from John P. Conrad and Simon Dinitz. 1981. The State's Strongest Medicine. In John P. Conrad, ed. *Justice and Consequences*. Lexington, Massachusetts: Lexington Books.

[7]Gail S. Funke, ed. 1986. National Conference on Prison Industries: Discussion and Recommendations. Washington, D.C.: National Center for Innovation in Corrections.

[8]Introducing another dimension of hope, John P. Conrad says that the prison should be a school of citizenship. *See* John P. Conrad. 1981. Where There's Hope There's Life. In David Fogel and Joe Hudson, eds. *Justice as Fairness*. Cincinnati: Anderson, pp. 16-19.

[9]American Correctional Association. 1993. *Gangs in Correctional Institutions: A National Assessment*. Lanham, Maryland: American Correctional Association, pp. 8-9.

[10]Interviewed in October 2000.

[11]Interviewed in November 2002.

Chapter Ten:

Corrections and a New Day in the Future

This book has presented an exciting story based on Frank Wood's accomplishments during his thirty-seven-year correctional career. During his two stints as warden of the Minnesota Correctional Facility, Stillwater, and the Minnesota Correctional Facility, Oak Park Heights, he developed a proactive approach to correctional administration, based on anticipatory methods of management. Wood was firmly entrenched in principles designed to create a humane and safe environment for staff and inmates. A very principled person, believing firmly in treating people with dignity and respect, he was able to excite staff with a variety of skills and talents and persuade them to become involved in this approach to managing prisons.

It was not long in Minnesota before correctional officers, caseworkers, sergeants, lieutenants, captains, and cell house directors became deputy wardens, wardens, deputy commissioners of corrections, and the commissioner of corrections. The Wood legacy continues, as they either continued the proactive philosophy in their institution or implemented this philosophy. In interviews throughout this book, they show their indebtedness to Frank Wood who was their mentor, confidant, and friend.

If that was all there was to the story, we can say, "Isn't this interesting what Wood accomplished in Minnesota?" Or "Frank Wood is a nice fellow; I am pleased that his work is being given this recognition." Or "So Wood is an extraordinary warden. Every now and then corrections comes up with a giant. They make their impact, retire or get out of the business, and the system goes on as before." Or "This proactive stuff sounds interesting; it is a shame that the social context is so negative about humane approaches." Or, perhaps even more cynically, "I would like to see his model work with California or Texas inmates."

What is promising about this philosophy of proactive management of correctional institutions is that Wood's approach is not the only model of proactive and anticipatory management philosophy in the nation. A number of wardens and heads of corrections system in other states are also implementing their own versions of this proactive model. Some of these individuals interviewed for this book reflect similar principles, philosophies, and implementation strategies to the Wood model.

What Was So Special about Frank Wood?

Frank Wood is unquestionably a remarkable human being. Endowed with a number of admirable attributes, including intelligence, charisma, a sense of calm, and a "presence," he brought a determination to accomplish the goals that he has set forth for himself. Charles W. Colson, the founder of Prison Fellowship Ministries, wrote this in a letter he sent to the author:

> *I'm so glad that you had a chance to get to know Frank Wood. He's one of the great wardens I've known over my 26 years in the ministry, and a wonderful, vibrant Christian. You said you weren't sure if your own faith was as strong as his; I'm not sure my faith is as strong as his. Frank is an unusual man.*

Frank Wood is clearly a winner! Jim Bruton suggested that if Wood took over the ownership of the Cincinnati Bengals, he would turn this woeful professional team into a winner within two years. He would surround himself, Bruton went on to say, with individuals who together with him would find a way to produce a winner.

When he was faced with a perennial loser, the Minnesota Correctional Facility at Stillwater, Frank Wood had to dig deep, but he found a way to restore order in the midst of great chaos. This experience at the edge helped him craft his proactive managerial philosophy. He succeeded there and later at the newly opened Minnesota Correctional Facility at Oak Park Heights for many reasons.

- He was a principled and moral person and staff respected that.
- He treated people with dignity and respect, and staff and inmates felt good about being treated that way.
- His model was well developed and, in fact, delivered what it promised: a safe and humane facility.
- He was a person who commanded enormous respect and was able to motivate staff to respond to this model of prison management.
- He was an excellent teacher, and staff felt empowered because of their associations with him.

There are times in which you really feel honored to know and to be associated with a person. Through the years, staff member after staff member felt this way about Frank Wood. Even after he retired from being the Commissioner of Corrections in Minnesota in 1996, staff members continued to think of themselves as carrying forth the Wood legacy.

For a model to work, it must be based on a sound philosophy or theory, must be communicated by a person or persons who has credibility and trust from others, and must have a fundamentally sound implementation strategy. All this was true with the proactive management philosophy that Frank Wood developed in Minnesota from 1976 to the time he retired in 1996. Correctional professionals throughout this nation, as well as other nations, owe Frank W. Wood a real sense of gratitude for what he has contributed to the field.

Will Proactive Management only Be a Flash in the Pan?

Cynics can parade a list of reasons why proactive management philosophy will have no long-term effect on corrections. Their reasons will probably be grouped in at least four categories.

The Time Is Not Right

There is no question that this is a hard time for correctional professionals. Beginning in the

1990s, with the "make prisoners suffer" politically mandated policies, correctional professionals opposed the intent of sending prisoners to prison for punishment (make imprisonment brutal, painful, and miserable) and the consequences of taking programming and recreational activities away from prisoners, of putting inmates in prison for longer periods of time, and of building more supermax prisons and high-security units.

This increased dosage of the "get tough" strategy was enough to discourage many correctional administrators. Then, in the early years of the twenty-first century, it got worse, with heavy fiscal cutbacks and budgetary shortfalls. Perhaps, corrections was not hit as hard as other systems of state and federal governments, but, nevertheless, the budget crisis has effected the operations of correctional institutions in nearly every state. Finally, the fear of terrorism, both at home and abroad, and the winds of war that terrorism brings to this nation make this an unlikely time for a new spirit to sweep through corrections.

Models Have Come and Gone in Corrections

Corrections historians could list the long litany of corrections models highly praised at the time, and then condemned or even ridiculed only a few years later. There was the Pennsylvania model of imprisonment, in which inmates were kept in absolute solitude during the course of their imprisonment. Equipped with a Bible, they were told to use their time of imprisonment as a time of penitence, in which purged of evil intentions they could go out and become useful citizens. The most consistent result of this form of imprisonment was that it drove inmates crazy.

There was the rival system of imprisonment in the nineteenth century, the Auburn Silent System. It was hard to imagine that this silent system, housed in an island of cells five tiers high and twenty cells long, with tiny cells seven feet long and three-and-a-half feet wide, could be perceived by anyone as a model to emulate. The silence was soon gone, but this system of imprisonment stayed and gave to corrections such "contributions" as the lockstep, striped uniforms, shackles, and the ever-present whip.

The Reformatory Model appeared next on the corrections scene. Proposed enthusiastically at the First Corrections Congress in Cincinnati in 1870, it was implemented at the Elmira Reformatory in 1876. In the next thirty years, reformatories appeared throughout the East and the Midwest. The reformatory movement did make some long-term contributions to corrections, including indeterminate sentencing, the payment of inmates for work, the supervision of inmates released into the community, a system of behavior modification, and the development of what later came to be parole. Nevertheless, it did not take its founder, Zebulon Brockway, long to become disillusioned and to begin to use brutal tactics against the youthful offenders. By the end of the nineteenth century, reformatories were widely recognized as brutal and repressive as prisons based on the Auburn system or other prison of the day.

The Medical Model was the next panacea that appeared on the correctional scene. Prisons began to be viewed as hospitals, where psychiatrists, practicing the medical model, could diagnose the disease of criminality and could prescribe a treatment for prisoners that would cure them of their disease of crime. Few corrections personnel felt that this model made any sense. Whatever prisons were, it was apparent to all, they were not hospitals. However, before this treatment could be dismissed, it was redefined into the rehabilitative ideal in the mid-twentieth century. Long before Martinson's 1973 "nothing works" thesis hit the presses, it was commonly agreed that rehabilitation's assumptions conflicted with basic human values, that rehabilitative philosophy did not work, and that rehabilitation was a disaster in practice.

It would be possible to discuss other corrections models proposed in the late nineteenth and twentieth centuries, implemented to some degree, and then rapidly forgotten. But the cynics have made their point: Corrections models proposed in the past do not have a good history. It is not long before they are discarded to the garbage heap of failed correctional ideals.

The Proactive Philosophy Worked in Minnesota for Reasons Not Present Elsewhere

Cynics can rightfully add that Minnesota is very unique and has a different correctional climate than is found elsewhere. They can say that the inmates in Minnesota's prisons are quite docile compared to those in California, Texas, New York, Illinois, or some of the Federal Bureau of Prisons' correctional institutions. What this means is that Minnesota has not had to deal with the levels of violence in its prisons that have been found in other states. Critics can quickly add that Minnesota has not had the organized prison gangs that so many other correctional systems have had to deal with in the past two decades. In addition, it can be argued that Minnesota has not had the degree of prison crowding that has been found in nearly every state. Moreover, critics remind their listeners that not every state has the financial resources that Minnesota has. Minnesota's resources have permitted adequate funding of its correctional institutions as well as the innovative architecture found at Oak Park Heights. Finally, critics could add that what Wood and his staff accomplished at Oak Park Heights is due in part to the fact that 45 percent of line staff had college degrees.

Corrections Has a History of Destroying Great Men and Women

The cynics at this point might make this concession: There have been remarkable men and women of great resolve in corrections in the past and even to the present. They could even agree to some extent on whom these corrections giants are. This list might include Alexander Patterson, who developed the borstal system, or training schools, in England; John Augustus, who was the father of probation; Thomas Matt Osborne, who developed the Mutual Welfare League, a pioneering effort in prisoner self-government; and Howard B. Gill, who developed a system of classification and treatment at the Norfolk Prison Colony.

Included in this list of corrections giants would likely be heads of corrections systems such as Richard A. McGee, who developed bureaucratic corrections in California; Kenneth Stoneman, who closed Vermont's only maximum-security prison; Lloyd McCorkle, who instead of building more prisons developed a network of satellites at other human services institutions in New Jersey; Kenneth P. Schoen, who was instrumental in laying out the principles of Minnesota's groundbreaking Community Corrections Acts; James V. Bennett, who created a professional bureaucracy at the U.S. Bureau of Prisons; Elayn Hunt who before her death was leading Louisiana corrections out of its dark ages; and Norman C. Carlson, who was widely recognized for his outstanding work as director of the Bureau of Prisons.

Cynics (once the listing was complete) might then conclude that in nearly every generation, since the first prison was established in this nation, a remarkable corrections pioneer emerged. Their theory or model of how a prison ought to be run was usually way before its time and met increased opposition from the various public. Sometimes, they were summarily dismissed by the political authorities, but, at other times, they became disillusioned and even resorted to brutal measures that they had long resisted. Consequently, the corrections professional standing alone simply has not done very well in taking on a repressive, brutal, and perhaps even corrupt system. The fact is, our cynics conclude, that a good person, no matter how good this person might be, cannot stand alone and make significant correctional change that is long lasting.

Does Proactive Philosophy Have Enough Support Today among Corrections Giants to Form a Critical Mass?

The good news is that even in a hard time for corrections, there are corrections giants from quite diverse correctional climates who are proactive in their leadership. As indicated by the interviewees in this book, their model may be similar to Wood's model or their model may be quite different. After all, we all bring to the table different backgrounds, talents, skills, and philosophical backgrounds. But within the variations are common themes:

- anticipating and preventing institutional problems
- desiring to make the prison as humane as possible
- restoring safety to the prison environment
- treating both offenders and staff with respect
- empowering staff
- developing an organizational team

Perhaps, it would be wise to stop for a moment and define what it means to be a corrections giant. Jack Crowley, a former corrections professional, defined a corrections giant this way:

> *Corrections giants can communicate the vision they have. This is not only the organizational vision but also their personal vision. You have so many stakeholders in corrections that it bends and puts pressure on compromising the personal vision. But if men or women in corrections are to be great, they must have the ability to communicate their vision and to maintain their vision and work the organization toward that. Most know that they will never gain 100 percent support, but they believe in the vision so much that they are able to rise above the day-to-day mundane operations.*
>
> *When they walk in the room, whether there is a riot going on or a Christmas party, their presence is known. They sort of light up the room because people have confidence in them. They never ever take the first story that is given to them. In the face of emergency and in the face of crisis, they are the calm in the midst of the storm. They seem to know when to get their hands dirty. They are part of the environment, but they seem to transcend the environment. They are able to communicate*

> *with power, and they always have the information they need to make informed decisions. They have very subtle ways of knowing what's going on in the prison. They know more what's going on than most staff, and they know more of what's going on in the prison than most inmates. They have a mystique about them. They can talk with the common person and then talk with the President and feel comfortable with both. They feel comfortable in most relationships. They are not afraid to walk alone in the yard. No one would ever dream of telling one of these giants, "Let me go and check it out" or "Let me go out with you." They may not be able or willing to talk about God or Jesus Christ or Mohammed, but most would say that they have a spiritual relationship with God. They also practice what they believe.*

Those who know Frank Wood well would say, "That sounds like Frank." Significantly, there are staff members in other correctional institutions across the nation who would say the same thing about their warden or superintendent.

Wardens' tasks are sometimes very difficult and as Frank Wood had to deal with chaos when he became a warden, many wardens find that the implementation of their visions of proactive philosophy is not easy. Even when they gained control of the prison environment, this is only the first step in implementing their vision. John Hurley, a former warden of the Federal Bureau of Corrections, reminds these wardens:

> *The warden truly (even sometimes in spite of existing as part of a lousy organization) does set the tone for the prison unit. Don't misunderstand; the warden can't accomplish a positive prison culture on his or her own. He or she must have a team in place that has the same vision, is loyal, and desires the same outcomes. However, if he or she is committed to the task, he or she accepts and acts like the "buck stops at their desk." Persistence is the key. Nothing gets done overnight and most good things don't come easy. Priorities need to be set, communicated clearly, adjusted if necessary, and most importantly accomplished. Roadblocks will almost always occur. The warden's task is to lead around, over, through, or underneath.*

The critical mass is a fascinating concept, which is based on the notion that movements need to gain a critical mass to have significant growth and development. The critical mass cannot be defined by any particular number, but one more (in other words, wardens proposing a proactive managerial philosophy) beyond the present group and the movement explodes and takes off. In discussing this notion of the critical mass, the hundredth monkey principle sometimes is cited with the notion that once this critical mass of the hundredth money is attained, then whatever is being proposed will explode in numbers. This hundredth monkey principle is explained in Feature 10.1. The fact is that this is probably a pseudoscientific myth of the Hundredth Monkey Phenomenon. Still, the point sociologically is valid: attaining critical mass appears to propel a movement and to expand its appeal and membership.

The answer to the question about whether there are sufficient numbers of supporters of proactive managerial philosophy to form a critical mass still unfortunately must be answered in the negative. There is support, which far exceeds those interviewed for this book, but still the movement is in its infancy, one that is lacking a critical mass.

Feature 10.1: The Hundredth Monkey Principle

The remote island of Koshima in the Pacific is home to the macaque monkey. A troop of these monkeys lives in the wild on that island. In 1952, something happened to the monkeys on Koshima, which has been the subject of intense research for decades. A group of scientists were researching macaque feeding behaviors and, as part of their experiment, set stacks of raw sweet potatoes in selected spots on the beaches of Koshima. Quite naturally, the potatoes were quickly covered with sand, presenting the monkeys with a dilemma: Every time they took a bite of these delicious new treats, they also got a bite of sand and grit.

One day, an eighteen-month-old female monkey named Imo carried a sand-covered sweet potato to a stream and solved the problem by washing it off before putting it into her mouth. She then taught this new procedure to her mother and to her playmates. The behavior began to spread. Slowly over the next six years—in full view of the team of scientists who set up the experiment (and without their interference)—monkeys on Koshima learned the procedure and taught it to others in the group: Wash the sand off food before eating it.

Then, something really extraordinary took place. By the fall of 1958, many of the monkeys on Koshima had already adopted the new washing behavior. An exact number is not specified, so let's take our cue from Watson and set that number at ninety-nine. Ninety-nine monkeys were now washing the sand off food before eating it. Then, one more monkey began to do it—the hundredth monkey. And the inexplicable happened-the behavior jumped. Suddenly and mysteriously, macaque monkeys on a nearby island began to wash the sand off food before eating it. The behavior kept jumping. It jumped to the islands surrounding Koshima, and then it jumped to mainland Japan, hundreds of miles away. The macaque monkeys there began to do the same thing—to wash the sand off food before eating it.

Source: Gwendolyn D. Galsworth. 1977. Visual Systems: Harnessing the Power of the Visual Workplace. *New York: American Management Association, pp. 276-277.*

The basic thesis of this book is that when enough wardens view themselves as proactive and operate their prisons similar to the principles described and explained in this book, then a sweeping change will take place in corrections. Regrettably, we are living in a dark time in corrections today, with all the advocates of repression who want to make the prisoners suffer in every way they can and with financial shortfalls affecting nearly every state. Yet, it is the author's belief and hope that from this disorder a new order will arise, and a new way of operating prisons will arise that will make them safer and more humane for both staff and inmates.

REFERENCES

American Correctional Association. 1993. *Prison Gangs.* Lanham, Maryland: American Correctional Association.

———. 2003. Juvenile and Adult Correctional Departments, Institutions, Agencies, and Paroling Authorities. Lanham, Maryland: American Correctional Association.

Bartollas, Clemens. 1981. *Introduction to Corrections.* New York: Harper and Row.

———. 2002. Invitation to Corrections. Boston: Allyn and Bacon.

Bruton, James. 2003. Inmate Incentive Programs. In Donice Neal, ed. *Supermax Prisons: Beyond the Rock.* Lanham, Maryland: American Correctional Association.

Carroll, Leo. 1974. *Hacks, Blacks, and Cons.* Lexington, Massachusetts: Heath.

Carter, Stephen L. 1996. *Integrity.* New York: Harper Perennial.

Clemmer, Donald. 1958. *The Prison Community.* New York: Holt, Rinehart, and Winston.

Colvin, Mark. 1990. *From Accommodation to Riot: The Penitentiary of New Mexico in Crisis.* Albany: State University of New York.

Conrad, John P. and Simon Dinitz. 1981. The State's Strongest Medicine. In John P. Conrad, ed. *Justice and Consequences.* Lexington, Massachusetts: Lexington Books.

Cornelius, Gary. 2001. *The Art of the Con: Avoiding Offender Manipulation.* Lanham, Maryland: American Correctional Association.

Cullen, Francis T., Edward J. Latessa, Renee Kopache, Lucien X. Lombardo, and Velmer S. Burton, Jr. 1993. Prison Wardens' Job Satisfaction. *The Prison Journal.* 73(June): 141-161.

Culbert, Samuel A. 1974. *The Organization Trap and How to Get Out of It.* New York: Basic Books.

DiIulio, John J., Jr. 1987. *Governing Prisons: A Comparative Study of Correctional Management.* New York: Free Press.

Duffy, Clinton T., as told to Dean Jennings. 1968. *The San Quentin Story.* New York: Greenwood Press.

Duffy, Gladys, with Blaise Whitehead Lane. 1950. *Warden's Wife.* New York: Appleton-Century-Crofts, Inc.

Earley, Peter. 1992. *The Hot House: Life Inside Leavenworth Prison.* New York: Bantam Books.

Ericksoln, Gladys A. 1957. *Warden Ragen of Joliet.* New York: E. P. Dutton and Co.

Frank Wood: He Worked to Keep People Out of Prison. 1966. *Star Tribune* Editorial, May 30, A20.

Funke, Gail S., ed. 1986. National Conference on Prison Industries: Discussion and Recommendations. Washington, D.C.: National Center for Innovation in Corrections.

Hawkins, David. 2002. *Power v. Force: The Hidden Determinants of Human Behavior.* Carlsbad, California: Hay House, Inc.

Irwin, John. 1980. *Prisons in Turmoil.* Boston: Little, Brown.

Jacobs, James B. 1977. *Stateville: The Penitentiary in Mass Society.* Chicago: University of Chicago Press.

Johnson, Robert. 1987. *Hard Time: Understanding and Reforming the Prison.* Monterey, California: Brooks/Cole Publishing Company.

Kantrowitz, Nathan. 1996. *Close Control: Managing a Maximum Security Prison: The Story of Ragen's Stateville Penitentiary.* Guilderland, New York: Harrow and Heston.

King, Roy D. 1991. Maximum-Security Custody in Britain and the U.S.A.: A Study of Gartree and Oak Park Heights. *British Journal of Criminology.* 31(Spring): 126-152.

Levinson, Robert B. 1999. *Unit Management in Prisons and Jails.* Lanham, Maryland: American Correctional Association.

Lawes, Lewis E. 1932. *Twenty Thousand Years in Sing Sing.* New York: A. L. Burt Co.

Linquist, Charles A. and John T. Whitehead. 1986. Guards Released from Prison: A Natural Experiment in Job Enrichment. *Journal of Criminal Justice.* 14: 283-284.

Lombardo, Lucien X. 1981. *Guards Imprisoned.* New York: Elsevier.

———. 1982. Alleviating Inmate Stress: Contributions from Correctional Officers. In Hans Toch and Robert Johnson, eds. *The Pains of Imprisonment.* Beverly Hills, California.: Sage Publications.

———. 1989. Metaphors for Prison Organizations and Correctional Officer Adaptation to Change. Paper presented to the Annual Meeting of the American Society of Criminology, Reno, Nevada, November.

May, John P., ed. 2000. *Building Violence.* Thousand Oaks, California: Sage Publications.

McKelvey, Blake. 1936. *American Prisons: A Study in American Social His-tory.* Chicago: University of Chicago Press.

Murton, Tom. 1976. *The Dilemma of Prison Reform.* New York: Holt, Rinehart, and Winston.

Orlando-Morningstar, D. 1997. *Prison Gangs.* Washington, D.C.: Federal Judicial Center.

Peters, Tom. 2002. The Missing "X-Factor": Trust. In Tara Gray, ed. *Exploring Corrections: A Book of Readings.* Boston: Allyn and Bacon.

Possel, Markus and Ron Amundson. 1996. Senior Researcher Comments on the Hundredth Monkey Phenomenon in Japan. *Skeptical Inquirer.* May/June: 51-52.

Ragen, Joseph E. and Charles Finston. 1962. *Inside the World's Toughest Prison.* Springfield, Illinois: Charles C. Thomas.

Roberts, John. 1997. *Reform and Retribution: An Illustrated History of American Prisons.* Lanham, Maryland: American Correctional Association.

Thompson, J. D. 1967. *Images of Organization.* New York: McGraw-Hill.

Toch, Hans. 1981. Foreword. In Lucien Lombaro. *Guards Imprisoned.* Elsevier, New York.

Useem, Bert and Peter Kimball. 1989. *Stages of Siege: U.S. Prison Riots, 1971-1986.* New York: Oxford University Press.

Ward, David A. 1995. A Corrections Dilemma: How to Evaluate Super-max Regimes. *Corrections Today.* 57(4): 104-108.

Ward, David A. and Kenneth P. Schoens, eds. 1981. *Confinement in Maximum Custody: New Last Resort Prisons in the United States and Western Europe.* Lexington, Massachusetts: Lexington Books.

Ward, David A. and Thomas G. Werlich. 2003. Alcatraz and Marion: Evaluating Super-Maximum Custody. *Punishment and Society.* 5: 53-73.

INDEX

Index of Names

Subject Index

About the Author

Clemens Bartollas grew up in Wheeling, West Virginia. He attended college at Davis and Elkins College and received his B.A. degree in history in 1958. In 1961, he received a B.D. degree from Princeton Theological Seminary. He returned to graduate school in 1969, after serving Presbyterian congregations for eight years. He received a Ph.D. degree in sociology from the Ohio State University in 1973. Bartollas included criminology in his sociological focus at Ohio State. For the four years he was in graduate school, Bartollas also worked full time at the Training Institution in Central Ohio, the maximum-security facility for older aggressive youths of the Ohio Youth Commission. He held various administrative positions, including Wing Director and Interim Director of Guidance. During one of the two years he taught at Pembroke State University, Bartollas ran work-release programs at a minimum-medium security prison in North Carolina.

Professor Bartollas has taught for the past thirty years and is in his twenty-third year at the University of Northern Iowa. *Becoming a Model Warden: Striving for Excellence* is the twenty-fifth book he has published, a number of which are in the field of corrections. Bartollas is probably best known for his works on juvenile institutions, juvenile delinquency, and juvenile corrections. In recent years, Bartollas has also become engaged in studying street gangs, both in the community and in prison contexts.